D1515298

How to Build a $100,000 Law Practice

How to Build a $100,000 Law Practice

JOSEPH T. KARCHER

Institute for Business Planning

IBP PLAZA, ENGLEWOOD CLIFFS, N. J. 07632

© 1976 *by*

Institute for Business Planning, Inc.
I.B.P. Plaza, Englewood Cliffs, N.J. 07632

*All rights reserved. No part of this book
may be reproduced in any form or by any
means, without permission in writing
from the publisher.*

Library of Congress
Catalog Card Number 75-39133

"This publication is designed to provide accurate and authoritative information in regard to the subject matter covered. It is sold with the understanding that the publisher is not engaged in rendering legal, accounting or other professional service. If legal advice is required, the services of a competent professional should be sought."

—From a Declaration of Principles jointly adopted
by a Committee of the American Bar Association
and a Committee of Publishers and Associations.

2nd Printing . . . . . November, 1976

Printed in the United States of America

ISBN 0-87624 207 7

WHAT THIS GUIDE WILL DO FOR YOU

"Any lawyer can make $100,000 a year from his practice—not just the $15,000 or $30,000 most stop at today. And he won't have to specialize to make it."

So says Joseph T. Karcher, one of the most successful lawyers in the country. This small-town lawyer built his practice well above $100,000 with methods so simple that any lawyer can do the same.

Now he reveals the secrets of his successful practice to you—shows you imaginative ways to break out of the rut and to boost your income dramatically . . . ideas so simple you'll wonder why you never used them before—that you'll never stop using when you see how big they pay off!

You'll find this Guide packed with ideas and approaches that give your entire practice a fee-boosting, client-building shot in the arm—with the practical how-to-do-it guidance you need to quickly and easily tailor these income-building strategies to your own practice.

For example, did you ever win a $100,000 verdict or settlement in an area of law about which you knew nothing when you took the case? Mr. Karcher did. He shows you how *any* lawyer can apply his method to win a large fee.

This Guide spells out dozens of such approaches and techniques that win "hopeless" cases . . . get bigger settlements . . . attract profitable clients . . . weed out weak cases . . . and make far more efficient use of your time, which in itself can put thousands of dollars of extra income in your pocket this year.

Mr. Karcher dispels forever the popular misconception that effective legal strategy depends upon surprise. He proves how using liberal discovery rules to the fullest promotes justice, hastens the collection of fees, and adds to income.

He reveals *eight powerful tools* for pre-trial discovery—shows you how to use each to keep in the driver's seat at all times, impress and startle your adversary, and get the kind of settlements that delight your clients and increase your fees.

You discover brilliant techniques that enable you to conduct a general practice—yet draw lucrative clients from all fields . . . prepare cases so they almost can't be lost . . . bill a client so he understands, appreciates, and gladly pays your true worth . . . recognize and cash in on collateral income opportunities . . . set any goal—including $100,000 a year and more income —and achieve it.

Joseph Karcher doesn't ignore the bread and butter of your law practice—the necessary but tedious, time-consuming details and paperwork that waste so much of your day. He shows you dozens of time-savers that get your work done in a fraction of the time—so you can achieve your $100,000 goal.

If you want proof that Mr. Karcher's techniques work, you have to look no farther than his own son—who, utilizing his father's methods, built his own huge practice in just five years.

About the Author

This book is unique and so is the author. Why did he write it? Read the Preface and you will learn his motivations. He was born in the family homestead on "Main Street" in a typical small American town, in modest circumstances. And yet, he succeeded in fighting his way up to success in several fields and to independent wealth as well—without the necessity of leaving "Main Street." He thinks that there is a moral in this story, and that practically every honest and honorable lawyer can duplicate his success with a little help. And he wants to supply that help.

After working his way through law school as a structural steel draftsman, he won an LLB in 1927 from (now) Rutgers Law School and a JD from Rutgers Law School in 1945. He started his law career by putting a note in the bank to cover his library and rent and leased modest offices in the local theatre building, which he later purchased. His rise in the profession was constant, progressive and sure until he came to be recognized as a success not only as a lawyer, but as an author, a public speaker and as a businessman and family man as well. He believes this book will enable every ambitious lawyer to emulate his example.

In addition to carrying on a heavy and successful law practice, he found time to author a dozen books and 40 or 50 published articles on history, government and law, and to lecture extensively as well. If that were not enough, he served in a variety of public and professional offices ranging from judge or magistrate in his home town to service in the New Jersey Legislature for three terms, as well as being a member of the Editorial Board of the *Journal* published by the New Jersey State Bar Association and a Parliamentarian of the New Jersey State Bar for a dozen years. This book reflects these multiple interests and activities and indicates how the alert and upright lawyer can likewise benefit from similar activities.

A recent reporter described the author as that "well-weathered, ruddy-faced, redoubtable 'Lion' of the law." You may very well agree with this colorful description after you have read this book. He is not a Clarence Darrow, a John W. Davis, or a Louis Nizer. Nor is he a Melvin Belli, an Edward Bennett Williams, or an F. Lee Bailey. And yet he has admired and emulated all of them in many ways and thus, perhaps, a little bit of all them has rubbed off on the "Main Street" lawyer—and it has paid off handsomely.

PREFACE

The title of this book is self-explanatory. It is a simple, clearcut, how-to-do-it book on the third most important subject in life—success. Incidentally, in my judgment the other two subjects are first, health and second, happiness. This book is addressed to those earnest, sincere and dedicated lawyers who really *want* to build a $100,000 practice and are willing to *work* for it rather than just *wish* for it.

A lucrative practice is within the reach of every competent and aspiring attorney today. However, it will not come to those who merely wait for the golden opportunity. Opportunities are made if you learn how to make them. You must be ready and prepared to exploit these opportunities when they present themselves. That is what this book is all about—how to prepare yourself for the opportunity—how to create these opportunities—and how to exploit and develop them to the fullest.

I believe that this book is unusual in that it summarizes, synthesizes and crystalizes many possibly well known facts and principles which the average practitioner may have overlooked or failed to recognize or to apply properly. I believe that I have presented a fairly simple system in this volume which, if properly applied, will help the reader achieve his goal. I say this because the ideas and principles expressed herein have all been successfully tested and used in my own law career which brought me from relative poverty to financial independence many years ago.

You may wonder why I wrote this book and how long it took in preparation. Personally, I have always been a buff for books. I have probably read more self-improvement books and how-to-do-it books than most of my contemporaries. I read them because I have as profound a respect for books as I have for libraries. I consider libraries the storehouses of all the knowledge and information developed and gathered through the centuries by the human race. I was admitted to the Bar and to the institution of matrimony almost simultaneously. The only book I took on my honeymoon was a book on "Law Office Management"—with my wife's blessing. Neither of us has ever regretted it.

The writing of a book cannot be forced either by the author or the publisher. It must spring naturally from the mind and heart. You must have a specific book in your system or you cannot produce it. The book under discussion has been more than 40 years in preparation. It has an important message. I feel I must tell it. In my judgment it is a lively, illuminating and fascinating story which embraces practically every sound, solid, reliable and honorable method I have learned or discovered and applied to help me personally build a $100,000 law practice. I want to help the reader do likewise. I think that this book will help achieve this result. If it fails to do so, I will be more disappointed than the reader.

In any event I believe that I have the duty—the moral obligation—to pass on to my contemporaries and to posterity any suggestions, information or advice which I may possess and which may aid them in developing a successful law practice at the earliest possible date in their careers. That is what this book is all about. Good reading—and good results!

Joseph T. Karcher

Sayreville, New Jersey
January, 1976

TABLE OF CONTENTS

Chapter 1

HOW TO USE THIS BOOK
TO ACHIEVE SUCCESS

Readers Are Natural Leaders . . . Lawyers Are Skilled Readers and Students . . . The Most Useful Book–the One that Makes You Think . . . Evaluation and Retention Important–Not Speed Reading . . . Admission of Ignorance–First Key to Wisdom . . . Your Greatest Investment Is in Yourself . . . Your Thirst for Knowledge Can Be Profitable . . . The World Always Respects the Man Who Knows What He Wants . . . Life Pays Only What You Demand . . . Ten Essential Requirements for Success . . . You Only Have to Know . . . Wide Array of Aphorisms . . . Steel Mogul's Ten Rules for Success . . . The Secret of Acquiring Patience . . . Concentration and Perseverance . . . The Power of Enthusiasm . . . Get the Other Person's Point of View . . . Model T. Makes Ford a Multi-Millionaire . . . Two Kinds of People–Lifters and Leaners . . . Do Your Job a Little Better . . . We Get Back What We Give Out . . . Walk the Other Mile . . . Ten Characteristics to Develop Success . . . Ten More Realistic and Practical Rules for Success . . . Let Yourself Be Overwhelmingly Absorbed and Engulfed in Your Work . . . Prepare for Your Opportunities and Know Where to Find Them . . . The Greatest Challenge of Your Life

1

Readers Are Natural Leaders

The mere fact that you have this book in your hands and are reading some of it is an excellent sign. What led you to peruse it is unimportant at this point. It indicates at least that you are a "reader" and being a reader you are a potential leader.

It was Macaulay who observed that he would rather be a poor man in an attic with plenty of books than a king who did not love books. The love of books is indeed a most valuable endowment. You do not have to be born with it either.

Lawyers Are Skilled Readers and Students

A lawyer should be "one up" on most people in their interest in reading.

Some people consider a lawyer's reading as dry, dusty, and uninteresting and as a chore he has to perform unwillingly. Not so! The lawyer who knows what he is about has long since learned that reading is the *open sesame* to larger knowledge, larger accomplishments, larger achievements and *larger income*.

The Most Useful Book—the One that Makes You Think

Your future attitude toward this book and the message it attempts to present may very well indicate whether or not in the future you will be a mediocre, a run-of-the-mill lawyer—or an outstanding member of the bar and a *success* in the true sense of the word. It is evident that even the title of this book has made you *think*. That in itself is one test of a good or worthwhile book. If it has made and will make you think, then it has served its purpose. I suggest you read the preface; thumb through the table of contents; read a few isolated quotes from some of the chapters before you commence reading any book. Even such a cursory examination of any volume should tell you instantly if it is a book which will start your mental processes.

Review briefly just how relatively few books have made you think intensely or extensively. Merely reading a book, however, is insufficient. You must follow through. You must read the book through. You must read it through several times! If it is a good book, you ought to review it annually for several years. Underscore the salient points that appeal to you! Don't worry about the resale value of a defaced book. Used books, irrespective of their present physical condition, command a very low price. If underscoring a book or making marginal notes in it or writing summaries at the end of a chapter will help you in retaining the initial ideas the book conveyed to you, then by all means do it! But most important of all—you must put into your daily practice the ideas and the suggestions which the book has given you.

Evaluation and Retention Important—Not Speed Reading

Merely reading a book is surely not enough. You must read it deliberately, thoughtfully, constructively, and with a purpose. Review again, if you will, the hundreds—perhaps thousands—of books you have read thus far in your lifetime. How many of them do you recall? How much of what you have read did you absorb, retain or *apply*? I urge you not to let the same thing happen to you with this book. Do full justice to it if you expect it to do full justice to you.

Admission of Ignorance—First Key to Wisdom

The greater the man, the more ready he is to admit that he does not know everything—even if he is a lawyer. The illustrious Thomas A. Edison is quoted as saying that mankind has not as yet learned one-tenth of 1 percent about practically anything! As Socrates said so many years ago, "Knowledge of our ignorance is the first step toward true knowledge." These basic rules apply whether we are dealing with such lofty studies as pure science or the more mundane pursuits of the lawyer on how to improve his income, make a living or build up a $100,000 per annum practice.

Your Greatest Investment Is in Yourself

It is also well always to bear in mind that the greatest investment you can make in life is the investment you make in yourself. Subconsciously we probably appreciate this fact, but we seldom state it or reflect on it. Every single additional item of useful knowledge we acquire enriches us, and our lives as well. But it enriches us either spiritually or materially only to the extent and in direct proportion to the extent to which we *apply and use* this acquired knowledge in our everyday lives. The more often you use this knowledge, the more familiar you will become with it, the more facile in its application to the solution of the problems which confront you and the greater and the richer the rewards which will flow to you.

The point to bear in mind is that you now must complete what you have commenced, i.e., read it—study it—use it—and profit by it!

Your Thirst for Knowledge Can Be Profitable

Even the average man seeks to improve or at least to preserve his health, his happiness, his work, his income and his life. You will note that included in this list are his work and his *income*. These elements are just as important, just as essential, just as laudatory and just as salutary as the others. There is nothing inherently mean, sordid, selfish or materialistic about trying to improve your work or increase your income, and this is true even if your ultimate objective is to reach or exceed a $100,000 income per annum figure. In fact, it is a healthy sign.

The World Always Respects the Man Who Knows What He Wants

The world takes its hat off to the determined man who knows what he wants and sets out to achieve it. Men with lesser strength, vigor and determination willingly step aside to let him pass, as he moves up the economic ladder. All that is really needed to get ahead in your efforts to build up your income is to acquire the knowledge necessary to know how to do it and the perseverance to continue your efforts until success crowns them.

Goethe put it this way: "Success usually depends upon two methods only—energy and perseverance." He points out that energy—real, genuine, dynamic energy—is a rare gift and when utilized, usually provokes not only hostility but opposition as well. On the other hand, he continued that perseverance "lies within the affordings of everyone, its power increases with its progress, and it rarely misses its point."

This is good reasoning and good advice indeed, particularly in the field of improving or increasing your income to the point where it reaches or exceeds $100,000 per annum.

Life Pays Only What You Demand

One of my favorite mottos which I had framed and hung in my office and near my desk where I could see it often is the one by Jesse B. Rittenhouse which I have abbreviated somewhat as follows:

My Wage

I bargained with life for a penny a day
and life would pay no more.

I worked for a menial hire only to learn—
dismayed
That any wage I had asked of life
Life would have paid!

Now these are inspirational thoughts indeed. But before you demand of life the full, ample, adequate—generous—wage you want for your work, you must first earn it. You must be worth it, you must be worthy of it. It follows that as your knowledge, your productivity, and your usefulness to your clients increase, your income will likewise increase to the point where you not only may dictate or command the fees you want for your work, but where your clients will gladly pay any wage you ask of life.

Bourke Cockran put it this way:

"The man who is successful is the man who is useful.
Capacity never lacks opportunity.
It cannot long remain undiscovered, because it is sought by too many anxious to use it."

Ten Essential Requirements for Success

Somewhere in my own varied reading, I once came upon a list of ten essential requirements for success in any line. As I recall them, they were as follows, but not necessarily listed in this order of priority: (1) Drive, (2) Broad interests; (3) Ability to organize; (4) Ability to rise to a challenge; (5) Self-reliance; (6) Ability to be realistic; (7) Intelligent use of time; (8) Stamina; (9) Originality of ideas; and (10) Knowledge gained through extensive reading and study. Study this list and you will find that these same ingredients play a very important part in what this book is all about, i.e., how to build up a $100,000 income and retain it year after year. Put into effect the system outlined in the chapters of this book which follow, and I predict that you cannot fail in achieving your objective. But you must want that objective intensely with an intensity which allows no interference. Marshall Foch once observed that the most powerful weapon on earth "is the human soul on fire." Henry Ford stated it in a much milder and equally effective manner when he said "It is my observation that successful people get ahead *during the time other people waste*." And Benjamin Disraeli said "The secret of success is for the man to be ready for his opportunity when it comes." This book will make you ready for whatever lies ahead.

"You Only Have to Know!"

For many years, another one of my favorite personal mottos was:

"You do not have to struggle.
You do not have to fight.
You only have to know."

I have followed this motto consistently all of my life. I have taught my children to honor and respect it. They have profited by it and are using it successfully today. It is still good, sound, common sense psychology or philosophy, but it is not necessarily the alpha and omega of success. The rules covering success are varied and manifold indeed. They vary almost in proportion to the personal whims, fantasies and philosophies of the author.

Wide Array of Aphorisms

I have a very simple, perhaps a homely, approach to all these rules for success. I recommend that you read them, study them and use them and follow them, but only to the extent that they fit into your own particular physical metabolism, personality and pattern of life. Most of them can certainly do you no harm. Many of them can do you a great deal of good—if you understand and apply them properly. By way of illustration, the three-pronged aphorism I began with is only partially true. It does point out the great impact—punch—power that *knowledge* does carry with it. But you will still have to struggle and fight—only not quite so hard. The possession of essential knowledge always makes the task easier and your prospects of winning the struggle substantially greater.

Steel Mogul's Ten Rules for Success

Charles M. Schwab, one of the most successful of America's tycoons, is reported to have suggested this list to insure success:

(1) Work hard.
(2) Study hard.
(3) Have initiative.
(4) Love your work.

(5) Be exact.

(6) Have a spirit of conquest.

(7) Cultivate personality.

(8) Help and share with others.

(9) Be democratic.

(10) In all things do your best.

The Secret of Acquiring Patience

This is not a bad list to follow. This list requires some analysis to determine its exact scope and purpose. But it can be modified to suit the needs of any aspiring lawyer and used to great advantage provided you have the requisite *patience*. The real secret of developing patience is to *do something else in the meantime*. This merely means that you set one specific problem aside temporarily—to work on another one. But when you are rested and refreshed, be sure that you return to the original problem again and again if necessary, until it is solved. Otherwise, you will not have the concentration and the perseverance which are also essential ingredients of success.

Concentration and Perseverance

Emerson said "The secret of success is concentration. Anything is possible to the man who knows his aim or end—and moves straight for it—and for it alone." And in more or less the same vein, Elbert Hubbard said "Genius is only the power of making *continuous* effort. The line between failure and success is so fine that we scarcely know when we pass it!"

While we are discussing concentration and perseverance it seems to me that we would be amiss or remiss if we did not also list *self-confidence*. This, says Samuel Johnson, is the "first requisite to great undertakings." Irving Berlin once observed that the only difficulty with becoming a success was that you had to keep on being successful. The lesson to learn to remain successful is that you must continue to work hard at being a success. Relax and you begin to retreat, to recede or to decline.

The Power of Enthusiasm

One of my own favorite and essential ingredients to success is enthusiasm. In my judgment, in any effort to achieve any objective, certainly one of the most important elements is enthusiasm. It is more potent than money, power or position. The real genuinely enthusiastic person can overcome prejudice and opposition alike; he ignores apathy and inaction; and finally storms the strongest entrenched citadel of his opponents and captures it.

Have faith in your objective, in its worth, in your capacity to achieve it, in your determination to achieve it and you will have the requisite enthusiasm for the task.

But sometimes it is not enough to have it yourself. You must spread it wherever you go. You must spread the enthusiasm like sunshine on a bright summer's day so that it touches and warms and strengthens and inspires and exhilarates everyone and everything it reaches. You will then find that the strength of your own enthusiasm has become infectious and that it strengthens your chances of achieving the victory you strive for in direct proportion to that enthusiasm.

If you can learn to harness and use this great spiritual and emotional force, it can also help you to win success in any field of endeavor.

Fred Williams said, "The longer I live the more certain I am that enthusiasm is the single most important of all traits or qualifications for success." Emerson is quoted as saying, "Every great and commanding movement in the annals of the world is the triumph of some enthusiasm."

Get the Other Person's Point of View

Men as disparate in their ideas as Henry Ford and Theodore Roosevelt had their own pet ideas as to what makes for success and sometimes they seem strangely alike. President Theodore Roosevelt said, "The most important single ingredient in the formula of success is knowing how to get along with people." Henry Ford said, "If there is any one secret of success, it lies in the ability to get the other person's point of view—and seeing things from his angle as well as from your own."

Model T. Makes Ford Multi-Millionaire

That is precisely how Ford was able to produce the most popular of all motor vehicles in its class in his day—the old Model T Ford—and become a multi-millionaire after he had reached age 50. His personal angle was to make money through making and selling cars, but he first figured out what the other fellow needed and wanted, i.e., a modest, inexpensive car which he could afford to buy, maintain, could learn to run, and which would run under almost any condition. This same technique applies in the field of law as well as in the field of the automobile.

Two Kinds of People—Lifters and Leaners

Ella Wheeler Wilcox in one of the most popular of her poems of that era said it like this:

> "There are two kinds of people on earth today
> Just two kinds of people—no more I say
> No, the two kinds of people on earth I mean
> Are the people who *lift* and the people who *lean*."

Believe me when I assure you that the ones who are successful—the ones who reach a $100,000 income—are the lifters, as the poem so aptly points out.

This is probably why Voltaire said, "Shun idleness. It is a rust that attaches itself to the most brilliant metals."

Do Your Job a Little Better

My own favorite single motto or formula for success is, "Do your job a little better than anyone else." This single rule applies with equal force on the farm and in the factory; in the streets and in the shops; in business and in the professions. It is merely a modification of the old rule of supply and demand. Quality survives just a little better than the next fellow's and is always in demand. It does not matter in what area this difference displays itself. It may be shorter or simpler; it may be more efficient or more effective. It does not matter just so long as it is better. In order to test yourself or test anyone else for that matter on this particular qualification, just pose these few questions on whether you can improve on your present methods in any of these respects. "Can I do it easier, quicker, pleasanter, safer, surer, in a more healthy manner, in a more satisfactory manner, in a more economical manner, etc.?"

We Get Back What We Give Out

Willingness to cooperate is another element which is frequently over-looked in the search for success. It is well to remember that in life we will get back only what we give out. Edwin Markham put it this way: "All that we send into the lives of others comes back into our own." It is true that it is sometimes more or less, but that does not destroy the validity of the rule.

Believe me when I tell you that the rule is inexorable.

Walk the Other Mile

One of the strongest admonitions in the Bible is not only to walk the requisite or usual distance, but to "walk the other mile." This means to make all reasonable efforts at resolving your differences, to become reconciled with your opponent, to show him every reasonable consideration—even to the extent of walking the extra mile. Too often in life we find persons who make a practice of being unreasonable to the point where it becomes a habit. It is a good policy always to meet your adversary at least halfway provided you can do so honestly and honorably and not compromise yourself or do your client any injustice, and still retain your self-respect.

I once observed a very prominent trial attorney settle a complicated and difficult case on terms which at one time seemed hopeless and impossible. When it was over, I said to him: "John, I was surprised that you were willing to humble yourself. I thought you had too much pride in your system to yield?" "Pride," he snorted, "I never let pride interfere with a fair and reasonable settlement. "I am here to get the best possible end result for my clients, not to bolster my own ego."

Ten Characteristics to Develop Success

I cannot pass up the opportunity of at least presenting a few of my own rules for success which I have formulated through the years:

(1) Develop personality.
(2) A well trained mind.
(3) Sympathy and understanding.
(4) Courage.
(5) Some knowledge of psychology.
(6) Some knowledge of logic.
(7) Ability to reason.
(8) Clarity of speech.
(9) Power of perseverance.
(10) A good character.

Frankly, the above list is not proposed as being complete, or all inclusive, or all exclusive. It is submitted primarily as a challenge in developing proficiency in these areas and will be definitely helpful to you in your search for a larger income. I have personally met and dealt with many successful lawyers who were not fortunate enough to possess more than 50 percent or 60 percent of them and yet they had achieved success.

Ten More Realistic and Practical Rules for Success

Some years later, I reviewed my original list of ten essential rules for success and revised it to make it much more realistic and practical. The ten rules I came up with are:

(1) Don't put leisure before work.
(2) Learn something new every day.
(3) Watch the net profits, not the gross profit.
(4) Don't hide your light under a bushel.
(5) Ignore trifles.
(6) Don't procrastinate.
(7) Sharpen your skills.
(8) Win the loyalty of your associates.
(9) Revise your routine to get out of a rut.
(10) Protect your reputation by protecting your character.

Follow these and watch your income reach the magic mark of $100,000 per annum—and exceed it!

Let Yourself Be Overwhelmingly Absorbed and Engulfed in Your Work

One of the greatest accomplishments in life is to achieve an inward satisfaction from what we are doing. It is a form of happiness which comes to us automatically, subconsciously, unbidden and unsought. Thus, as we become more and more proficient in our work, we achieve accomplishments and self-sufficiency and in most, if not all, cases almost incidentally and automatically we deserve and receive income above the average, and eventual wealth as well. This progression is inevitable.

Nor does this mean that you have to have a one-track mind or live exclusively in a single rut. In fact, to achieve real genuine success and happiness, you must develop an honest interest in practically every other facet of life simultaneously. But this interest will naturally and necessarily be a much more subdued and modest one and will be pursued at a lesser tempo than your major concern, namely, the profession of law which you have selected as your preferred career for your life's work, as well as for your livelihood.

Prepare for Your Opportunities and Know Where to Find Them

This book is intended not only to prepare you for your opportunities, but to show you how to go out and *find them,* and, if necessary, to *create them.* Some wit once observed that too many of us are out in the backyard looking for a four-leaf clover when our opportunities are knocking at the front door and receiving no answer. Another wit said that even if we answer the knock at the front door we would probably not recognize opportunity and welcome him in with open arms, but would more likely dismiss him as a house-to-house salesman.

The Greatest Challenge of Your Life

Through this book, I hope to give you the greatest challenge of your life. The challenge of:

(a) Thinking
(b) Planning
(c) Dreaming
(d) Working
(e) Striving
(f) Building
(g) Creating
(h) Achieving.

These are the very well springs and building blocks of life. They are what makes life worthwhile. Incidentally, they also assure a substantial, and in fact, a lucrative income. They lay the foundations for the $100,000 per annum practice. When the time comes when you can say to yourself "I made it—now I can relax and rest on my laurels," you may think you will be happy, but you may be the most unhappy man in the world. Life may have lost its zip, zest and tang—its challenge, its inspiration, and its aspirations. You may indeed have ceased to live for all intents and purposes. I hope that this book not only offers you a great challenge, but shows you how to meet it.

Chapter 2

HOW TO ORGANIZE,
DEPUTIZE, SUPERVISE

A Lawyer's Stock in Trade Includes More than His Time and Advice . . . Average Man Uses Only 25 Percent of His Capacity . . . Six Rules Guaranteed to Produce More Work . . . How to Organize the Day . . . Always Use the Same Secretary on the Same Case . . . Utilization of Multiple Law Secretaries . . . Establish Ideal Appointment Hours . . . Organize the Title Closing . . . Avoid the Luncheon Myth . . . Let the Autonomic Nervous System Do Some of the Work . . . Active Tray Emptied Many Times a Day . . . The Friend Who Failed to Follow the Rules . . . Problems of the Sole Practitioner and Large and Small Partnerships . . . 60-80 Percent of Work Can Be Deputized to Laymen . . . Deputizing Work Is No Sign of Weakness . . . Deputize All Non-Professional Work . . . Typical Title Transactions from Contract to Closing . . . Making a Person Think . . . Don't Be an Iceberg—Try Surfacing . . . Supervision Skills Essential . . . The Captain of the Ship . . . The Orchestra Leader Analogy . . . There Is No Such Thing as Little Things . . . How "A Little Thing" Won an Important Verdict . . . Picking the Proper Personnal . . . Working With and Through People . . . How to Keep the Organization Operating at Full Capacity . . . Material Recognition Important . . . Praise and Appreciation More Important

A Lawyer's Stock in Trade Includes More than His Time and Advice

Lincoln coined the most overworked motto in law offices across the nation, i.e., "A lawyer's time and advice are his stock in trade." It was a false

13

generality as most generalities are. I long ago supplemented it by adding ''plus his brains, his eloquence, his sweat and tears.'' This was to remind me that *increased productivity* applies in law, as well as in industry, and this involves work. The secret of accomplishing the greatest amount of constructive, effective work lies in the ability to organize, deputize and supervise.

Each man may have his own ideas and methods. It is unimportant from what sources these may have been derived. It has been said that originality is simply a pair of fresh eyes. It is advisable always to be on the alert for new and better ideas and methods; to study the old ones; to supplement, amend or modify the old ideas to give them a new and fresh approach to present day problems. Eventually, you should have a modern, compact, and efficiently operated office. Without this base, a $100,000 annual income will be difficult to achieve. With it, this is not only possible, but logical and probable. Theodore Roosevelt said: ''Nine-tenths of wisdom consists in being wise in time.'' So start now in acquiring this increased wisdom.

Average Man Uses Only 25 Percent of His Capacity

Andrew Carnegie was one of those astute fellows who learned early in his career how to organize, deputize and supervise. He also learned early that work played an equally important part, but that it really should not be called work—because none of us ever begins to work to his fullest capacity. He is quoted as saying ''The average man puts only 25 percent of his energy and ability into his work. The world takes off its hat to the man who puts in more than 50 percent of his capacity. It stands on its head for those few and far between souls who devote 100 percent of their capacity to their work.'' I believe that this rule covering the average man is much more prevalent in the legal profession than in most other walks of life. My objective is to change that rule so far as it affects the average lawyer. I hope to inspire him to *think* about the wonderful potential which lies within his still undiscovered and unused capacity. ''Great thoughts, reduced to actual practice *become* great acts,'' says Hazlett.

Six Rules Guaranteed to Produce More Work

Every accomplishment in the world since time began has depended upon organization. From the building of the pyramids to the landing on the moon, organization was the magic secret of its accomplishment. It can also be yours in increasing your income to the $100,000 per annum mark. Someone once observed that the greatest things in the world have been done by those who *systematized their work* and *organized their time*. I have a few very simple rules for putting these lofty thoughts and eloquent phrases into practice, in getting more work done in less time. Here they are:

(1) Set a goal—*now*.
(2) *Start*—from where you are.
(3) Conserve your time.
(4) When you tire, rest, but come back to the task.
(5) Eliminate the irrelevant.
(6) Finish the job—positively *finish it*.

Note the simplicity of these rules. "Set a goal—start—conserve time—stick to it—finish it." Victor Hugo said: "He who every morning plans the transactions of the day—and follows out that plan—carries the fine thread that will guide him through the labyrinth of the most busy day." The goal you set may take various forms. My favorite method is to draw lists of work to be completed on a daily, weekly, monthly and long-term basis. These should be compiled regularly from your daily schedule. It takes but a few minutes to list on a yellow pad in chronological order the 5 or 10 items selected from the weekly or monthly list, and start work on them now. Bear always in mind as you review and select the items that it is much better to pay close attention to matters before they become critical and involve a crisis, and prepare for them in advance by anticipating them. This is much better than waiting for the crisis to happen. Lowell says: "Attention is the stuff that memory is made of—and memory is accumulated genius."

How to Organize the Day

By way of illustration, I would like to indicate a typical day in my own office. The first step in any organized day should be the adoption of the program or schedule indicated above. The mail is first sorted by a trained employee into several categories and routed to the individuals who have charge of the specific matters covered. The remaining first class mail is then stacked on my desk in a neat pile. This mail is reviewed quickly. A further process of elimination and routing is continued. Simple notes on the margin refer them to the person handling it with appropriate instructions directly on the letter, or on a supplemental memo. Those items to be handled by me are retained. New items of work are added to the daily, weekly, or monthly lists referred to later. The mail frequently determines the priority of the work scheduled for the day. An effort is made to answer or otherwise dispose of all first class mail promptly the same day as it is received. The answers may not be actually typed the same day, since the secretary will have to fit them into her own schedule of priorities, but at least they will be dictated, off the executive's desk, and on the way to organized action.

Always Use the Same Secretary on the Same Case

Having analyzed the mail, having routed it to other employees with instructions, set up my own daily goal, I can now summon one secretary after another to take dictation. As time goes on, you will find that if you have two or three secretaries, you can assign one of them to a particular specialty, such as title work, litigation, estate work, or the like. In like manner, the same secretary should be assigned to a special case, or a special client, as she acquires a greater familiarity with the subject matter. I guarantee that this method will make every employe more efficient and more productive.

Utilization of Multiple Law Secretaries

Former New Jersey Attorney General, David T. Wilentz, who gained world wide attention through his masterly prosecution of Bruno Richard Hauptmann in the famous Lindberg Kidnap Case was visiting my office one day on a matter of mutual interest. In the course of the visit he chided me pointedly on the fact that I had three (3) personal law secretaries. I countered by pointing out that he had six (6). He retorted by saying, ''Yes, but I have five other lawyers to keep them busy!'' I then pointed out to him that the late Arthur T. Vanderbilt, former Dean of the New York University Law School and later Chief Justice of the New Jersey Supreme Court, always seemed a little proud that he could keep four (4) law secretaries busy without the slightest difficulty. Anyone who knows Justice Vanderbilt's personal record knows that he was a prodigious worker and left behind him as a heritage a newly organized, complete court system that was for many years a model for most of the remaining states to follow. From this I take it, there should be no reflection on a lawyer if he is a little more industrious than his contemporaries.

Incidentally, Mr. Wilentz's own record showed him also to be a prodigious worker and one of the most successful lawyers in the nation. He now supervises the work of more than 20 or 30 lawyers.

Establish Ideal Appointment Hours

The time saving devices in law offices are limited only by the imagination and inventiveness of the attorneys. I have several of my own which have saved me countless hours and have proven both helpful and *profitable*. The first one is that I schedule all appointments for three specific times of the day, viz: 11:30 a.m., 1:30 p.m., 4:30 p.m. These hours may be changed to fit the individual metabolisms of the individual attorney, but the basic theory behind them remains the same—to save time. Each of these hours can be advanced to 11:00 a.m., 1:00 p.m. and 4:00 p.m., depending upon the number of appointments or the length of time involved. These specific hours accomplish several desirable objectives. You will note that the morning appointments are scheduled at the end of the morning. This prevents unnecessary interruption while the mail is being analyzed, routed, answered, or otherwise disposed of. It also leaves the balance of the morning for concentrated dictation when the mind is fresh and most productive. Scheduled so close to the noon hour, the interviews will be reasonably brief. An effort is made to limit each interview to 10 or 15 minutes. If the client overstays, a concealed buzzer under the desk can be effective. The secretary who hears the buzzer knows what to do. She rings me to remind me of the next client waiting for me or of some other urgent appointment. As my bell rings, I stand up and usually the client realizes that the interview is unfortunately ended due to other commitments. I then graciously escort the client to the door and bid him goodbye.

Organize the Title Closing

There is a consistency and a uniformity in most of our office functions which indicate *organization*. By way of illustration, let us consider the matter of a routine real estate closing of title. Go into any average law office while such a closing is in process and you will have no way of indentifying the buyers from the sellers, the attorneys from the laymen, etc. In our office, this problem has been simplified. The person closing the title sits at the head of the library table or conference room table. The buyers are always on the right. The sellers are always on the left. Counsel for the buyers flank the person in charge of the closing on the right, while counsel for the sellers flank that individual on the left. The real estate brokers are usually at the end of the table. If a lien holder is also present, his position is next to the brokers, etc. This *physical arrangement* renders any title closing more efficient, more economical, it avoids confusion, expedites the operation and saves considerable time. Why so few other lawyers have not adopted this simple method is difficult to perceive. I recommend it heartily as one of the best methods of securing organization of your office operation.

Avoid the Luncheon Myth

The idea that much valuable work can be accomplished at a luncheon is a myth. I have found the luncheon appointment to be one of the greatest time wasters devised by man—rather than a time saver. If you are polite, you usually wait until the luncheon is over before getting into any serious discussion of the problem intended to be discussed. The ultimate result usually is that the parties overeat, overdrink and over-extend the luncheon hour. The result is that, while the occasion is socially delightful, it is economically wasteful.

The value of the 1:00 or 1:30 p.m. appointments is that you will be able to fit them in at the beginning of your afternoon schedule. Hence, you avoid unnecessary interruptions, are able to concentrate directly on your dictation or legal research through most of the afternoon. As to the 4:30 p.m. appointment, once again it is at the end of the day. The bulk of the work is behind you. These interviews can even be arranged to extend a little longer than those in the morning or early afternoon. There is always one sure "assist" in terminating them, i.e., the office staff departs and the client himself is due home for dinner and so are you. Thus, as the day closes, you have accomplished an orderly, compact, constructive work-filled day with a minimum of distractions and interruptions, and yet the clients have had their choice of three separate hours for their appointment, presumably for their convenience.

Let the Autonomic Nervous System Do Some of the Work

The above outlines are only a few of the many systems which may be devised to suit the individual attorney. Personally, I carry my organization even to the point of organizing the top of my desk, with its wooden "outgoing" tray file, the two wire files, the center and side drawers so that I can find everything I want or need almost automatically. This includes not only pens and pencils in the usual place, but a half dozen other essential items running from paper clips to postage stamps. It is a provable fact that the autonomic nervous system can be trained to perform most of the mechanical functions of the body without wear or tear upon the mental or emotional reserves. These acts and functions are not limited to such complicated items as playing the piano or driving a car which are turned over to the autonomic nervous system regularly. Most of the remaining acts and functions you perform at your desk (except that of actual thinking) fall into the same category.

Listing some additional time savers: I never go or send a messenger anywhere where a postage stamp will perform the same function; I never walk from one office to another when an intercom will do the job better; never keep an out-of-office appointment without first having my secretary phone ahead and confirm the fact that I am expected. These and dozens of other seemingly simple items will save you not only minutes, but hours of time in the course of a day, a week, or a year.

By way of illustration, a valued client, a real estate developer, came into the office with a poor grade blueprint of an old real estate development, which he was trying to sell. There were several prospects in different cities. He had only the one print and it was an old one. The surveyor who laid it out was dead, and the whereabouts of the tracing were unknown. I realized that any letter from him or me offering the property to these prospects would be futile without the print. I advised the client not to worry that I would take care of everything.

After he left, I wheeled my desk chair and secured a mailing tube which had been neatly tucked away for just such a requirement. To the old print, I clipped a new note reading ''(1) one cloth tracing off (2) make 4 black and white prints from tracing.'' I slipped it into the mailing tube, closed each end with a strip of scotch tape, took a regular imprinted mailing label from my center drawer and addressed the tube to a blueprint house at the county seat. I then placed it in my ''outgoing'' tray file. It was as good as mailed and delivered.

Within a few days, the old print came back to my desk, plus the tracing with 4 crisp white and black prints. A secretary was summoned. Letter and maps were dispatched to the prospects. The development was sold—and all without leaving my desk.

Active Tray Emptied Many Times a Day

The ''outgoing tray file'' referred to is a simple procedure I am particularly fond of. I am aware of the fact that the use of tray files with incoming and outgoing mail, etc., has been in use for centuries, but to me it is the simplicity of my system which appeals to me particularly. On the left hand corner of my desk, there are always two wire tray files, topped off with a wooden tray file. They are sacrosanct in my office and should be in the office of every lawyer or other executive. The two wire trays on the bottom are for clearing my desk of all matters disposed of. When I have finished with a matter for the day or for the time being, I slip it into these wire tray files and thus clear the desk whether it is a single sheet, a bulging file, or a book. Every employe knows that when they see *anything* in these wire trays it is to be taken out and returned to the file or the library forthwith. But the wooden tray is even more important. Every item of work, every memo, every written instruction is placed in that tray directly without leaving the chair behind my desk. Not once a day, but a dozen times a day, that tray file is emptied and routed for immediate action. Every employe has been trained to keep that tray empty all day. The fact that it is empty is my personal signal that all work I have dispatched is in process.

The Friend Who Failed to Follow the Rules

I once had a friend who lived in a town immediately to the east of my community and who maintained an office in the town immediately to the west of my community. We had conducted business dealings for years by phone, correspondence and in person. One of his inherent weaknesses was that he had violated practically every rule of efficiency that I lived by. He insisted on "dropping off" some letter or documents as he passed my office. Many times I admonished him that he should conserve his energy, but he assured me that it was just as simple to deliver personally. And, believe it or not, on each visit, he would complain of how busy he was—how he had trouble keeping office appointments and meeting his schedule, etc. I regret to advise that he has now passed on. His death was indeed untimely. He had exhausted himself with needless expenditures of energy. The lesson to learn is that you should let the post office deliver a letter for you even if you pass the client's door four times a day.

Problems of the Sole Practitioner and Large and Small Partnerships

In achieving a $100,000 per annum income, the sharp question arises as to whether you can do it as a sole practitioner. If you have to take in a partner, you have to double that gross income to achieve that objective. Statistics show that the bulk of the lawyers practicing in the U.S.A. are so called solo practitioners. There are, of course, a wide variety of partnerships consisting of two or three partners up to a half dozen or more. A firm must consist of 50 or more partners to be considered a really large partnership and these are usually limited to the metropolitan areas. However, this book is not intended for these larger firms. It is addressed primarily to the sole practitioner and the smaller partnerships where the members do not exceed six or so partners. It is my view that the suggestions herein set forth are equally applicable to all lawyers in this category. There is one point that is clear. I do not believe that it is physically possible for a sole practitioner to achieve or exceed a $100,000 per annum income with just one secretary. He will be more likely to achieve it with three or four secretaries and, particularly, if one is a para-professional and is able to become in effect his office manager, bookkeeper and accountant.

The employment of a bright young attorney, recently out of law school, is also recommended. This can add greatly to the volume of the work which can be carried on by the sole practitioner without unduly burdening his overhead. These young employes have frequently developed into able and competent associates and eventually into partners if a partnership is desired. It is in these areas that the rule of "watching the net profit and not the gross profit" applies particularly. I have personally tried all systems mentioned and have evaluated each of them from the standpoint of which method is the most likely to produce the largest net returns for a person of my particular characteristics.

60-80 Percent of Work Can Be Deputized to Laymen

From this background of actual experience, I can say that by proper organization a lawyer can deputize up to 60 percent or 80 percent of his work to non-professionals or para-professionals without losing effective professional control of his practice—or his income. I have observed that any lawyer (or any executive for that matter) who is always busy is usually taking personal charge of a mass of details that can probably be done twice as well by a subordinate in half the time. The point is that the lawyer's emotional energy and mental powers should be conserved for the important matters which are strictly professional.

Deputizing Work Is No Sign of Weakness

Walter Lippman is quoted as saying: "It is never a sign of weakness when a man in high position delegates authority—to the contrary it is a sign of his strength and of his capacity to deserve success." I would add a word: Frankly, unless he does learn to deputize, he will never actually succeed in law or in any other profession or any walk of life for that matter.

By way of illustration, I have never employed a legal stenographer without immediately having her apply for and become a fully qualified Notary Public. All expenses are borne by the office. Her value to the office and her efficiency in doing her work are immediately raised. If she is given an affidavit to prepare, simultaneously she can be assigned the task of contacting the affiant, making an appointment for him to come to the office ane executing the affidavit before her. She then takes the jurat, impresses her official notary seal and places it on the attorney's desk fully completed as she ushers in the client. This procedure in itself cuts down the time involved for the interview by more than 50 percent in most instances. In complicated cases where corrections have to be made in the affidavit, the story may be different, but in the average case the operation can be handled more smoothly, accurately and efficiently if the secretary is also a qualified notary.

Deputize All Non-Professional Work

The same thing applies to the preparation and execution of deeds, bonds, mortgages and the like. In such instances, it is also wise to have the secretary remain throughout the closing since she is familiar with every document as she has typed them. She is undoubtedly also familiar with the closing statement because she has prepared it and typed that also. In view of her familiarity with all of this detail, she is the most logical person to draw all of the checks for paying off the liens and encumbrances and fixing the net consideration. If she has had even a smattering of training in bookkeeping and accounting and has been carefully taught and trained to follow an orderly, systematic routine procedure at a closing of title, you can depend upon it that the drawing of the checks will be done more efficiently and accurately than if done by the attorney himself. It may be that the attorney will insist upon signing the checks personally, although in many law offices a trusted secretary can also be given power of attorney to sign the checks as well. However, when this is done, the attorney handling the title closing should double-check the amounts of the checks and see that they correspond with those called for in the closing statement. This is the extent of the supervision required. This is a classic illustration of how to deputize the routine paper, non-professional work to others, leaving the attorney free to supervise the overall operation of the title closing.

Typical Title Transaction from Contract to Closing

By way of illustration, if your office handles a great deal of real estate title work, the lawyer himself could easily become bogged down in the minutiae involved in what should have been established as a routine procedure. I once checked and listed the steps involved in an ordinary title matter from the initial contract to the final closing. The items listed ran to something around 30 or more. Of these items, only a half dozen or so required professional attention. The contract must be formulated by the attorney, but there is no reason why its transmission, submission, execution, receipt of deposit, or earnest monies, etc., cannot be deputized to a competent secretary. The abstract of title, or title binder, can be ordered by a secretary. There is only the reading and the examination of these documents which require professional skill. Likewise, in ordering the various upper court lien searches, municipal lien searches, etc., only the reading of these requires professional skill. As to obtaining pay-off figures on liens and encumbrances and drawing up closing statements, this is not actually work for an attorney. It may be done much better by a secretary, particularly one with a background in bookkeeping and accounting. Drafting the final documents, such as the Deed, Bond, Mortgage, Affidavit of Title, Estoppel Certificate, etc., is the work of the attorney—but only as far as dictating and checking are concerned. The actual work of producing them is purely stenographic and clerical. Setting up the date and time and place of the closing with all the various parties is certainly not professional work. Hence, it can be safely and legitimately—and I might say confidently—delegated to a well-trained, mature, responsible secretary.

The problem is finding and training such personnel, but it certainly can be done with a little effort. The vast majority of lawyers come eventually to depend upon such secretaries. The difficulty is that the lawyer usually wastes or fritters away the time and effort he has thus saved, instead of ploughing it back into constructive work in his own office that actually requires personal expertise. It is this last habit which must be developed if you wish to achieve the magic figure of $100,000 per annum. *Capitalize on the time saved*.

Making a Person Think

But all of this organization and deputization requires the ability to think. Someone once said that one of the greatest achievements in life is to make a person *think*. Studies show that the average person will do practically anything to avoid thinking. This aphorism is generally thought to apply only to the principal, i.e., the attorney or other professional, but this is not true. The resistance to thinking is common to all of us, including our office personnel as well. Thus, we have a two-pronged objective. The first is to cultivate the habit of thinking ourselves, but it is equally important to train our office staff as well to think. The more we think and the more they think, the more efficient the operation of the office will become and the greater the volume of work which can be accomplished and the larger the increase in fees which may be anticipated from said work.

Don't Be an Iceberg—Try Surfacing

More people than is realized go through life like icebergs, with only 10 percent showing above the surface and 90 percent concealed. These observations also apply to the executive and his personnel as well. It is unfortunate that this is so, but the trick is to do something about it. As more of the person rises to the surface, the greater his potential for work, for achievement and for happiness. The iceberg metaphor is another way of saying that most of us, the boss and the employee alike, utilize only about 10 percent of their innate natural capacity. The remaining 90 percent lies submerged, inactive, dormant. Our aim as intelligent, thinking executives must be to reverse this trend in both ourselves and our employees. Let's sear this single thought in our conscience and in our memory. Let's resolve that we will develop at least 50 percent of our full potential in our daily work. I summon you—I challenge you—to this objective and this achievement!

Supervision Skills Essential

All the organization and deputization may come to naught if the overall operation is not properly supervised. Supervision is the key to a successful office operation. As a member of the Bar and licensed to practice law, an attorney has a duty to his client. He may assign as much of the *detail work* as he cares to, or is able to, but the ultimate responsibility for the *legal* services *always* remains with the attorney. It is the attorney who is the principal. This responsibility cannot be delegated. Thus, it is neither possible nor proper to assign legal work to a subordinate without retaining direct control of the ultimate net results. It may be all right to assign some of this detail work without maintaining any direct control on "how" the work is accomplished. But the attorney must always retain full and absolute control as to the net results in order to discharge properly his personal professional responsibility.

The Captain of the Ship

I often liken my duties in running an office to that of a captain of a ship. He must stick to the bridge, keep a weather eye out for all objects which might constitute a menace to navigation; he must gauge the weather; "box the compass"; issue the orders; delegate authority; enforce discipline; keep the crew happy; and yet bring the ship safely into port with its cargo intact. I sometimes facetiously say that I feel like the captain of a sinking ship—but this is merely to alert all hands to pay strict attention and to make sure that each one is performing his or her assigned task to the best of his or her ability.

The Orchestra Leader Analogy

To carry the analogy a little further, the head of a law office, large or small, is like an orchestra leader in many respects. He has a fine organization under the control of his baton. Each section knows its function—the bass, the woodwinds, the string section, etc. They follow his orders. He seeks perfect harmony. His ear must be attuned to the whole symphony and yet it must be acute enough to hear the slightest false note not only in any one section, but coming from any one player or instrument. This capacity for detail is the secret of a successful orchestra presenting a successful recital. The lawyer is trying to produce the same results in the field of law with trained personnel in various fields, but he must also be on the alert to detect the first evidence of defects or discordance so that it can be remedied immediately.

"A good executive," says Lawrence C. Powell in his *A Passion for Books*, "sees minutiae with one eye—visions with the other. He is both galley slave and dreamer." Some less imaginative and eloquent a writer put it more bluntly when he said that a genuine executive is a fellow who decides on something quickly and then directs somebody else to do it.

There Is No Such Thing as Little Things

Some sophisticated attorneys may attempt to brush off at least some of the suggestions and recommendations I advise as "old hat" or out-of-date, or too simple or too trivial to be concerned with, etc. To all of these persons, I have a simple answer, i.e., you are the one who will be the loser if you do not follow these admonitions. I know that these ideas will work and pay big dividends, for the simple reason that I *have used them all profitably*. I would be the first to concede that some of the ideas advanced may seem too small or simple or obvious or well known. But the difficulty is that perhaps for this very reason the average attorney fails to put them into practice. The old adage says that "perfection is no trifle, but trifles make perfection." Looking backward through the rich experience of years, I am amazed as to how many successes I achieved in so many varied fields of endeavor by observing the so-called "little things." I now conclude that in law at least there are no such things as little things. They are all important.

How "A Little Thing" Won an Important Verdict

By way of illustration, I once defended two young men charged with rape. The complaining witness was a mother who was given a lift in the defendant's auto late at night with her 14-year-old daughter when their own car broke down and they were stranded in an isolated area. Her story was that she was coerced into submission by the threat that the two defendants would otherwise molest her innocent 14-year-old daughter. The case was featured in the press as the "honor rape" case. The two defendants were almost convicted. There was one single small element which I had observed throughout the three-day trial, i.e., that the mother had permitted the poor, innocent, unsophisticated, 14-year-old daughter to sit in the front row of the courthouse along side of her throughout the three days of lurid testimony.

In summation I argued strongly—and effectively—that if the complaining witness was so solicitous for the protection of her daughter it certainly would have extended to a similar solicitude to save her from the sordid and embarrassing details brought out in the trial. I pointed out that it would have been just as easy to have the daughter wait in the corridor, or in an anteroom, or even in the judge's chamber, until her brief testimony was required. It was a seemingly trivial point, a small item, but it carried the day and there was an acquittal. Hence, one of my cardinal rules for all lawyers to follow—is to watch the little things and the big things will fall into proper place.

Picking the Proper Personnel

From all of the foregoing, it is clear that organizing, deputizing and supervising will not produce results without the proper personnel. The world is full of unsure people who seem afraid to share their know-how with others for fear that they may be training their own successors. This is an unsound attitude indeed. I believe that training a subordinate is the only way to win promotion yourself. You can make a career out of a job or you can let the job weigh you down and get you into a rut. It is well to admonish your employees occasionally that those who do *only* what they are paid to do seldom get paid any more.

Another one of the secret weapons of a really successful executive is not only to use all of the brain power he may have personally, but to arm himself with as much additional brain power and talent as he can beg, borrow or otherwise persuade—and hire it and harness it to his own objectives. Always remember that brain power and talent are too scarce a commodity to waste or overlook. But there is a corollary to this rule also. If you find that you have over-estimated the man or woman whom you have employed; that they are definitely the wrong persons; that they don't fit in with your overall scheme of things;—get rid of them fast! Pay them an extra week or two weeks or even a month, if necessary—but don't let them stay under any circumstances. If you do, it will cost you infinitely more in the long run.

Working With and Through People

I am thinking of the person who cannot get along with his fellow workers, who cannot work with them, or through them. In my judgment, such a person is not an asset, but a liability to any organization, large or small. This ability to get along with people works both ways. The executive must possess it also, or he really doesn't have executive talent. John D. Rockefeller once said: "I'll pay more for the ability to handle people than for any other ability under the sun." Dr. Murray Banks, the humorist, psychiatrist and lecturer, put it this way: "The art of getting along with people is more important than all the knowledge and skill that a person can develop in or out of school."

How to Keep the Organization Operating at Full Capacity

And so with your office work properly organized, deputized and supervised; with the proper personnel properly selected and trained—how do you keep such an organization functioning at full capacity? The answer is to raise their morale, their *esprit de corps*, make them like their work and more of it. This can be done in several ways, such as by rewarding them materially and showing them genuine appreciation.

However, this requires team work. It requires joint effort all along the line for "our office," or "our firm," or for "our case." Charles Buxton says: "Success is due less to ability than to zeal. The winner is one who gives himself to his work—body and soul." This capacity and energy must be transmitted to each member of the staff. There can be no laggards; no clock watchers; no one who does not have firm faith in the firm and pride in its reputation, its record, and its accomplishments!

Hard work never hurt anyone, either the boss or the employes. Former Chief Justice Charles Evan Hughes is quoted as saying "Men or women do not break down from overwork—but from worry and excesses and abuses not associated with their work." And I would add to that—from not having enough to keep them busy in more worthwhile work which they really enjoy doing.

Material Recognition Important

But, aside from an effort to keep your personnel healthy and happy and their morale and *esprit de corps* high, under no circumstances can you overlook the all-important factor of proper material compensation. They should and must be paid at least just a little above the prevailing compensation paid for similar work in the same locality. They should be given a bonus, not only at Christmas or New Year's, but occasionally when they have worked particularly hard on some special case—provided the efforts have produced satisfactory results. Fringe benefits in the way of a 5-day-week schedule; adequate vacation; and an occasional extra weekend or holiday off; pensions; life insurance benefits; hospital and surgical care, thrift savings and the like all help to keep an office staff contented and happy. Incorporating the firm in a Professional Association will make the most of these tax-deductible under I.R.S. rules.

Praise and Appreciation More Important

But over and above all this, I believe that the personal touch—the showing of appreciation for the work performed and the loyalty shown is even more important than monetary return. Charles Schwab is quoted as saying that when his workers showed particular effort or loyalty "he was generous in his appreciation and lavish in his praise." These are indeed words to live by. They can mean so much in the life of an earnest, sincere, dedicated worker striving to do a good job. Hence, I try never to fail to jot down on work submitted to me the accolade of "good," "fine," "very good," or "excellent," before I return it to him for some minor correction. In some cases, I go further and write "wonderful" and on some rare occasion "thank you for doing such a good job." It takes so little and it means so much. Try it sometime and see what happens!

Chapter 3

HOW TO CONDUCT A GENERAL
PRACTICE—YET DRAW CLIENTS
FROM ALL FIELDS

Never Admit You Lack Qualifications . . . The Retainer with Reservations . . . Contingent Fee Agreement . . . Provide for the Right to Bring in Trial Counsel or Execute Substitutions . . . Make Preliminary Research of Law Involved . . . Shall I Bring in Special Counsel? . . . The Possible $100,000 Verdict Attracts Me . . . List Yourself as Counsel by Letter or Suit . . . You Too Can Be an Expert . . . A Problem Well-Stated Is Half Solved . . . Another Illustration of a Case Requiring Special Expertise . . . Distress of Homeowners Leads to Taking Case–and Winning . . . Preparation for Trial Will Disclose Your Capacity or Lack of It . . . You Are More of a Specialist than You Think . . . Inherent Dangers in Referring to Other Attorneys . . . Railroad Cases Usually Considered a "Specialty"

Never Admit You Lack Qualifications

One of the favorite admonitions of the criminal trial lawyer is "never plead guilty." If you are offered an important case in any field, never, never admit that you lack the qualifications to handle it. Yet I know many attorneys who go fearfully through life actually afraid to handle anything more difficult than a title closing or a simple estate. You must first overcome this negative attitude if you ever expect to make the grade and reach or exceed $100,000 per annum.

Always bear in mind to begin with that you have been issued a license to practice law by your own sovereign state. This presupposes that you have the requisite education and training to be entrusted with the handling of all of the legal affairs of your client. There are no restrictions or limitations imposed upon your practice, except those which are self-imposed. Few if any states recognize specialization in a particular field of law. Specialists are self-made, self-constituted, self-appointed. You don't need to recognize their expertise—at least at this stage. I recommend that you always accept the retainer, with certain built-in reservations.

The Retainer with Reservations

These reservations need only be slight ones. They can be spelled out clearly in the retainer form. One of the first forms I designed for personal use and used effectively through the years was a retainer form. It has been modified slightly as new conditions developed. The basic form was one to cover the handling of personal injury claims on behalf of the plaintiff. The blanks indicate that the fees charged were to be subject to negotiation. Thus, while an ordinary auto negligence case might command a fee of 33-1/3 percent, a slip and fall case might command a 40 percent fee. If the case was even more difficult, such as one covering libel and slander, products liability or the like, it might conceivably be higher. In recent years some states (including New Jersey) have placed certain restrictions and limitations not only upon the amount of the contingent fee to be charged, but spelling out the items of expense which may be advanced by the attorney for the client before the net amount of recovery is determined for the purpose of calculating the ultimate fee. It is therefore, imperative that you check your own state laws and regulations before you use any specific retainer form. The following is the one we used for many years, until recently when the New Jersey Court took over control of contingent fees. Following it is a modernized form of Retainer intended to conform to the Supreme Court's new regulations.

CONTINGENT RETAINER AGREEMENT

WHITE, BLACK & BROWN, P.A.
COUNSELLORS AT LAW
61-65 MAIN STREET
ANYVILLE, N.J. 08872

To: WHITE, BLACK & BROWN Esqs.   , 19___

Dear Sirs:

In consideration of your acceptance of our case and agreement to handle same for us as long as you conceive it to be advisable, and to exercise your best efforts to effect collection of same;

We, the undersigned, hereby retain you as our legal attorneys and our attorneys-in-fact to prosecute any action or actions and/or to compromise to settle any claim or claims we may have against

and/or
or any other person, firm or corporation whomsoever, because of damages suffered by us arising out of or sustained on or about
at
as a result of

It is mutually agreed that your attorney's compensation for services rendered in our behalf in this matter shall be a sum equal to_____% of verdict obtained (plus taxed costs) or gross amount recovered or compromised upon on settlement. It is understood and agreed that you as our attorney are to advance incidental costs of Court up to trial, and other expenses and disbursements incidental thereto except the following: compensation or reimbursement for lay witnesses and expert witnesses; physical examinations; surveys; photographs; depositions; and all other similar items of expense, including taxed costs in the event of an adverse verdict.

Any and all disbursements or costs advanced by you are to be reimbursed to you out of claimants said_____%

share of any gross amount recovered. It is also understood that our doctors, hospital, auto repair bills and all similar consequential damages are to be paid out of claimants said_____% share of any gross amount recovered.

All services and disbursements on appeals are to be extra. You are to have full discretion as to substitution of attorneys or referring matter to your associates or special trial counsel to handle for you.

We hereby expressly release you from any and all liability in the event that you are not successful in the handling of this matter which may not be covered by any professional liability insurance you carry to protect clients.

_____ L.S.

WITNESS:

_____   _____ L.S.

CONTINGENT FEE AGREEMENT

1. Name of Client (Claimant)   Tel. No._____
   Address of Client (Claimant)

2.   hereby retains the firm of WHITE, BLACK & BROWN, P.A. (A Professional Corporation), whose address is 61-67 Main Street, Anyville, New Jersey 08872, for the purpose of representing him/her with reference to a certain incident which occurred on or about the ____ day of _____ , 197_as the result of which the said Client (Claimant) sustained personal injuries and property damage.

3. Client (Claimant) acknowledges that he/she has been advised of his/her rights to retain the services of an attorney under and by virtue of which he/she would compensate the attorney on the basis of the reasonable value of his services regardless of the outcome of said case, but the Client and the Attorneys have agreed that the Attorneys shall be paid a contingent fee in accordance with Rule 1:21-7 (c) as follows:

   (a) 50% on the first $1,000 recovered;
   (b) 40% on the next $2,000 recovered;
   (c) 33-1/3% on the next $47,000 recovered;
   (d) 20% on the next $50,000 recovered;
   (e) 10% on any amount recovered over $100,000 and
   (f) Where the amount recovered is for the benefit of an infant or incompetent and the matter is settled without trial the foregoing limits shall

apply, except that the fee on any amount recovered up to $50,000 shall not exceed 25%.

4. Should the Attorneys fail to effect settlement of said claim or to win a favorable verdict for the Client (Claimant) in the event of suit, the said Plaintiff shall not be required to pay for the services of the said Attorneys but shall nevertheless be liable to reimburse the Attorneys for all lawful disbursements made by the said Attorneys in connection with the said suit including cost of depositions, expert medical and technical witnesses, etc., including taxed costs in the event of an adverse verdict.

5. The aforesaid contingent fee shall not be computed on the basis of the gross recovery but on the net recovery only, after deducting all costs and disbursements in connection with said suit, including investigation expenses, fees for medical or technical experts, depositions, costs of briefs and transcripts on appeal and any interest included in any Judgment by virtue of R.4:42-11(b).

6. The above listed fees shall include all legal services rendered by the Attorneys on any retrial, review proceedings or appeals but nothing herein contained shall be deemed to require the Attorneys to take such proceedings except by mutual agreement between the parties.

7. The Attorneys reserve all their rights under R.1:21-7 (f) to make application to the Assignment Judge on appropriate notice to the Client (Claimant) for such additional fees as the Attorneys may deem fair, equitable and just in the event they deem the fees above provided for as inadequate.

8. The Attorneys agree to continue to handle this claim for the Client (Claimant) for as long as they may deem it advisable but expressly reserve the right to withdraw from the case on appropriate notice and leave of the Court if necessary. They also reserve the right to bring in associate counsel for the purpose of preparation or trial if they deem same necessary and to also execute Substitution of Attorneys in the event they deem such proceedings advisable.

Signature of Claimant

Dated:_____   _____
Signature of Spouse of Claimant

Dated: _____   _____
Signature of Attorneys

**Provide for the Right to Bring in Trial Counsel or
Execute Substitutions**

You will observe that these forms cover several somewhat unique features. First the attorney agrees to handle the case only so long as *he* conceives it to be advisable. However, it is well to note that in some jurisdictions now you must obtain court leave to withdraw when suit has been instituted. You will next observe that the form makes the attorney also the attorney in fact and gives him the right to compromise, i.e., settle the claim, although we have never exercised this right. You will note further that all the ethical requirements prohibiting attorneys from actually financing litigation are rigorously observed. The attorney agrees to advance these funds and expenses but is entitled to reimbursement. The attorney does not acquire any direct interest in the subject matter of the litigation. Note also a recital of the obligation of the client to eventually pay the fees of the expert witnesses and even the taxed costs in the event of an adverse verdict.

Probably the most single significant point covered by the retainer (other than fixing the fees) is the provision that the attorney is "to have full discretion as to substitution of attorneys or referring matter to associates or special trial counsel." Finally there is the precautionary provision expressly releasing the attorney from any and all liability in the event the case is lost. It concludes by an assurance to the client that our office is covered by professional liability insurance to protect the client. This type of retainer practically gives the attorney *carte blanche* authority in many areas. It is, of course, urged that this discretion be exercised with extreme caution and always in the best interests of the client and within the spirit as well as the letter of the Canons of Ethics. Meanwhile the attorney should feel free to accept the retainer of his services in any case, even if it is a complex one involving a class action such as a stockholders' suit or on behalf of the defendants in an anti-trust suit, if you are ever fortunate enough to be retained in a litigation of this type. But check your own state laws on attorney-client relationships by all means—and conform.

Make Preliminary Research of Law Involved

The first step would be to immediately research the law. It need not be exhaustive. A cursory examination may suffice for the moment. This should include at least a review of the applicable state and federal statutes involved; the court rules likely to be relied upon by either side and a hasty review of the decisional law of your own jurisdiction as found in the Digests of your own state, Corpus Juris Secundum, A.L.R. etc. By this means you will have fortified yourself with knowledge of the gravamen of the proposed action and the essential ingredients of the suit. Based thereon, in drafting the complaint you will be able to set forth a valid cause of action (or several of them) which will be invulnerable to attack or dismissal on the grounds that it "fails to set forth a valid cause of action."

Shall I Bring in Special Counsel?

I have a vivid recollection of handling a large, complex and extremely important suit in substantially this very manner. To tell the entire fascinating story in all of its details would take a volume larger than this one. I can only recite the barest details. A committee of irate citizens representing some 50 homeowners whose homes lay within a half-mile bend of the South River called on me one evening. Their purpose was to complain bitterly about the industrial pollution of the river by three prominent industries whose plants lie upstream. They claimed that the odors emanating from the stream were so bad as to cause nausea; that the river was discolored and unfit for any recreation or commerce and that occasionally fumes arising from the river actually caused the paint to peel from their homes! They sought my advice as to their rights and my legal assistance in enforcing them.

The Possible $100,000 Verdict Attracts Me

I had belonged to several trial associations at the time. It was not unusual for speakers to talk on such subjects as "How I Won My First $100,000 Verdict." These talks naturally appealed to me. I realized that even one such verdict per annum would supply 33-1/3 percent of my objective of a $100,000 per annum practice. Verdicts of that size were unusual in my jurisdiction at that period—and still are. The thought occurred to me that here was a case which should bring at least $100,000 gross with so many plaintiffs. Had I realized at the time the volume of the work involved I probably would have shied away from the burden. Instead I excused myself for a half hour from the meeting with the committee, went into the library and did some swift legal research. It is amazing how much law can be located even in a half hour when you need it. I returned and accepted the case. Two years later and after being shuttled back and forth between Federal and State Courts several times and having answered some 13,000 interrogatories, my clients finally settled the suit for an even $100,000. A later suit involving the same defendants, but with different plaintiffs, produced an additional $150,000 or a composite of a quarter of a million dollars. And this from an area of law which was novel at the time and in which I had no particular familiarity or expertise.

List Yourself as Counsel by Letter or Suit

The first step after you have accepted a retainer to represent a client in a difficult suit is to get yourself listed as counsel of record. This may be done either by formal letter to the defendants or their attorneys or by filing suit. Frankly, I prefer the latter since it then gives you substantial, if not absolute, control of the litigation. It forces all parties to deal with you directly. Any settlement by payment of damages thereafter is subject to the lien of your attorney's fees. Their collection will usually be enforced on your behalf by the court having jurisdiction of the suit.

Having filed the suit, you can then pursue the matter aggressively on four separate fronts: (1) intense additional legal research; (2) exploring the possibility of an amicable settlement; (3) an intense search for factual data to support your claims, and the locating of expert witnesses to back up your contentions; and (4) preliminary search for one or more legal associates or trial counsel whom you might eventually need, but solely for the purpose of ascertaining their availability and to formulate terms on which they would handle it for you.

If these four avenues of investigation are pursued properly, I can assure you that one of these four things will occur eventually viz: you will either (1) determine that the case is hopeless and withdraw; (2) settle it; (3) bring in outside counsel as associates for reinforcement; or (4) refer or forward the case outright to some other law office with the facilities and competence to handle it.

You Too Can Be an Expert

Andrew Carnegie is quoted as saying "Immense power is acquired by assuring yourself in your secret reveries that you were born to control affairs." The same philosophy can be applied to assuring yourself of your individual capacity to handle personally an important case which at first seems overwhelming to you. Personally I have never let myself be overly impressed by so-called experts. I have looked upon many of them with a skeptical if not jaundiced eye. I always recall Ben Stolberg's definition of an expert as one "who avoids the small errors as he sweeps on to the grand fallacy."

Books can be extremely helpful in making you something of an expert in your own right on almost any subject if you are willing to do some intense reading and research. No case is properly investigated or prepared until *you have read all of the data* available to you in that particular field. Books still are the chief source of knowledge and of power. Apply yourself with sufficient diligence and you can become an expert in your own right on practically any subject on earth. There is hardly an important case which has passed through this office upon which I have not developed at least a certain degree of expertise in order to handle it properly.

A Problem Well-Stated Is Half Solved

Before you can make an intelligent judgment on your own individual capacity to handle a given case, you must understand it thoroughly. In particular, you must comprehend the specific problem involved. Next you must envision the modes or methods available for the solution of these problems. At this stage it is well to recall the old adage that "A problem well-stated is half solved."

Sometimes a problem can be fully stated in the complaint. Frequently this is not true because at this stage only the affirmative favorable side of the case is stated. In most jurisdictions, under modern procedure it is permissible to plead conclusions of law, and not necessarily the facts upon which they are predicated. Hence, it is more likely that the problem can be better stated in a detailed legal opinion in which all of the pros and cons are carefully reviewed, analyzed and weighed. I find that in submitting a resume of a case to a prospective expert in a given field, I am more likely to state the problem fully and accurately than in any other manner. In any event, I have found that the old adage is indeed true.

Many times, somewhere along the line as I am dictating a synopsis of the case and the problems involved, the solution becomes almost self-evident. In some instances the problem is insoluble and this likewise becomes self-evident. In my judgment there is no better way that I am aware of, of analyzing a set of facts and conclusions, than through dictating them seriatim in this fashion. Even when the solution, or lack of solution, is in equipoise, it leads to the essential investigation of the "missing links" in the chain of evidence. It sometimes points up the imperative need for one new expert witness in a specific field who may be able to supply the missing ingredient which can spell the difference between victory or defeat.

Another Illustration of a Case Requiring Special Expertise

I recall another case in which I was called which required specialized expertise in the field of local property taxation. Both state and federal constitutional questions were involved for good measure. Up to this point I had never made any pretense of specializing in any of these fields. I had always represented myself as an ordinary county-seat type general practitioner—and still do. In this case the clients were certainly frank enough because they gave me a ten-page written opinion by a distinguished member of the Bar in a different section of the state (with his bill annexed) in which he rejected the case on the grounds that it was hopeless. He marshalled his facts, he cited the law with book and verse and came to the ultimate conclusion that he could not, and would not, undertake the task of defending this group. I read the opinion with considerable interest.

Very briefly, and perhaps to oversimplify the case, it involved 120 homeowners in New Brunswick, New Jersey, who had contracted to purchase homes constructed by the U.S. Government to provide essential housing for employees in certain war industries. Under the terms of the contract with the federal agency, the houses were to be exempt from local municipal property tax until the purchasers made their final payment. At this point the deeds were to be delivered and recorded. Thereafter, with title no longer in the federal government or one of its agencies, the property would naturally and automatically become subject to city taxes.

The group of homeowners organized themselves into the Lincoln Gardens Civic Association. They were dissatisfied with the alleged poor municipal services they had received while the properties were tax exempt—which they claimed were practically nonexistent. They stoutly contended that by not making the last few payments due the Government, title remained in the U.S. Government and the property continued to be tax exempt. In today's terminology, this would probably be called a tenant's or taxpayer's strike. The U.S. Government, apparently in desperation, attempted to waive the last few payments and vest title in the occupants by recording the deeds. This impasse went on for years while the tax liens mounted. The homeowners' claims had been heard in summary proceedings and arguments for Writs of Certiorari by the New Jersey Supreme Court on at least two occasions. The U.S. Supreme Court had passed upon it on at least one occasion. In all instances, the courts had rejected the claims of the owners and declared the property subject to taxation.

Distress of Homeowners Leads to Taking Case—and Winning

Normally I would not have had the courage or audacity to touch the case for a variety of reasons. However, the city had commenced tax foreclosure against the homeowners. A climax had been reached. It was a case of paying up these large accumulations of back taxes or losing their homes. Some were out of work while others were in extremely modest circumstances. The president of the organization was a very persuasive gentleman by the name of James J. Chance, Sr. Eventually I acceded to his pleas. Several years later we had won the case on a series of technicalities. I had earned a very substantial fee of approximately $37,000 on a 10 percent contingency basis. But most important of all I had become a recognized expert in the field of municipal taxation.

I do not want to leave the readers frustrated trying to figure out how the victory was won. To begin with, it developed that the title of the state statute under which the tax foreclosures were being conducted failed to meet the then constitutional requirement that the title alert the public to the general content of the law. This enabled us to get an injunction restraining the prosecution of the pending foreclosure suits. During the delays which ensued we were able to get help from the Congress in passing an amendment to the statutes covering insured FHA mortgages which made these properties eligible for guaranteed loans. We then negotiated with the city for an abatement of the interest on the liens. The principal tax claims were eventually settled for approximately 50 percent. The city was paid the amount due with mortgage funds representing the proceeds of the guaranteed mortgages, and everyone was happy.

Preparation for Trial Will Disclose Your Capacity or Lack of It

Assuming that you do accept a difficult case in a new field and that you have filed suit and that you now control the litigation—it usually takes a year or two at least before it is reached for trial. During this period you will be busily occupied on many aspects of the case. This will include the exchanging of interrogatories and answering them; taking depositions and counter-depositions; making motions and answering counter-motions, and perhaps writing briefs on each or all of these proceedings. If there is anything which will convince you as to your capacity to complete this litigation successfully under your own power, it will be this pretrial discovery and preparation for trial. If you feel that you have gone beyond your depth—and you cannot settle it—this is the time to exercise your rights under your retainer. You may bring in such associates or trial counsel as you deem necessary. Or you may even execute a Substitution of Attorney on a formal basis. There will still be ample time for the new counsel to complete the pretrial preparation and go to trial if necessary. Should you elect to pursue these latter courses, by all means alert your clients to what you are doing and the basis for your action. You may frankly admit the real reason for your withdrawal and assure your clients that they will now have the benefit of two attorneys instead of one. Or you may prefer to find that you are too pressed with other matters and are unable to give this particular case the time it requires and deserves. In any event, be sure that you alert your clients to the fact that they will be dealing with other attorneys rather than yourself.

My final advice would be never to wait for an ultimate decision on bringing in associate counsel until the Statute of Limitations has run. It just might be too late to retrieve any serious mistake you might have made.

You Are More of a Specialist than You Think

In the few instances when I did bring in a so-called specialist to try a case for me, I was disappointed more often than not. I always had the feeling that I could have tried the case equally as well by myself. Instead of relaxing and letting the substituted counsel carry the burden alone, I redoubled my efforts to assist in the preparation and presentation of the case in order to justify my client's initial confidence in me. Thus the client did indeed have the benefit of two attorneys. The difficulty was that I had surrendered a substantial portion of my own fees. Incidentally, in many cases the fee that was left after paying trial counsel was disproportionate to the time and energy which our office had expended up to the point where substituted counsel came into the case.

This always reminds me of my first experience when I was elected to the Assembly, the lower House of the New Jersey Legislature. On Inauguration Day all of the members of that august body went to the Assembly Chamber to take their oath of office and to hear the Governor deliver his annual message to the Legislature. It was always an impressive affair. The members were in formal morning attire complete with Ascot ties. The Chambers were banked with expensive floral tributes from well wishers. I looked about me in awe.

Realizing that I was only a simple country lawyer from a small community and a medium-size county, I could not help but wonder "How did *I* ever manage to get in here?" A few weeks later after I had the chance to observe the endowments of my fellow members of the Legislature, I was sometimes inclined to ask "How did *they* manage to get in here?" It is much the same with the so-called specialist in handling certain phases of legal work. He does not always measure up to his reputation or to your expectations. So if you are reasonably confident that you can handle a matter yourself, effectively and without prejudicing or jeopardizing your client's rights or interests, do not hesitate to do it. Generally speaking, that is precisely how the reputed experts became experts in the first place.

Inherent Dangers in Referring to Other Attorneys

The danger in referring your cases to other attorneys is that sooner or later your clients are going to raise serious questions as to your capacity to handle cases in a particular field. For a while you may be able to retain your practice by the pretexts heretofore set forth, i.e., that you are too busy, that they will be getting the services of two attorneys, etc. But after a while you may find that when a really important or attractive case comes along, they may bypass your office and go directly to the competing office to which you had previously referred their case. This could have a serious impact on your objective—the $100,000 per annum practice.

On the contrary, if you accept all cases, and handle all cases, your reputation for all-around competence also travels. If you are able to handle these cases successfully, that news will also spread rapidly. Thus, while you may be admittedly a general practitioner, your clients will not hesitate to bring all of their legal problems to your door—not just the small, the mediocre or the hopeless. Once you actually hit the top and have achieved a $100,000 per annum practice there is considerably less danger in referring cases to younger or less busy attorneys. Your clients know that you are competent, successful and *busy*. They will appreciate your overall supervision of the case even if you permit the handling of the actual trial work by someone else of your selection.

Railroad Cases Usually Considered a "Specialty"

Another example: Railroad law like Admiralty, Aviation, etc. is considered one of the specialties requiring some additional expertise. We had a case come in involving a woman on her way to her doctors for a final examination and discharge following major surgery, whose car came in contact with a dark-colored, unlighted freight car as it was being pushed across a single track grade crossing on a city street at night. The crossing was unlighted and unmarked except for an old fashioned, wooden, faded "saw-buck" sign. Her car was dragged some 50 to 100 feet. She suffered severe injuries to the cervical and lumbar spine; was confined to a hospital for six weeks and completely disabled for eight months. The railroad denied liability claiming she ran into their train.

We began to "bone up" on railroad law; read the applicable statutes and cases as well as some leading text books. Then we invested in a few cassettes and listened to them. As a result of this research we were certain of at least one thing, viz: we had to depose the entire train crew. We did this promptly using train phraseology like old pros. The information developed was illuminating to say the least.

The depositions disclosed that while the track was owned by one railroad and leased to a second, it was being used by a third. The operation involved the drilling, weighing and spotting of cars for a single industry; that if the 11-car train had been shortened to 8 or 9 and made two short trips, there would have been no need to "foul" the public crossing; that a flagman was sent to the center of the roadway with only a low-watt lantern and a single flare; that before he stopped the westbound traffic and turned his attention to the east, his lone flare had burned out; that the engineer did not wait for a "come ahead" signal but continued across the street without stopping (in violation of the railroad's own printed rules); that there was no bell or whistle sounded. To compound the matter, the defendants had permitted a large industrial building to be built very close to the tracks and roadway and a "Plant Entrance" sign to be erected in violation of local zoning laws, further impairing a driver's visibility.

With these facts in our possession and established on the record, all defendants contributed to a satisfactory settlement. We earned a substantial fee without calling in any special counsel.

From the foregoing it should appear self evident to any ambitious lawyer that it would be unwise to decline to handle a novel case solely on the basis that you have not had experience in that particular field. As indicated, the prudent course to follow would be to secure a written retainer with the reservations I have previously outlined, which would enable you either to bring in special trial counsel as an associate, or execute a full substitution of attorney to an expert in this field of your own selection. I have found that in most instances a case of this kind can be settled on a satisfactory basis for both the attorney and the client long before the Statute of Limitations has run.

Chapter 4

HOW TO DEVELOP THE FULL POWER
OF YOUR PENCIL

The Magic of the Pad and Pencil . . . Routing the Memo from File Tray to File Tray . . . Fixing Sole Responsibility . . . Sometimes Memos Annexed to Supporting Data . . . Memo Pads Used in Home, Auto, etc. as Well . . . "Thoughts Should Be Secured" . . . Why Burden the Memory? . . . Preserve Rejected Thoughts . . . Tape Recorders Ideal for Other Uses . . . Larger Memos Also . . . Single Sheet–Single Message . . . Don't Say It–Write It . . . Need for Delegating and Fixing Responsibility with Follow-up . . . No System Infallible . . . Some Sample Memos . . . The One-Line Memo or Message . . . Financial Benefits from Use of Memos Immeasurable . . . The Follow-up Schedule Serves as Tie-in . . . A Few Words Capture the Thought . . . Sample of the Follow-up Schedule . . . Cancel Out Items on List as Completed . . . Remainder of Five Daily Follow-up Lists Consolidated into Daily Schedules . . . Daily Schedule Constitutes Core of Important Substantial Matters Which Are Likely Money Makers . . . Recent Readers Digest Article Endorses Similar Program

The Magic of the Pad and Pencil

If I were asked to specify the one single item of equipment or supplies in my office which has proven the most effective and efficient aid in running the office, I would unhesitatingly say a 5″ × 8″ plain unprinted memo pad—and a tray full of sharp pencils. Perhaps I would also have to add to the above the miniature clip board with the tear clasp at the top. This permits the insertion of two or three of these pads under the clasp at one time, and the memo note can be torn off evenly and cleanly with a mere flip of the wrist, because the tear clip is *exactly as wide as the pad*.

Through the years, I would estimate that several hundred thousand, more or less, penciled memos have been written by me, torn off quickly along the knife edge of the clamp and put into the out-going wooden tray on my desk to set my written orders into immediate motion.

Routing the Memo from File Tray to File Tray

These plain white bond pads are ordered by the gross. With 50 pages to a pad, you have 7,200 pages. These in turn provide approximately 25 written memo instructions per day for 300 working days in the year. I know that I use at least one-half this amount and perhaps more in the course of a year. Simple and commonplace as they may seem, I have found that they work magic. Printed forms, with written legends and boxes to put check marks in, all seem less effective and less dynamic. This is probably because they are less personal as contrasted with mine. I attribute much of the success of running a modern, effective and efficient office to the constant daily use of these short personal written orders.

The date or even the day of the week can be indicated with two simple numbers at the top. The person to whom the order is directed can be identified by his or her initials written clearly and large at the top. Thus my notes are addressed to TS, EW, LR, MM, MGP, NH or Alan or John. Every employee is instructed to pick up these notes or memos or orders *regularly* from the wooden tray file on my desk; take them out to the row of similar wooden tray files lined up on the top of the steel files.

Fixing Sole Responsibility

These steel files in turn are lined up in the office occupied by the secretarial or stenographic pool. Each secretary or stenographer has her own tray. Their instructions are to remove every item from the tray as soon as they observe it. This arrangement has been found even more efficient than placing the memo or order directly on the secretary's desk. In some instances where this procedure had been followed they got mixed up with other files, correspondence and memos, or actually got lost or overlooked. In this manner each secretary is made responsible for her own work and for carrying out the instructions from the time the item is put in her individual tray.

Sometimes Memos Annexed to Supporting Data

Loose memos or orders are in the majority by far. But these same standard-size memo sheets are also used to clip to a letter; a file; a map; or a book to shorten the message and to deliver the essential data to the secretary simultaneously. In my judgment these written memos are the mainspring of the entire office operation. Their value has been proven many times over. Some of my associates who have left my employ to start a practice of their own have adopted the same system with equally good results.

One of these men left the office to become an Assistant Prosecutor or an Assistant D.A. where he rose quickly to prominence. When asked as to what he attributed his rapid promotions, he candidly expressed the belief that it was this simple system which he introduced into a busy office. He proceeded at once to use the same simple memos as a means of issuing orders or instructions covering every aspect of his work. Incidentally, he was the only one on the staff or in the office who was doing it. His superiors were curious as to how he could get out a maximum of production within a minimum of time and with a minimum of errors. He frankly admitted that his only secret weapon was his written memos. He was promoted on the spot to a better job at a substantial increase in salary. Today, he heads his own very successful law office with associate lawyers—and they *all* use this same system.

Memo Pads Used in Home, Auto, etc. as Well

Outside the office these pads are equally effective. I use the same size and style for uniformity. It is common knowledge that standardization was one of the secrets in the industrialization of this nation. I am a firm believer that the theory of standardization extends even to the use of office pads. At home a pad and pencil are placed strategically at many points; along side of each phone; on an end table along side of my favorite chair in the library; on a night table along side of my bed, etc. These pads are used not only to write memos directly to the office staff and to my law associates, but to myself as well.

"Thoughts Should Be Secured"

Bacon said "A man would do well to carry a pencil in his pocket and write down the thoughts of the moment. Those that come unsought are frequently the most valuable and should be secured, because they seldom return." I have found this to be true. Whether it is an office chore; an item of office maintenance; a new idea for handling a case; or some abstract thought which might be found useful at some time—it should be jotted down at once. Be certain that you limit one item to a page. In this manner these memos can be placed on your desk each morning and rerouted through the same standard process upon your return to the office. Unless they are captured immediately they are usually elusive and may not return again for weeks or months, if they ever do return.

Why Burden the Memory?

Hence, it is my suggestion that you never rely upon your memory no matter how retentive or redoubtable it may seem to be. The weakest lines by the shortest stub of a pencil are stronger and more powerful than the best of memories. In addition, why burden your mind with minutiae which can be so safely recorded and stored on a simple 5″ × 8″ sheet of white paper. Always bear in mind that small memos can precede big events.

Preserve Rejected Thoughts

It was Emerson who said "A man should learn to detect and watch that gleam of light which flashes across his mind from within . . . yet be dismissed without notice, his thought—because it is his! . . . yet in many works of genius we recognize our own rejected thoughts—as they come back to us with a certain alienated majesty." I am sure that all of us at some time or another have recognized some new idea or thought expressed by another, which we recognize as precisely the same as one which had flashed through our own mind—and which we had failed to capture at the time and put down in writing.

Tape Recorders Ideal for Other Uses

In this modern age there has been a progressive movement in all offices toward the tape recorder. I use them myself extensively. They are excellent for many purposes. However, in my judgment they lack the flexibility of the short hand-written memo. Hence, I would not attempt to substitute the tape or the cassette for the immediate orders of the day. Some of the other drawbacks for this use of tapes are obvious: They must be inserted in an appropriate machine to be played back; listened to; transcribed—and all this before they are put in operation. My recommendation, therefore, is that you save the tape recorder for use in more extended documents. They are ideal for dictating legal memos, briefs, extensive itemized bills, etc.—but not for the telegraphic order you wish carried out immediately.

Larger Memos Also

I would not want the reader to think that you can operate an efficient law office by limiting your writing to 5″ × 8″ memos. Our office also consumes large quantities of 8-1/2″ × 14″ canary yellow pads as well. But these are reserved for more extended memoranda and more detailed and comprehensive instructions. I recall one evening I decided to jot down a ''few'' interrogatories which I would want to dictate or to turn over to a secretary to type up the next morning on a pending case. Before I had finished, I had filled ten pages of these 8-1/2″ × 14″ papers—and this was only the rough draft.

Single Sheet—Single Message

I say that the use of this type of memo, and processing them in the manner indicated, will prove to be one of the most effective and economic methods of controlling the operation of your office. In fact I am almost willing to guarantee it. It is imperative, however, that one message or order or instruction covering one subject matter be put on a single sheet. If the message requires more than one sheet it is, of course, all right to use two or more. However, the point to be borne in mind is that no two separate messages pertaining to two separate cases should ever be included in the same memo. This can prove fatal. I say this because you run the risk of having one of the instructions overlooked, ignored or lost. It also complicates the follow-ups; the responsibility for completing the order; the filing of the memo itself for later use in billing, etc.

Don't Say It—Write It

One of our large local industries had some pads printed up similar to the ones I have described. The only difference was that they used them horizontally instead of vertically and they had a heading imprinted. This heading across the top embraced a single admonition: ''Write It—Don't Say It.'' Frankly this is the very message which I am advocating so vigorously. Incidentally, it was the multi-million dollar and eminently successful E. I. DuPont de Nemours & Co. plant at Parlin, N.J., which was using it.

Need for Delegating and Fixing Responsibility with Follow-up

In the first place this type of memo definitely delegates responsibility. The initials at the top constitute a preemptory order that the responsibility for carrying out this specific instruction rests solely and exclusively with the individuals addressed. They have it on their desk *in writing*. They do not file it. They keep it there until the task assigned is completed. At that point they draw a heavy diagonal line across the memo page and return it to my desk with the single word "done." Thus we have accomplished several very desirable things, i.e. fixed responsibility; given a written order, in a permanent form which is unlikely to be lost; which can serve as a constant reminder until the task is completed. When completed the report comes back to the executive as evidence of its completion.

At this point the memo may be either discarded as complete or marked "file" and put in the wire tray from which it will automatically be filed in the appropriate folder as a record of the work done. Quite frequently these memos are accumulated in the file as a source of items to be included in the eventual tabulation for billing, as outlined in a later chapter.

No System Infallible

Incidentally, no system is infallible. I once had a law associate to whom I assigned instructions through these memos. There were days and weeks when all these memos were not returned with the distinguishing and reassuring diagonal mark across them. I began sending repeats. The same thing happened. Finally in desperation I began making carbon copies of the memos and retaining my copy. There were still no results in some cases.

At last I confronted my associate with these facts. I reminded him that under no circumstances was any memo to be destroyed, filed or returned to me until the work was done. I then asked him what he was doing with these written memos I issued to him so frequently. He assured me that he was following my instructions precisely and implicitly. I found this difficult to believe. I even suggested that if he had retained them all his office or at least his desk would be bulging with them.

Fortunately for both of us he sought and found employment elsewhere shortly thereafter. In clearing out his desk I regret to advise that his desk was indeed bulging with these memos. His system of merely retaining and sitting on them is the only method I know of which can effectively stymie or cancel out all the good that can be accomplished through written memos. Thereafter, I made it my personal responsibility to follow up on all memos at least once a week.

Some Sample Memos

Memo A

October 1,

TS:

Re: <u>Blank to Anyville Savings</u>

1. Phone attorney for seller and
   clear closing date.

2. Set up closing.

3. Get check from bank.

Memo B

November 15,

EW:

Re: <u>Estate of Fred Holmes</u>

1. Phone Mr. Wood

2. Have him come in and sign attached forms.

3. Take his jurat.

4. Mail back to bank.

5. Use usual form letter of transmittal.

<u>Memo C</u>

December 5,

LR:

Re: <u>McCarthy vs. R.V.R.R.</u>

1. Acknowledge pleading on card.

2. Prepare usual statement of amount
   of damages claimed.

3. $100,000 for First Count—
   $20,000 for Second Count.

4. I will dictate letter of transmittal.

<u>Memo D</u>

January 4,

MM:

Re: <u>Cross Riparian Grant</u>

1. Correct attached affidavit.

2. Mail to Mr. Cross for examination
   and correction.

3. Carbon copy to Mr. W.

4. Return copy to my desk.

Memo E

February 15,

MGP:

Re: Proceeds of Sale of #100 Main St.

1. Draw refunding bonds for two legatees
   named in the Will.

2. Prepare checks to cover.

3. Have beneficiaries come in to sign.

4. Take acknowledgment.

5. Have them see me before they leave.

Memo F

February 25,

NH:

Re: White vs. Bluehaven Lanes

1. Call engineer H.S.

2. Ask him to inspect parking lot
   and furnish report to us.

3. Supplement our answers to interrogatories
   by letter showing H.S. as additional expert.

The above are merely illustrations of a simple process for doing what many attorneys would convert into a major project. These six memos which would take not more than ten minutes to write can set up more than six hours of work for intelligent personnel trained to do it.

The One-Line Memo or Message

These samples will give you some idea of the breadth and scope of these memos. A little note can sometimes pack a big wallop. The memos shown are long ones. Numerous ones consist of a single line. Here are a few illustrations:

1. Serve Summons on Gorman Trucking—issue process to Sheriff.
2. Re: Mystrena v. GMC—Please bring in file for dictation covering Complaint.
3. Please locate map of S & F property and place on my desk.
4. Send form letter to bank on withdrawal from Edith Smith case.
5. Switch deposit ad to 5-1/4% ad in all papers for Anyville Savings.
6. Put in P to P call to Mr. Nicols of P.R.R. at 9:00 a.m. sharp.
7. Post October 13th for motion in Como vs. Black.

Most of these notes are prefaced with "please." Occasionally they sound a little too peremptory and I go back and insert "please." Even such a small item as this can have a salutary effect upon the celerity with which an instruction is carried out—and particularly the spirit in which it is done. Let your employees know that every act, every word of these memos is directed toward the common cause of insuring that the office is operating at a profit rather than a loss.

It was Bacon who said, "Reading maketh a *full* man—conference a *ready* man—and writing an *exact* man." Be sure that your instructions are *exact,* because they are going to be carried out in exactly and precisely the manner in which you have set them forth.

Financial Benefits from Use of Memos Immeasurable

If I were to attempt to catalogue all of the purely technical and strategic advantages the use of these written memos has gained me through the years, it would take a book several times the size of this volume. The financial benefits through their use have been literally immeasurable. By way of illustration: On numerous occasions we have succeeded in filing suit on behalf of our client *first,* in a two-car collision case. This has given us the distinct advantage of placing our client in the roll of the plaintiff instead of the counter-claimant. This in turn has carried with it the advantage of opening first and closing last to the jury. This in turn has frequently resulted in favorable verdicts in our favor where otherwise there would have been a "no cause" verdict or a standoff with both sides being denied verdicts.

Every busy lawyer is inclined to put off whatever he is able to, until a later date. Sometimes these matters are postponed a day or two longer than they should be. The result? His client comes into the office clutching the summons and complaint just served on him—when the reverse should have been the case. If you cannot dictate the complaint promptly, just write a memo which says in effect:

Jan. 1,

EW:

1. Be sure I dictate complaint in
   Pawlowski vs. White Construction Co.
   tomorrow A.M. sure.

2. Bring in your file early.

Using memos in this manner and for this purpose can definitely improve the office operation and increase the profit margins as well. *Just test it for a week!*

The Follow-up Schedule Serves as Tie-in

I have told you about deciding on a work schedule each morning from the typed up lists on your desk of work to be done. I have already outlined the effective use of 5 × 8 white bond pads—when you have the time and the opportunity for completing the short message or instruction on the spot—and when you have the pad immediately available to you. Now I would like to tell you of the connecting link which supplements and in fact ties these two processes together. We call it the "Follow-up Schedule."

I take a page from one of these canary yellow legal pads and with three folds I bring it down to where it presents four narrow, equal-size surfaces on each side. These sides are then used for one- or two-line memos or *reminders to myself*. Each fold will accommodate at least ten such memos or 40 to a side. In emergencies the opposite side will take 40 more, or a total of 80, on a single folded sheet!

I carry such a folded page with me always, usually in the inside pocket of my jacket whether it is a sport, casual or formal jacket. I concede that you may be considered slightly eccentric, if in the middle of a black-tie affair you surreptitiously pull a yellow folded sheet out of your jacket and furtively jot down one or two notes—but don't let that worry you. You may even be admired for your dedication to the obligations of your profession. If you worry about it, you may even do it in the men's room.

If you do not happen to be wearing a jacket, this page can be easily folded over to fit in either a vest or trouser pocket. I always put the date across the top of the page. Then I jot down on single or double lines memos or messages or reminders to myself, immediately as they penetrate my consciousness.

A Few Words Capture the Thought

I have found that unless you do it promptly—immediately—the thought or idea will vanish and escape you. Each line is given a number in chronological order, so that you may refer to them either in dictation or instructions by these individual numbers. No attempt is made to put them down in any special sequence or priority. There is time enough for that later. These lists are reserved for matters which cannot be disposed of or effectively assigned with a short memo on the 5 × 8 white pads or when none are available or near at hand. A single fold of my yellow sheet is usually adequate for the period from the closing of the office at 5:00 p.m. to the time it opens at 9:00 a.m. After all, ten line items can cover a lot of ground. But for weekends I usually use two, three or even four of these folds, since I write rather large. If the normal weekend includes a holiday, I sometimes find myself starting to use the reverse side as well. This usually means that the list by this time now exceeds 40 items.

Some skeptics may say no; but I say yes—if you lead a very active life. My interests usually fall into three broad or general categories—Professional, Public Interests, Personal—but the sorting out of these into priorities, categories, etc. does not have to be done by you. That is precisely why you have skilled, trained secretaries.

Sample of the Follow-up Schedule

As I write this chapter during a weekend at home, I have my "old reliable" folded yellow sheet in my pocket or near at hand. It already has a dozen items jotted on it. The dozen items will undoubtedly grow to 30 or 40 before Monday morning:

"Follow-Up Schedule"—April 4,

1. Send congratulations to retiring Judge.
2. Send attorney N.T.C. copy of first Will.
3. Follow-up on spare time secretary, Susan K.
4. Have medical expert examine Mrs. Jensen.
5. Notify Irene D. of trial date.
6. Have J.B. serve Order to Show Cause.
7. File Proof of Service with Clerk.
8. Set up appointment with F.C. re estate planning.
9. Post date for address to Historical Society.
10. Have J.B. research law on corporate dissolution.
11. Prepare Resolution for VFW.
12. Follow-up on opening shore home.

When I arrive at the office Monday morning, I will pull out the list and put it on my desk. The items listed will be checked rapidly. I may place an asterisk in the left hand margin for those items which must be taken care of immediately. I will not classify them into any particular categories. This will be done eventually by a trained secretary. Those marked with one asterisk will be disposed of as soon as the day's mail is segregated and dispatched and my work schedule for the day is decided upon.

Cancel Out Items on List as Completed

When the secretary or stenographer is summoned to come in, even before or immediately after the high priority items on my day's schedule have been dictated or otherwise been taken care of, I will take up with her the list of some of the 40 new items I have listed "on my follow-up schedule" and particularly those marked with an asterisk. Many of them can be disposed of quickly by writing the usual instructions on a 5 × 8 white sheet or by dictating a short instruction to the secretary which she will keep open and appropriately marked in her pad until completed. Other items can be disposed of by dictating memos to other members of the staff which are too long to be written in long hand, or will not fit on a 5 × 8 white sheet. Many or most of these will be disposed of that very morning or at least by that day's end. As each item on the list is taken care of by my dictation, I draw a heavy black line through that item obliterating it so it is no longer legible. It is a source of great pleasure and satisfaction to be able to strike out ten or 20 or more of these items so listed. We call this "clearing the deck" for more extended and laborious items requiring extensive time, research or preparation.

Remainder of Five Daily Follow-up Lists
Consolidated into Daily Schedules

Usually I bring to the office each day one of these *follow-up schedules*. Some may have no more than four or five items on them. Others may have up to 30, 40 or more. Each morning the new list is handled the same way with the objective to strike out as many as possible. The remaining items on the list of the day or days before are also quickly reviewed. Additional information may have come in enabling me to dispose of and strike out additional items. Thus at the end of the week there may be as many as five of these follow-up lists on my desk—all of them with a number of items still remaining undisposed of. These five lists are now turned over to a secretary with instructions to type up on flat yellow sheets captioned "Daily Work Schedule" and place on my desk for attention the following Monday morning.

Daily Schedule Constitutes Core of Important Substantial
Matters Which Are Likely Money Makers

As the process is repeated each week, these separate daily work schedules are before me to guide me on deciding the program for the day. No special priority is indicated. By a process of elimination, the remaining items on the Daily Work Schedule constitute items which cannot be disposed of by simple memoranda; this means that they require more legal research or preliminary discussion or consideration before they can be attacked and disposed of.

These items constitute the hard core of matters of substance which would require perhaps an hour or more of concentrated review of files and extensive dictation. Usually, they constitute the more important matters in the office —the ones where substantial fees can be earned and collected. Thus by the process of "clearing the deck" for action, we now have a list of items before us, *all of top priority*. They are not only the ones demanding prompt or immediate action, but they are also the cases which will guarantee the build-up of a $100,000 law practice. You cannot afford to ignore them or shunt them aside. They will remain on this flat yellow sheet on your desk until they are disposed of. The pleasure of striking out the smaller and simpler items on the follow-up schedules is nothing compared to the down-right joy you will experience in striking out and obliterating the larger items on this daily work schedule and collect the fees earned!

Recent Readers Digest Article Endorses Similar Program

Recently the *Readers Digest* published an article entitled ''The ABCs of Saving Time—or How to Get Control of Your Time and Your Life.'' It was a digest or condensation of part of a full length book written by a professional efficiency expert. He called for the preparation in the office of ''To Do Lists'' and of assigning A-B-C priorities to each of the items listed. The author reported that interviews with successful men and women clearly established that most of them attributed most of their success and particularly their ability to get so much done in so many various fields of endeavor in such limited time available, to the preparation and maintenance of the so-called ''To Do Lists.''

The *Digest* thought so much of the simple ideas discussed in the article that they not only published it in a regular issue for their 25 million to 30 million world-wide circulation—but actually offered *reprints in quantities* for those who wished them. I respectfully submit that my system is far simpler and far superior from the name of the list down to the results accomplished. Besides, my ''follow-up list'' has a built-in method of ''clearing the deck'' for action by disposing of short simple matters and thus automatically establishing priorities for the far more important and profitable matters to be included in the ''daily work schedule.'' In my book, every item on the daily, weekly and monthly work schedule *has a priority until it is done*.

Chapter 5

HOW TO SELECT YOUR CLIENTS—
DON'T LET THEM SELECT YOU

Weed Out the Weak Cases Early . . . Be Diplomatic and Compassionate with Every Client . . . Every Client Deserves Understanding and Empathy . . . See the Client Promptly and Make Him Welcome . . . When You Withdraw from a Case, Always Do It Gracefully and Regretfully . . . Scrutinize the Case Some Other Attorney Wants to "Refer" to You . . . The Type of Cases Which Are Usually Money-Losers . . . Give the Client the Best You Have . . . "With All the Help the Law Allows" . . . Trunk Sewer Line in Valley Leads to Eminant Domain Case–Chain Reaction Leads to String of Eminent Domain Cases . . . Every Client's Property Was Unique . . . Your Best Advertisement Is a Satisfied Client . . . The Power of Word-of-Mouth Recommendation . . . How to Process an Estate, So as to Attract Other Estate Business . . . Make Yourself Indispensable to Your Client . . . The Fate of Some Clients Who Ignored Advice . . . The New Product with No Pilot Plant . . . The Legal-Engineering Advice that Saved $50,000 and Earned a Good Fee . . . How to Save a Client $30,000 and Earn a Good Fee . . . Consolidate a Hard-Core of Desirable Clients . . . Select Good Clients–Charge Them Only in Proportion to the Good You Do Them

Weed Out the Weak Cases Early

This chapter title may sound a little unrealistic to the young lawyer just starting out—and it probably is. Initially, the newly-admitted practitioner may take practically anything that comes along—and usually does. He considers it a matter of self-preservation and perhaps an opportunity to gain experience. Both are admittedly laudatory objectives. The difficulty is that the public are also usually aware of the inclination. With this thought in mind, they sometimes "shop around" to secure the services of the attorney who they believe will do the job at the lowest price. Other clients come to him because they are relatives and expect a substantial discount. Others come with worthless claims. Still others with claims so complex and troublesome that no other attorney wants to handle them. Thus, the average lawyer starts off with a group of clients and cases which almost foredoom him to economic, if not professional, failure. The trick is to weed these cases out as diplomatically, but as effectively and above all, as promptly as possible. Johnson is quoted as saying in effect, "No one but a blockhead writes except for money." I would paraphrase this to read, "Only a blockhead (or an idealist) practices law except for money."

Be Diplomatic and Compassionate with Every Client

But it is to be borne in mind that it is the cases which are undesirable and not the clients. The clients and the potential clients are to be cultivated assiduously. The undesirable cases are to be shunned whenever and wherever possible. As the evangelist says, "You hate the sin, but not the sinner." A client with a poor case may have a $50,000 or $75,000 personal injury case in his family the next week, or the next year, or someone in his family may inherit a substantial estate. In any event, the client himself may gain sufficient affluence to buy a home or a tavern or engage in some other occupation or enterprise which might be productive of an attractive and worthwhile fee. Therefore, it is always well to bear in mind that if you want to succeed in any line of business, politics, or the professions, "no one is so insignificant that you can afford to have him for an enemy." Putting it another way, a friend turned enemy is the worst kind; he works harder at it and more intently.

A lawyer occupies a somewhat unique position in the everyday lives of most people. Like the doctor, he is something of the father image. He is a recognized leader in the civil, social and political life of the community. Moreover, he is, or at least should be, a paragon of civic virtue. But more important still, he is a "Counselor" first and an "Advocate" second. His counseling is to help his clients avoid the pitfalls that might otherwise befall them. He is the advocate dedicated to extricating them from such dilemmas as their foibles and other misjudgments may have led them into.

Every Client Deserves Understanding and Emphathy

When a client calls on a lawyer, the client is usually in trouble. His mortgage is being foreclosed; someone has defrauded him; he has suffered a fire loss; his child has been struck by a car; he has struck someone with his car; his son has been arrested; the Government is threatening to sue him for tax evasion; his wife is divorcing him; etc., etc. The list is endless. With this type of menace and tragedy pending, is it any wonder that he enters the law office with a sense of fear and trepidation? It is the lawyer's task to help him—and so the help should begin the minute he enters the office.

There is nothing more exasperating than to go into an office and find that as you enter it, all of the office staff suddenly get interested in files, or arrange their desk, or consult their records. Invariably, they seem to turn their backs on you as you enter in order to consult each other. Don't let this happen in your law office. Have your staff greet a prospective client with courtesy and solicitude. Next have them inquire as to the purpose of the visit and make him comfortable with a feeling that he is welcome and should feel at home until the attorney can see him.

See the Client Promptly and Make Him Welcome

When the lawyer does see a client, it should be as promptly as possible. I once was kept waiting in an office while the person I came to see dictated letters, phoned his broker, and talked to his associate about a prize fight they had been to the night before. This attitude is an invitation to failure. Always remember this "desk-side manner" is extremely important. So, have your secretary usher in the client promptly. Invite him to sit down and be comfortable while he tells you his story. Be encouraging and evince solicitude for his welfare from the very beginning. Start out with some such greeting as "So, what is your problem—I hope it's not too serious.", or "Now, what can I do for you?"

And when the client tells you his story, listen—even though you may not intend to take the case. This man is here because he needs help. He's picked you because he has faith and confidence in you. He needs sympathy and understanding. Even if you eventually don't take the case—the few minutes it takes to listen may pay large dividends later. If the case looks reasonably attractive, have him sign a conditional retainer. If it looks questionable, tell him you will have to think it over and advise him by letter promptly. If the case looks utterly hopeless, tell him that you are sorry that you cannot help him. There are many ways of saying "no." The gentle, kindly, considerate method is always preferable, and costs no more than the brusque, curt, brush-off. Better still, refer him to some other attorney who needs the business more than you do.

When You Withdraw from a Case, Always Do It
Gracefully and Regretfully

Here is an illustration of the letter we have used effectively for years. We call it the "bowing out gracefully letter." It reads as follows:

Dear Friend:

We have given careful and personal consideration to the above matter which you would like us to handle for you.

We regret to advise that at the present time we have so many other cases already pending in the office that we are afraid we would not be able to give your matter the proper time and attention which it would require and which it undoubtedly deserves.

Under the circumstances we simply could not undertake this additional work and do full justice to it. We are, therefore, giving you this formal notice in order to afford you ample opportunity of retaining some other attorney to represent you in this case.

Trusting that at some other time we may be in a better position to serve you, and with every good wish for success, we remain,

Faithfully yours,

Scrutinize the Case Some Other Attorney
Wants to "Refer" to You

Long ago, I had an older lawyer teach me a bitter lesson I never forgot. He was a prominent, distinguished, and very able lawyer with a heavy practice in an adjacent community. He did the kindness of referring a case to me involving a local family in my own town. The case involved minors, seduction, incest, illegitimacy, etc., etc. I should have suspected from the start that it was a "lemon." Instead, I was naive enough to assume that my esteemed contemporary found that he was too busy to handle this important case; had implicit confidence in my ability; and had thus entrusted the case to my care to be sure I won it. I won it all right, but at the cost of alienating a family that was prolific enough to have relatives and in-laws in every section of the community and wide sections of the county as well. I once figured out that the $500 fee paid me eventually cost me, in good will, approximately $25,000 in fees I would have earned otherwise. Later, this aging Counselor advised me—"It's the cases that you don't take, rather than the cases that you do take, that determine your success as a lawyer." To this, I say, "Amen."

The Type of Cases Which Are Usually Money-Losers

From this bitter experience, I learned that there are specific groups of cases to avoid at all costs, unless you are desperate and need the fees to survive, until a good case comes along. Here are some of them:

1. Paternity Cases—unless the parties are wealthy.
2. Commercial collection cases.
3. The average marital dispute.
4. Private boundary line disputes.
5. Cases involving complex state and federal bureaucratic red tape.

Sound reasons for rejection of a paternity case are too obvious to need elaborate explanation. Both sides will hate you whether you win or lose. Such cases are charged with too much emotion and usually pay poorly. Commercial collection cases are usually not much better. The percentages fixed by the forwarders are usually low, and pursuing these claims frequently engenders bitterness as well. Frequently, there are counter-claims based upon a failure of consideration, inferior merchandise, erroneous bookkeeping, or downright fraud. The claimant is usually a nonresident while the defendant is a resident. In large cities, where the defendant is a hard-bitten shopkeeper or a businessman and the volume is large and the amounts of claims are substantial, it may be all right to handle this type of legal work for a while to help pay the rent and office overhead. My advice is to let collection agencies handle the smaller items for you for your own peace of mind and so that your time and talent and energy can be applied to more profitable and attractive work.

Marital disputes usually fall into two categories roughly. One is where the parties are engaged in one of their habitual spats. They do not want a divorce—or even a separation. If you take either side, you will be wrong —because there is bound to be a reconciliation within a day, a week, or a month at the most. Moreover, you will probably not be paid, and both sides will condemn you. The other type is the cleancut, matter-of-fact, businesslike divorce where both parties conceive that they made a mistake and would like to get out from under as soon as possible, with the least acrimony and recrimination. This last type can be handled profitably. The first type should be avoided at all costs.

Boundary line cases are usually "tempests in a teapot." The value of the land in dispute may be negligible. The cost of litigation may very well exceed the value of the land in dispute many times over. I suggest that you recommend that both sides hire their own surveyor and work out the settlement of the dispute themselves. Assure them that you will gladly draw up the deeds of exchange when the matter is amicably settled.

I do not want to specify any particular state or federal bureaus whose bureaucratic red tape should persuade you to avoid them. They vary from area to area. Some of them are well-known to the average practitioner. Unless you have a substantial volume of practice and can process a half dozen or more claims simultaneously, this type of claim can constitute a net loss to the average office. Hence, the average lawyer would be well advised to avoid them unless the amounts involved are so substantial as to make the handling of them clearly worthwhile based upon the anticipated fee.

Give the Client the Best You Have

Thus far the tenor of this chapter has been more or less negative when it might have been positive. The only way to be able to select your clients rather than have them select you is to give them a little more dedication, a little more devotion, a little more service and a little more results than any other attorney that they have ever had before. Do this and these clients are yours for life, as well as "their heirs, executors, administrators, precessors and assigns forever."

It is a simple rule and yet it is absolutely basic. These are the things that clients dream of and crave. When they receive them, full measure, pressed down and running over, their natural response is loyalty. By this type of service to a client, I do not mean to imply in the slightest degree that the attorney would do anything improper, unethical or illegal. I mean only that you give your clients the best you have to offer—every last ounce of dedication, devotion and loyalty you are able to render them within the spirit and the letter of the law. This is what they retained you for and this is what they are entitled to.

"With All the Help the Law Allows"

Just as Senator Arthur Vandenberg once gave a gift to his secretary with this felicitous note annexed, "With all the affection the law allows."—you give to your clients "all the dedication the law allows." If you do this, you won't have to worry about losing your client; you will have the client worried about losing you.

I have used this system consistently with valuable clients; clients who I believed were worthy, deserving people who needed my services, were able to pay for them and most important of all, *were willing to pay* for them to the full extent of their fair and reasonable value. Some attorneys may discount this method by asserting that they are lawyers only, that they do not make policy, and that hence, their services should be limited to the legal aspect of the questions only. My answer to this is that there is scarcely a facet of life today which does not have legal overtones, legal highlights or legal consequences. These factors alone justify an attorney in contributing his aid in the solution of any problem which involves any of these legal aspects.

Trunk Sewer Line in Valley Leads to Eminent Domain Case—
Chain Reaction Leads to String of Eminent Domain Cases

An illustration I can cite is a case where a trunk sewer line was going through the valley. They needed a 100-foot right of way. Purchase of most of the small parcels was negotiated, but when it came to the larger parcels, it was not so easy—since the valley was dotted with brickyards and sand, clay and gravel pits. Since I was already doing legal work for the owners of one such tract, I was assigned the task of handling the first substantial condemnation case involved, almost automatically. I always believed it was *how* I handled that one case that started the chain of events. I gave my clients the type of service I have described. The result was an excellent settlement which was highly gratifying to them. I had accepted the job on what I considered a fair and reasonable fee. I advised my clients in substance to have the Authority make the top dollar offer they were willing to make and that I would then handle the case on a one-third contingency on whatever I could obtain for the owner over and above the last top-dollar offer.

Through some quirk of fate, the offer was low. The Authority was adamant. They apparently expected that their offer would be rejected and they wanted some leverage for bargaining. The case was finally completed. The price they paid was roughly $96,000 more than their top offer. Since my fee was one-third of the money obtained, my office earned a $32,000 fee, but this was just a starter. The property owners recommended me to the property owners on either side of them. A chain reaction was started and before it stopped, our office represented practically every large property owner in the valley and each case was handled on the same terms.

It seemed that each of the succeeding properties involved was larger than the one which preceeded it. By degrees we did indeed become specialists in the field of Eminent Domain. Normally, there are three standards of appraisal to go by:

(a) Fair Market Value—based on comparable sales.
(b) Reproduction cost less Obsolescence and Depreciation.
(c) Capitalized Income Approach.

The most frequently used one is the Fair Market Value and this is usually considered binding although the price may fluctuate moderately. There is a single important exception to even the Fair Market Value, i.e., if you can prove that your property is *unique* (irreplaceable), in such instances, you are not bound by the Fair Market Value. Strange as it may seem, in all of our cases, the property was *unique*. If you have any doubts, just ask the owners.

Every Client's Property Was Unique

There is another rule that if you claim uniqueness, because of underlying minerals, such as clay, sand, gravel, stone, etc., you may *not* introduce evidence of the estimated quantities of these deposits as they are determined by borings as part of your damages. But there was no rule or court decision that said that you could not show these astronomical quantities as proof that this property was indeed *unique, and its actual market value increased proportionately*. In this manner we were able to assist the expert appraisers in estimating the amount by which the Market Value was increased by virtue of these large quantities of mineral deposits. The expert witnesses—the appraisals, etc.—may have been, and indeed were, thoretical and hypothetical, but nevertheless, in less than a year, fees from these condemnation cases alone reached the magic figure of $100,000 (that is before overhead and taxes). This may sound like an isolated situation, but there are many similar or analogous opportunities merely waiting to be discovered by the alert lawyer who is prepared to recognize an opportunity and exploit it to the fullest extent.

Your Best Advertisement Is a Satisfied Client

These illustrations are not given in any spirit of boasting, but merely to show how a wide-awake lawyer can take advantage of special situations, developments, and public improvements, in his area. Such opportunities are numerous.

The alert attorney who capitalizes on them by giving dedicated service to his client, just a little bit better than the client expected or could have obtained elsewhere, can profit by them. It is true (as of this writing) that lawyers are barred from advertising by virtue of their own self-imposed Canons of Ethics, but the best advertisement a lawyer can develop or project is a satisfied client.

Modesty is not one of the usual characteristics of any lawyer. I have met relatively few who could really qualify. Some feigned it—but it fooled no one. In a strange city, my wife had an intuitive feeling that she could recognize an attorney almost anywhere, and this was not due to his innate modesty. Attempts at false modesty sometimes are an indication of the exact opposite. If you have done a good job for a client, you have a right to be proud of it and to let the client know you are proud of it. Perhaps some of your pride and enthusiasm will rub off on him, and he may in turn pass it on to a relative or friend.

The Power of Word-of-Mouth Recommendation

All of this leads up to this point: The beauty of finding a good, well-to-do client whom you are able to serve efficiently and profitably is that this can, and usually does, lead to other clients of the same or similar type. This is what I mean by selecting your clients rather than have them select you. Each of the clients we had acquired in this manner, through the condemnation cases, led to others. In most cases, they were of the well-to-do caliber with corporate, estate and investment problems. The eventual results on our practice and our profits were foreshadowed, and foreseen and indeed guaranteed.

How to Process an Estate, So as to
Attract Other Estate Business

By way of illustration, the corporation whose land holdings were most adversely affected by the 100-foot right of way became a permanent corporate client. Most of the officers and directors also became clients of the office. We were invited to join the Board of Directors but had to decline because of a possible conflict of interests with competing clients. When the founder of the company died, we were retained to handle the estate, even though the will had been drawn in another office. Once again, we introduced some special services. By eliminating some of the pro-forma red tape; eliminating unnecessary appraisals and inventories, using a stipulated informal final accounting, instead of going through the formality of a court procedure, we were able to close out the entire estate in nine months or in one-half of the time period permitted by the statutes and rules of court.

The fact that all of the beneficiaries were adults contributed to this happy end-result. Each of the beneficiaries as he signed his final Refunding Bond and Release to the Executors of the Estate, and received his rather substantial check representing his net share of the residuary estate, became a fast friend, a booster for the office, and a potential client. In fact, our office receipts were augmented through one such estate, by a fee that approximated 25 percent of the target of $100,000 which we were shooting for at that time.

The death of the founder's wife followed shortly. Then the wife of the Secretary-Treasurer of the Corporation. Next his aunt, his uncle and his sister all passed on. This office inherited a backlog of desirable estate work directly traceable to the first estate we had handled so efficiently and satisfactorily. Since there were no minors involved in any of the estates, we were again able to handle each of the estates in the same, simple, expeditious manner as we had handled the first one, with the same advantageous side effects.

Still later, the corporation owned by this founder decided to sell out all of its holdings in separate parcels. We became counsel for the company in each of these sales. Still later, the company decided to liquidate and to distribute its assets to all of its remaining stockholders. Once again, our office became co-counsel. Each of these proceedings brought in an attractive fee and contributed substantially to the office income which by this time had long since reached and passed the magic mark of $100,000.

Make Yourself Indispensable to Your Client

I have sometimes observed a lawyer permitting a client to take a false or dangerous step in a business matter which could be treacherous, if not disastrous. I have inquired, ''Why don't you warn them of the potential dangers involved?'' and they usually respond, ''I am a lawyer, not a business executive or a tax expert. I don't inject myself into other people's business. I have been retained to offer legal advice only. My job is to tell them what the law is.'' If there is one thing I most heartily disagree with, it is this impersonal attitude toward a client. The real secret in selecting your clients is to give them everything you've got, if you are able to contribute something constructive to the solution of their problems and particularly if it has legal overtones, as most of them do.

Sometimes a client is too close to the problem to envision it impersonally and you can do it for him. You owe it to him. Usually, he will not resent it. He will welcome it. If he is the ''prima donna'' type, who resents good, sound, logical advice when it is offered to him, then you wouldn't want him for a client in the first place, because he is doomed to failure from the start and you are doomed to poor fees or no fees. Only an intelligent, progressive, successful and satisfied client will pay good fees. Thus, I recommend that you make yourself *practically indispensable* to your client in the solution of his problems. He'll not only love you for it but he will pay you well for it. Sometimes a client even sends a "fan letter" of appreciation when he sends his check to cover fees!

The Fate of Some Clients Who Ignored Advice

I once served as counsel for a large corporation. I learned that a tract of 120 acres of land with valuable sand and clay deposits lying adjacent to this client's land could be acquired for $1,000 an acre or $120,000. I wrote to the president of the company, with a copy to each of the directors recommending that it should be purchased at once even if they had to borrow the money. The president and engineer held a hurried conference. They were fearful of zoning regulations, of setback lines, of taxes to be paid on idle lands, etc. They stayed up most of the night preparing an adverse report to the Board recommending that the tract should not be purchased. A few years later, the persons who did buy the tract took about one-quarter of a million dollars of sand off the surface along and then sold the tract at $8,000 an acre. It pains me to tell you what happened eventually to the first company. But the company that actually bought it is now in the multimillion-dollar class and one of the soundest enterprises in the area. Incidentally, we now serve as counsel for this company.

The New Product with No Pilot Plant

Another corporate client was about to launch into a new enterprise. They had the land and the buildings. It was a new and untried product. Their technical advisors assured everyone that the material could be manufactured at $2.95 a ton; that 200,000 tons could be manufactured annually. This could be sold at $3.95 a ton for a net profit of $200,000 per annum on this one product alone. I was only a lawyer serving as counsel, but as I heard these reports on this project, I could not help but have grave doubts about its success.

The project seemed too roseate to be true. I pointed out that there had not been sufficient research and that the process had never been tried on a commercial basis; that it could create nuisances which might result in expensive litigation, etc., etc. This last point was my excuse for contributing my views on the subject. The investment was to be approximately one million dollars. I suggested that the proper course would be to invest $100,000 in a pilot plant before rushing into the project. My suggestions were ignored.

One day when I missed attendance at a board meeting, they had a demonstration of the new product being made with an oversized grill, costing less than $100. The decision to go ahead with the construction of the plant, based upon this demonstration, was approved; and a most illogical site was selected. The plant was eventually constructed and placed in operation, but unfortunately, every prediction I made came true. The product it produced was good, and finally commanded a price on the market of $8.95 a ton, but it cost $9.95 a ton to produce. There were nuisances galore and litigation galore and the project was eventually abandoned and the plant torn down, which, incidentally, cost twice the original estimate.

The Legal/Engineering Advice that Saved $50,000 and Earned a Good Fee

Another illustration: I once represented a company that sold a large site for a multi-million-dollar factory. Estimates had been compiled covering site preparation, road construction, utilities, including storm drain, etc. Because of a slight change in the terrain made by the purchasers through artificial fill, this resulted in blockage of some of the natural water courses or ditches resulting in a serious drainage problem. At one time, this even threatened to undermine large buildings and jeopardize millions of dollars of investments. The purchasers threatened to sue our clients for all damages.

I consulted with our clients who were familar with the terrain. They expressed the opinion that these water courses had carried much of the run-off in a northwesterly and northerly direction to a nearby creek and eventually to the river. They were certain that a filling in of these courses caused the blockage to arise and that their re-opening would be the solution. Various engineers representing the buyers, the builders, and the various sub-contractors took an opposite position. They were adamant. They expressed the opinion that the flow of this water should be due south for a considerable distance and thence due west—all at my client's expense. There was an impasse. The structures were in danger. Approximately $50,000 of additional expense on the part of my client was involved.

I retained the service of an independent hydraulic engineer. I took two or more hours to go over the grounds with him on foot. Based upon his observations, I wrote a seven-page comprehensive opinion. The report concluded with the statement that unless the buyers opened the water courses and led the waters directly west and north, our clients would hold them responsible for any and all damages. The secret of this solution was that I knew the terrain from boyhood, and my common sense told me that with a river to the north and a creek to the west, the drainage certainly had to lead in that direction and not due south. Eventually, the buyers agreed that our hydraulic engineers were right. The $50,000 was saved and our clients were happy to pay us a fee of $5,000.

How to Save a Client $23,000 and Earn a Good Fee

Another illustration—a tavern owner once called upon me and advised that he was thinking of open-listing it and advertising it for sale. I inquired as to the asking price and was advised that he thought "$70,000 was about right." Now, any selling broker would rightfully charge 10 percent, leaving the owner with $63,000 net and we would have earned $700 closing fees, maximum. From past experiences and from handling similar transactions in the area, I knew the place could bring in at least $95,000 at a private sale and I told him so. In fact, I knew several clients who were prospects, in the market for just such a place. I gave him their names. Eventually, one of them bought the property for $93,000. My client had saved $23,000. Instead of the $700 closing fees, we billed him for a very substantial fee and he paid it gladly.

Consolidate a Hard-Core of Desirable Clients

In summary, I would like to suggest that the secret of success in practice is to avoid the money-losers at the very start. Don't accept them. If you have made the mistake of getting into them, get out of them promptly. Withdraw completely if the case seems hopeless or worthless. Give them to some young lawyer with more time available for the case. Eventually, you will consolidate your clients into a hard-core of worthwhile clients who have the ability and willingness to compensate you properly. Give these chosen people the best you have to offer!

Select Good Clients—Charge Them Only in Proportion to the Good You Do Them

There is a very old saying that the real secret of wealth is to get a great many people contributing even a small amount of money to you regularly. This is the underlying theory of huge food and other chain stores whose profits seem low compared to their gross receipts. This rule does not apply to private practices, particularly law. I have found that in the field of law it is much better to cultivate good clients with real problems, who can afford to pay you a substantial fee. However, always be sure you charge in accordance with the good you are able to do them. In this manner, you will be selecting your clients and you will not be letting them select you.

Chapter 6

HOW TO PREPARE A CASE
SO IT WON'T BE LOST

No. 1 Rule for Winning . . . The Six Tests of a Sound Case . . . Three Reasons for Getting a Comprehensive Statement Signed . . . The Blueprint for Proper Preparation . . . Outline of Steps to Be Taken in Every Negligence Suit Before Suit Is Instituted . . . The Police Report and the Investigating Officer . . . Get Official Driving Records of Each Party . . . Photographer and Surveyor on Site Within an Hour . . . Another Case: Dirty Windshield and Thrown Boots . . . Locating the Witness and "Nailing" Him Down . . . A Simple Technique for Getting Signed Statements . . . How to Prove Liability When Your Client's Emergency Police Car Runs into Another Vehicle . . . Covering the Neighborhood for "Sights and Sounds" . . . One Picture Is Worth 10,000 Words . . . How to Establish Negligence Against a Driver of a First Aid Ambulance . . . Photographs Do It . . . Photographs of Scenes and Cars Essential . . . Getting What You Need from the Attending Physician . . . Furnish Attending Physician with Your Own Report Form . . . The Shy and Retiring GP . . . Bring in the Specialists if You Need Them . . . Is the Driver Insured or Financially Responsible? . . . Obtain Experts in Other Fields . . . Aerial Photographs Can Help . . . The Trial Brief and Request to Charge . . . Prepare Them to Try Them!

No. 1 Rule for Winning

An old-time practitioner and one of the best in his field, once told me that the No. 1 rule for winning a case—any case—was preparation and *more preparation.* It sounds simple. It can be and should be simple—but the trick is to follow the rule. You must do it assiduously, indefatigably, religiously. If you do so, the case will be won. If you fail to do so, in all probability, the case will be lost or settled at a fraction of its true worth. This rule is as inexorable as death itself.

The Six Tests of a Sound Case

My first recommendation is that you analyze each case carefully as it comes in. If possible, see the client personally and conduct the initial interview yourself. There is no better way to evaluate a case than to see the client face to face; hear his story; explore the weak points as well as the strong points; test him with a little cross-examination on the crucial points.

This procedure will put you in a sound position to determine; (1) do I have a case?; (2) will the evidence hold up in court?; (3) will the client make a good impression on the judge and jury?; (4) is the liability strong enough to win?; (5) are the plaintiff's injuries serious enough to warrant a substantial recovery?; (6) is the defendant financially responsible and able to pay a substantial judgment?

Three Reasons for Getting a Comprehensive Statement Signed

If you get favorable responses to these six questions, have the retainer signed promptly. At the same time, have the plaintiff or the plaintiff's spouse sign the Authorization to Obtain Medical Data and a similar one for wage losses. While you are interviewing the client, evaluate the case and appraise the prospects of a substantial recovery. Do it thoroughly, but don't attempt to write down everything that is said at the first interview. Sometimes it pays to have the interview tape-recorded and have a stenographer transcribe it. However, this is time-consuming and frequently time-wasting.

I have found it is satisfactory just to jot down the high spots. *Who, what, when, where, why* and *how* are still the key questions in listing all the facts. Then, after the client has left, call in a secretary and dictate a complete resume of the case in the form of a "statement by the plaintiff." Have it typed up and mail an original and copy to the plaintiff for review. Ask him to check it, correct it if necessary directly on the original, sign it and then mail back the original, retaining the copy for his personal records. Provide a self-addressed, stamped envelope to insure its return.

In this manner, you have accomplished several significant things in one operation by; (a) committing the interview to writing; (b) converting it into a statement upon which you can rely in the further handling of the case; (c) forming a basis for refreshing the client's memory several years later when the case is reached for trial.

The Blueprint for Proper Preparation

Now that the die is cast, the intense preparation must begin; not tomorrow, not next week, or next month—but now—*today*! To guarantee that each step is done properly and promptly, we analyze each case to determine the best method, to determine the facts and how to prove them.

The following is a typical list which is more or less standard for personal injury cases. Similar ones are prepared for each type of case:

OUTLINE OF STEPS TO BE TAKEN IN EVERY
NEGLIGENCE SUIT BEFORE SUIT IS INSTITUTED

1. Take plaintiff's statement of the case in detail.
2. Have plaintiff sign retainer (with usual conditions).
3. Have plaintiff sign authorization to obtain hospital data.
4. Have plaintiff sign authorization to obtain medical data.
5. Have plaintiff sign authorization to obtain wage data.
6. Obtain copy of Police Report by paying requisite fee.
7. Interview police officer who investigated case—promptly.
8. Contact Motor Vehicle Department to verify registration, driver's license and ownership of cars involved.
8a. Locate and preserve all demonstrative evidence available.
9. Make a list of all known witnesses and interview *promptly*.
10. Visit scene of accident so witnesses statements will be clear.
11. Canvas neighborhood of accident carefully to locate additional witnesses.
12. Order or take photographs of cars (professional size—not snapshots).

13. Order or take photographs of scene of accident.

14. Visit hospital for copy of its records.

15. Write attending physician for report and request information be treated as confidential.

16. Write all consulting physicians for copies of their reports.

17. Investigate insurance or financial responsibility of defendant.

18. Write U.S. Weather Bureau re weather and lighting.

19. Order survey by licensed surveyor—with colored map for court use.

20. Arrange to retain experts in all fields involved.

21. Get aerial map of location when distance, sound, smell, etc., is important.

22. Have charts prepared showing difficult computations.

AFTER SUIT HAS BEEN INSTITUTED

1. Propound interrogatories on all defendants.

2. Serve Demand for Admissions (where appropriate).

3. Take depositions of parties (and selected witnesses).

4. Prepare medical brief.

5. Prepare trial brief.

6. Prepare request to charge.

7. Prepare settlement brochure with final demand.

The Police Report and the Investigating Officer

You will note that you have already taken care of items 2 to 5 at the initial interview. The claimant's statement you may anticipate shortly. Since the insurance carrier usually starts out with a police report, we do so likewise. Today, most police departments furnish a copy of a report designed by the state motor vehicle department, at a nominal fee. The report will indicate most of the facts required including time; place; condition of weather; of the roadway; speed of vehicles; skidmarks, etc. It will also give a history of the owner, driver, passengers, etc. Some of these reports even include rather detailed sketches with measurements of the final location of the vehicles to certain fixed objects. Still others include brief statements of both drivers; lists of injured persons and sometimes even lists of witnesses.

All of this material can be extremely helpful. As "leads" in the investigation and preparation of the case it is absolutely indispensable. The key man to see is the investigating officer. Interview him at once. He may resist being questioned and refer you to his reports. But don't let this dissuade you or your representative. There may very well be additional information in his possession which can be helpful. If more than one officer participated, interview them all. Usually the officers will not give you a signed statement so it is futile to attempt to secure one. In fact, it might be harmful to press the point. You can prepare your own statement of what they said when you get back to your office.

Get Official Driving Records of Each Party

While the police report will furnish the names and addresses of the owners and drivers of the respective vehicles, it is still advisable to verify this data. A simple inquiry to the State Motor Vehicle Department or similar agency will suffice. I would also recommend that you get a certified copy of the driving record of each party. These records are not competent evidence in themselves. However, they can be extremely helpful when, by way of illustration, you are taking the deposition of a driver and he knows that you have his official traffic record showing one-half dozen traffic convictions ranging from speeding to running a stop-street sign. While you are about it, get your own client's driving record as well. You may find it equally interesting.

If the injuries are sufficiently severe to disable the plaintiff and he has been admitted to the hospital for treatment, some of your investigative procedure may not necessarily follow in the chronological order given. If you have been called into the case by relatives or close friends shortly after the accident occurred, an immediate visit to the scene of the accident can be far more productive of valuable demonstrative evidence than a visit to the hospital.

Photographer and Surveyor on Site Within an Hour

By way of illustration, we were retained by telephone shortly after a boy of 10 or 12 was struck by a car while crossing the street near his home at 3:30 p.m. on his way home from school. As soon as the caller hung up, we phoned a local photographer and engineer, or land surveyor. Within an hour they were both on the scene. Skidmarks cut in the highway were clearly visible although it was a heavily-traveled street. Skidmarks made by the left wheel were 75 feet long while those made by the right rear wheel were less than 60 feet in length. They led directly up to the painted crosswalk and stopped. This demonstrative evidence was not only photographed within one hour of the accident and while there was still sufficient daylight to accomplish it, but the skidmarks were measured by the local engineer and land surveyor and recorded in his field book for later charting by him on a map of the scene. These items were almost conclusive in establishing; (a) that the boy was indeed on the cross-walk; (b) that the car was traveling at an excessive rate of speed, and; (c) that it had defective brakes.

Another Case: Dirty Windshield and Thrown Boots

Another case involved a fatal accident in which a farmer was struck and fatally injured as he was crossing the highway near midnight on his way home on foot from a nearby village. A slight rain was falling and the roadways were muddy. We were not called into this case until the next morning. There was still time to have our investigator inspect the site and the car, and interview the ambulance driver and Coroner.

The site established that the farmer was crossing at a low spot or a "dip" on the highway. At this point, the highway had alternately high and low spots with undulating rises and falls. As a result, it appeared that the car was also apparently in an adjacent low spot immediately north of the scene of the accident. Thus, the decedent did not see the driver's headlights and the driver's headlights did not pick up the figure of the farmer crossing the street until it was too late.

But more important still, an inspection of the defendant's car at his home by the police on the next morning revealed that the windshield was so dirty as to make visibility difficult, if not impossible. And a test of the windshield wipers showed that they were not operative. Moreover, the ambulance driver stated that the body had been thrown more than 20 feet at the time of the impact. It was also ascertained that the decedent's boots were found some 20 feet beyond the body. It was an isolated section and there were no eye witnesses. But even without any eye witness, we were able to secure a favorable verdict with the circumstantial evidence we had managed to locate and preserve. Liability was based on; (a) poor visibility due to terrain; (b) dirty windshield; (c) inoperative wipers, and; (d) excessive speed in view of the time, place, and circumstances as evidenced by the thrown body and thrown boots.

Locating the Witness and "Nailing" Him Down

Next in order is locating any witnesses and interviewing them promptly. This is not always an easy task. Witnesses are a strange breed indeed. While some are willing and anxious to help, others are not only reticent but in some cases, invisible and unable to locate for interview. Some can be persuaded to talk; others become even more taciturn and reluctant if they are pressed. And there are still others who may become actually hostile.

Unfortunately, it is the responsibility of the lawyer or his representative to locate these witnesses and ascertain what they know about the case. If they solemnly declare that they saw nothing and know nothing about the case, this factor at least eliminates them from the picture.

It is the surprise witness whom you have not located; one who you did not know existed, who can destroy your case. Be sure you locate him. Enlist him in your cause if the facts warrant it—or at least interview him and neutralize him by his denial of any knowledge of the case. Only then can you be sure that he will not appear with evidence that might demolish your theory of the case and result in your client's case being thrown out of court.

A Simple Technique for Getting Signed Statements

We have developed a novel technique for the handling of witnesses which has proved quite helpful. Its only novelty lies in its simplicity. We mail them a brief, simple form and ask them to fill it in and return to us. We deliberately avoid the so-called legal cap or legal size paper, heavily embossed legal stationery, etc. Instead, we use the plainest type of imprinted stationery and envelopes and it seems to disarm them. Here is the form on *plain paper*.

WITNESS STATEMENT

RECORD OF ACCIDENT

We will greatly appreciate it if you will answer each question fully, and return to us.

Did you see the accident?_____

Where did it occur? (Streets)_____

Give position of cars after accident. _____

_____

Was anyone injured? Who?_____

Did you see any damage to automobiles?_____

Please give full account of accident as witnessed by you. _____

_____

_____

_____

WITNESS STATEMENT
RECORD OF ACCIDENT
(Continued)

Who do you think was to blame for the accident? _____

_____

WHY? _____

Please give the names (and addresses, if possible) of any other persons who witnessed the accident. _____

_____

What is your full name and address? _____

_____

_____

Dated: _____

      Admittedly, it is far from perfect. The conclusion of law at the end; i.e., "who do you think was to blame for the accident and why" will probably be particularly painful to the good lawyer—but we have been agreeably surprised by the amount of fair-minded helpful people who have returned this form to us. On some occasions, they have even included facts to back up their views of who was at fault. If the statement looks promising, we send an investigator to the witness's home and conduct a personal interview. Even if the witness denies any knowledge of the case, we still feel this is worthwhile since we have effectively neutralized the witness in any event.

How to Prove Liability When Your Client's Emergency Police Car Runs into Another Vehicle

      We once had a case in which a police car was pursuing what was believed to be a fleeing hold-up man. It was at night so the red turret light on the roof of the police car was flashing. His siren was also sounding. As he climbed the crest of a hill, he was confronted with a passenger car in front of him. It was stationary in the middle of the road apparently preparing to make a left turn into the driveway of his home. Unable to stop, the police car struck the partially-turned vehicle a crashing blow, veered sharply to the right and struck a tree, severely injuring the police officer.

      It was obviously an extremely difficult case in which to prove liability. If the driver of the passenger vehicle had heard the siren and seen the flashing lights, it was his statutory duty under the law to yield to the emergency vehicle by pulling his vehicle to the right and stopping immediately. Instead, this driver had remained out in the dead center of the road and was pulling his car to the left.

Covering the Neighborhood for "Sights and Sounds"

In order to establish liability, we sent out our man to canvass the entire neighborhood. He went up and down each side of the street, house-to house and interviewed every occupant. The area covered was one-half mile *before* the scene of the accident and one-eighth mile *beyond* the scene. We were amazed at how many people were out visiting; in the basement doing the laundry; taking a shower; listening to opera on the radio, etc. It seemed as if the reasons for *not* hearing the siren and *not* seeing the flashing red light were as numerous as the inventive mind of man could conceive. But in that distance, we were fortunate enough to find at least six persons in the one-half mile before the site and two persons in the one-eighth mile beyond the site who positively swore that they heard the siren and saw the lights of the police car.

This was more than sufficient to raise a jury question. It permitted the jury to draw the legitimate inference that if eight people heard and saw the siren and light, the defendant certainly should have. Incidentally, the jury was out five hours and the verdict was a divided vote of 10 to 2. But once again, intensive investigation and preparation paid off.

One Picture Is Worth 10,000 Words

Photographs have probably won more cases and lost more cases than any other single item of demonstrable evidence. Whichever side you are on, they are definitely a must. And don't just be perfunctory about it and order photographs of the cars and scenes. Use some imagination. Recall the old Chinese proverb that one picture is better than 10,000 words.

We had another case involving an emergency vehicle also. In this case, however, it was an emergency ambulance which was responding to a call one Saturday afternoon in the summer. The vehicle struck and killed a 9-year-old boy as he rode his bicycle out into the roadway in front of his home. This case involved the use of many photographs as proof.

How to Establish Negligence Against a
Driver of a First-Aid Ambulance

Suing a First-Aid Emergency Squad and the driver of its ambulance, when they themselves are on an errand of mercy, is no easy task and yet we undertook it. It developed that the street in question was really a quiet, narrow, shady lane through a heavily-wooded, rural/residential area. The errand of mercy, however, was hardly an emergency. It only involved a boy with his foot caught in the sprocket of his bicycle. Further investigation revealed that there was also some evidence that the emergency squad was competing with another emergency squad whose headquarters was actually closer to the scene and could have reached the site safely and quickly.

In any event, the defendants' driver claimed that they had been summoned to this accident; had responded promptly; had entered this shady lane at a lawful speed of 35 m.p.h. and had continued at that rate for approximately one-half mile. At this point, they alleged that suddenly and without warning, the boy had pulled out in front of them. We sent our photographers out with instructions to take pictures of every home on each side of the street. It developed that there were actually four on one side and five on the other side in the one-half-mile stretch before the accident was reached. Some of these homes were near the roadway while others were some distance away. Luxurious foliage, trees, bushes, evergreens, etc., cast shadows on the road. The road itself was rough, poorly surfaced, narrow and winding.

Photographs Do It

On the stand, the driver of the ambulance was confronted with the fruits of our extended investigation. In seried order, each photograph of each home was shown to the witness from #1 to #9. He was asked in a casual manner if; (a) it was a residence; (b) facing on the road; (c) occupied by a family; (d) which usually contains some children; (e) that it was a Saturday and a holiday and the children would be presumed to be at home rather than at school; (f) that the weather was pleasant, and it might be anticipated the children would be out playing; (g) that the roadway was narrow and rough and winding and shady; (h) that many children ride bicycles; (i) that children of tender years are sometimes inclined to ride out of their driveway suddenly; (j) that younger children are not expected to have the same comprehension of danger as adults; (k) that, in fact, law does not require it of them; etc., etc.

With this background or foundation firmly established, the witness was next asked if he was; (a) aware of each of the factors above set forth that day?; (b) if he kept these factors in mind as he operated his large, powerful machine along the roadway; (c) and finally, if he was aware of them, and had them in mind, *what precisely did he do personally to make reasonably certain* that he would have his powerful vehicle under reasonably safe control in the event that one of those children on one of those bicycles rode out of the driveway of his home that afternoon. His only answer was that, ''I kept my vehicle within the legal speed limit.'' But that answer was not enough. And the insurance carrier covering the ambulance paid substantial damages to the parents for the death of the boy.

Photographs of Scenes and Cars Essential

It is always imperative to at least have photographs of the cars and the scene. They can be used very effectively in both the direct and cross-examination of all witnesses. Jurors have come to expect them. It is difficult to conceive of preparing a case properly without them. Photographs of injuries to the person are also helpful sometimes. Their principal virtue is in preserving and presenting, visually and graphically, various swellings, lacerations, scars, and other deformities, in the process of settlement. At the trial, they usually serve only to establish conditions which previously existed. These photographs are sometimes excluded from evidence by the court on the grounds that the purpose of the present inquiry is to ascertain the present condition of the plaintiff.

Getting What You Need from the Attending Physician

Each doctor involved in the case should be contacted promptly by letter. We use this method to; (a) make it a matter of record that we are on the case; (b) that no reports are to be given to anyone else without a written authorization signed by the claimant; (c) that we need his *preliminary* report as promptly as possible; (d) that his fees will be fully protected; (e) that he will also be paid for his reports and for all additional time he may spend in follow-up examinations and follow-up reports.

We point out precisely what we need; (a) his examination; (b) his diagnosis; (c) his treatment; (d) his prognosis; (e) his fees to date; (f) his estimated future fees. We frankly state that his prognosis may be left open or ''guarded'' since otherwise he may close the door to any complications or setbacks which may develop in the progress of the case.

Furnish Attending Physician with Your Own Report Form

Long ago we found that the use of our own medical report forms facilitated the task of obtaining any form of report from a busy doctor. Here is a fairly simple form which we found effective. Similar forms can now be purchased from most establishments furnishing legal forms.

MEDICAL REPORT

INJURED CLAIMANT

Name_____Age _____ Address _____

Occupation_____ Employed by _____

HISTORY

Date of Injury_____ 19__ How did patient say injury occurred?

_____

_____

Are you the family physician?_____ If not, give the name of family physician

DIAGNOSIS

Complete description of nature and extent of injury_____

_____

_____

TREATMENT

Describe treatment given _____

_____

Was patient confined to hospital? _____

Name of Hospital _____

X-RAYS

Date Taken _____ 19___Where taken? _____

By Whom?_____ Findings _____

CONTRIBUTING FACTORS (IF ANY)

Are symptoms from which patient is suffering due entirely to this injury?__

_____

Has previous sickness, injury or disease contributed to disability?_____ If so,

give your opinion as to extent_____

_____

PROGNOSIS

Is patient able to attend to any part of regular or any other occupation?_____

If so, state nature of work he can do now _____

Is patient working now?_____Where, if known _____

Has patient received any permanent injuries?_____If so, give nature and

degree of permanency_____

Give your estimate of disability from work FROM DATE OF ACCIDENT:

   Total Disability_____ weeks _____days _____

   Partial Disability_____ weeks _____days _____

MEDICAL REPORT *(Continued)*

Number of treatments to date: Office_____ Home_____

Hospital_____

Date of Your First Treatment_____

Date of Your Latest Treatment_____

Amount of Your Bill to Date_____

Estimate of your further treatments, if any_____

Remarks (Use Reverse Side Also)_____

_____

_____

Date of this report_____ Signed_____ M.D.

Graduate of_____Year_____ Address_____

Telephone_____City_____ State_____

The Shy and Retiring GP

It sometimes happens that the attending physician is anti-claimant. This is readily understandable since the average physcian has a great deal to do with insurance companies in the normal course of his practice. They use his services regularly in processing conventional health or life insurance applications. Some insurance companies may even suggest that his name is under serious consideration for permanent appointment as their "official examiner."

Other doctors are regularly retained for examinations, reports and testimony on behalf of the defendants, or rather their insurance company in a specific area. Doctors know that these assignments can be productive of regular and lucrative fees. As a result, they are bound subconsciously to build up at least some resistance to the claimant's side. This is particularly true if their treatment of a claimant may involve extended court appearances, with consequent interruptions in their busy practice.

Bring in the Specialists If You Need Them

In preparing a case, the attorney must be constantly on the alert for this type of physician. Such doctors can definitely ruin a case. I have had clients sitting across the desk from me with classic symptoms of whiplash or cervical sprain, who had been given no treatment whatsoever for these conditions up to several months after the accident from which they arose. The doctor's reports did not even mention these symptoms or complaints. In cases of this kind, the lawyer must act swiftly and decisively, if necessary.

Have the patient request the family physician to call in a neurosurgeon for consultation; insist that he take X-rays of the cervical spine. If the general practitioner resists these requests, do not hesitate to send the patient to some competent specialist for a complete examination, diagnosis and report. Make it clear that this does not mean that the attending physician is being superseded—not at all. The general practitioner should still remain in the case to follow-up with the patient regularly as his attending physician and have the specialist report to him regularly until the specialist's work is completed and he is referred back to the attending physician for ultimate discharge. Tact and diplomacy will be required.

Is the Driver Insured or Financially Responsible?

At an early date, it is well to investigate the insurance coverage of the defendant to determine if a claim has to be filed under the Uninsured Drivers' Fund. A Dun & Bradstreet or other credit report is also advisable in order to ascertain his financial responsibility in the event he has inadequate PI insurance coverage or in the event there is a possible disclaimer by his insurance carrier.

If weather conditions are, or may be, a factor in the case, official reports from the nearest weather observation station should also be obtained. We once had a case where a waitress in a luncheon concession in a drug store slipped on some ice at the side door as she was going out to dispose of some debris in the trash cans adjacent to the door. She suffered a depressed fracture of one of the lumbar vertebrae. We sued the owner of the drug store who let out the luncheon concession. We joined the owner of the building alleging structural defect on the roof, gutters and leaders which caused a small pool to form just outside the door.

There were many sharp issues in the case. But the sharpest of all was the question of whether the temperature had fallen below the freezing point and the ice had formed long enough to put the defendants on notice, actual or constructive, of its presence. We called two experts from the two nearest weather observation stations. The jury was convinced of our version of the facts and awarded a verdict of $60,000. We attribute much of the success of this case to the skillful use of the official weather reports.

Obtain Experts in Other Fields

But if experts on the factual allegations are important, so are experts on the medical proofs to establish damanges. Be sure to secure a recognized and competent expert in each specialty covering the injuries involved. In death cases, use an economic analyst who can project the potential earnings of the deceased for the period covered by his working-life expectancy. This is the only sound way of calculating the potential loss in such a manner as to take into consideration everything from fringe benefits to inflation, and then discount the final gross figure at today's value. This form of proof has now been recognized as legitimate and proper in a number of states. It should be recognized and utilized in all states.

Aerial Photographs Can Help

On occasion we have found aerial photographs of great help in the preparation and presentation of a case. Sometimes a simple, single plane view, or three-quarter view or an isometric view fails to develop the particular or peculiar aspects of a case. When you run into this problem, do not hesitate to invest an extra $100 or so in the aerial photograph. You will never regret it when the verdict comes in for $40,000 or $60,000 in a case which otherwise might have been lost.

The Trial Brief and Request to Charge

Factual preparation is only part of the story. Legal preparation is equally important. If the case is difficult, or complex, prepare a trial brief by all means. The judge will be favorably impressed and so will your adversaries. But more important, you will have a degree of self-confidence in your case that is beyond price. You will radiate that sense of confidence. Your opponents will recognize it and so will the jury. This work on the trial brief can wait until suit is actually started.

Draw up a set of "Requests to Charge" as you prepare the trial brief. That is the proper time to do it. Don't procrastinate on the theory that new and unanticipated points might arise during the trial. If they do, the solution is simple. Draw up a supplemental set of "Requests to Charge" and submit them to the Court as well.

Prepare Them to Try Them!

And so, may I reiterate that the secret of winning a case is to prepare it properly. And the secret of preparing it is to do it promptly, logically and chronologically as I have outlined here. If you merely promise yourself to do it, it will never get done. If you vaguely hope that it will get settled, it won't get done, and the chances are it won't get settled. My admonition is, prepare every case as though trying it was inevitable. In that way, you can't lose—whatever happens—or at least, you shouldn't!

Chapter 7

HOW TO PREPARE A CASE
TO INSURE SETTLEMENT
90% OF THE TIME

Well Prepared Is Half Settled . . . More Tools Today to Promote Settlements . . . The Eight Best Tools for Pretrial Discovery . . . Set the Tone of Your Practice by Your Pleadings . . . The Tax Foreclosure Case . . . Buyer of Lien Fights Redemption . . . Welcome Demands for Medical Examinations . . . Propound Interrogatories Promptly . . . Follow-up Vigorously on Answers . . . Demand Responsive Answers Under Threat of Court Sanctions . . . Depositions–The Important Key to Preparation and Settlement . . . Method, Manner and Extent of Depositions Mark Your Strength as Adversary . . . Use Office, Courtroom or Convention Room if Necessary . . . Remember the Opponent's Summary of the Depositions–His Conclusions and Recommendations . . . The Burnt Hands Case . . . Use of All Tools Fixes Liability and Assures Recovery . . . Use Qualified Technical Experts . . . The Typical Technical Expert's Report . . . The Uncertified Nondescript Scaffold Plank that Broke . . . Start Exploring Possibility of a Settlement Early . . . Can Use Settlement Brochure for Trial Guide . . . Typical Settlement Brochure . . . Form of Summary of Injuries and Out-of-Pocket Expenses . . . Detailed Letter Analyzing Elements of Damage . . . "Specials" Not Proper Guide to Settlement Value . . . When the Firm Offer Is Finally Secured . . . Five Tested Steps to Persuade a Client to Accept . . . Five More Softening-up Steps in a Tough Case . . . Try for Settlement Until the Bell Sounds–Then Go in There Fighting

Well Prepared Is Half Settled

It is well to bear in mind that a case properly prepared is as good as half settled. Also remember that from 70 percent to 90 percent of all matters in litigation seldom go to trial. Up to 90 percent of personal injury claims are settled. But there is no virtue in a settlement *per se*. Anyone can settle a case if he wants to throw it away. The magic is how to obtain "the adequate settlement." By that I mean how to obtain as much or almost as much as if the case were tried. Hence, the task before you is convert damages into dollars, with a minimum of cost, discomfort and delay to your clients.

More Tools Today to Promote Settlements

In today's practice and procedure there are more tools to force a satisfactory or attractive settlement than ever before. The Federal Court Rules long ago adopted liberal provisions for pretrial discovery. They have been enlarged many times since. Most, if not all, of the state courts have adopted the federal system for liberal discovery. This procedure has been frequently referred to as the "Race for Disclosure." Prior to these new rules the old fashioned method was to follow the "Race for Concealment." Much legal strategy depended upon surprise. This led to the employment of technicalities and frequently to a miscarriage of justice. So we begin with the premise that the liberal discovery rules are intended to prevent surprise and promote justice. If our case is just, we have nothing to fear by disclosure. So let's use it to the fullest—if we want to promote justice and hasten the collection of our fees and the added increment to our income.

The Eight Best Tools for Pretrial Discovery

Among the tools most commonly used are: (a) demands for admissions; (b) demand to furnish documents; (c) to submit to examinations and inspections; (d) to answer interrogatories; (e) to submit to oral or written depositions; (f) to conduct counter depositions; (g) early settlement conferences; (h) pretrial conferences, etc., etc. We know that our opponents are going to use all or most of these—so why merely wait to meet the crisis? Anticipate it by carrying the offensive to your adversary.

These tools have teeth—so let's use them promptly. This will not only impress your adversary, it will startle him. But there are many other advantages to be gained since you can pick the time and place and terms of meeting *your demands,* if you are the moving party. Why expose yourself to being dunned, and perhaps threatened, by your adversary and subjected to motions to compel answers under penalty of dismissal or other sanctions by the court. You are in a position where you can follow this procedure if you wish. But don't carry it too far or you will cut off all opportunities of enjoying the mutual and reciprocal respect and cooperation which one attorney should extend to another.

Set the Tone of Your Practice by Your Pleadings

You can set the tone of your practice by your initial pleadings. In many jurisdictions today you may plead mere "conclusions of law." You can omit the facts if you wish to. But to do so in all cases seems shortsighted to me. They will come out eventually. This method of pleading seems the antithesis of the full disclosure theory. So why not plead at least some of the essential facts in your initial pleading. This is particularly applicable when you have some strong persuasive ones to plead, i.e., "that the defendant was physically unfit to operate a motor vehicle, lost control of his car, crossed the median strip to the wrong side of the highway and struck the plaintiff's standing vehicle with great force and violence, demolishing the vehicle and seriously and permanently injuring the plaintiff."

Is not this much more impressive than saying that the defendant so negligently, carelessly and recklessly operated his motor vehicle as to cause same to collide with the motor vehicle of the plaintiff damaging the vehicle and injuring the plaintiff? But if you do elect to frame your pleadings in this more detailed manner of pleading facts, it is advisable to be absolutely certain that you can and will prove these factual allegations. We have no less an authority than Abraham Lincoln who once admonished a fellow lawyer, "Never plead more than you have to—because someone may make you prove it." This advice may have been appropriate for the days preceding our present liberal discovery rules. They certainly do not seem to apply today.

The Tax Foreclosure Case

We once had an interesting case where a client named Albert Henry owned 20 acres of meadowland fronting on the river. He neglected paying the local property tax for a few years and a stranger bought the tax lien at a municipal tax sale. The purchaser proceeded to wait the statutory two-year period before starting his suit in the Chancery Division of the Superior Court for the purpose of perfecting his title by foreclosure.

Incidentally, about this time, the state elected to construct a highway which would cross at or near this meadowland tract. Its value rose astronomically. Henry tried to redeem from the purchaser of the lien. The holder of the tax sales certificate rejected the offer of redemption. He denied that Henry was the legitimate owner or had the right to redeem. Henry came to us for advice and protection.

We filed suit promptly. Our complaint set forth in chronological order the devolution of title for the past 60 years. This involved various estates both testate and intestate; payment of the taxes for years; the conduct of the tax sale for delinquent taxes; the lapse of two years; the attempt to redeem; the rejection of this proffered payment; varied exchange of correspondence, etc., etc. The suit produced no results.

Buyer of Lien Fights Redemption

The defendant retained one of the largest and most prestigious law firms in the state. They filed an answer setting up a general denial. This was followed by the use of some of the steps in discovery discussed above. They began by serving on us a Demand to Furnish Copies of Documents. They went methodically through our complaint and demanded that we furnish them the written copy of every single document we had referred to in the complaint.

This was a tough assignment. It was using just one of the manifold discovery tools—but using it with a vengeance. We as plaintiffs had no choice but to accede to the demand. We were forced to comply with every item covered. But the results, for us at least, were magnificent. These documents were extensive and voluminous and ran to some 200 or 300 pages. The costs of preparation approximated $1,000. But as we prepared them—we also prepared our own air-tight case.

So much so, that when the case was eventually called for trial, the Trial Court reviewed the documents we had submitted and entered judgment in favor of the plaintiff on these very proofs. Fortunately, they complied with, and conformed to, the requirements of our Evidence Act to make them competent evidence. Incidentally, the state highway did go through these lands. As a result, the plaintiff was in an excellent position to pay a very substantial fee for services rendered not only in filing the original suit but in representing him in the condemnation suit which followed.

Welcome Demands for Medical Examinations

The demand to submit to examinations and inspections can also be used effectively by both sides. The defendant usually demands medical examinations early and often. As part of our preparation of a case, we have no objection to this procedure. In fact, we welcome such demands. In our judgment it is a good sign that your adversaries recognize the seriousness and importance of your case. Cooperate when such demands are made upon you, by all means. The danger sign is when the defendant is disinterested in your client's physical condition.

But when we send our clients to submit to these medical examinations we usually have a representative of this office accompany them. This sometimes gets the examining doctor miffed—but we feel that it is worth it. Our representative makes a mental record of everything that happens from the time the claimant enters the doctor's office until he leaves. The 40 minutes he sat in the waiting room is clocked. The fact that the nurse took the history in a perfunctory manner is noted. We make it a practice to send a female representative with a female claimant so that she may be admitted to the examination room.

The time taken for the examination itself is also noted. The questions asked by the doctor and the claimant's responses are noted. If there are involuntary cries of pain or other discomfort, a mental record of these is also made. We have observed that our method has produced a strikingly large number of favorable reports on our clients—even from the defendant's own examining physician. But don't carry this method of surveillance too far. Most examining physicians are so reputable and responsible that they can be trusted to forward a fair and frank report with your office representative merely sitting in the doctor's waiting room and acting solely as "chauffeur" for the claimant.

Propound Interrogatories Promptly

Once a suit is started be sure to issue your interrogatories immediately. But most counsel for defendants make a practice of serving defendant's interrogatories on the plaintiff concurrently with their answer. Take a page from these hardy practitioners and do likewise. Serve *your* interrogatories as soon as counsel for the defendant enters an appearance on the record. In many jurisdictions standard forms are now provided by the Rules of Court. They are usually adequate for the average case but it is best to supplement them by a few pointed and well-chosen additional questions which point up the strength of your own case—and the weakness of the defendant's. Thus, you carry the fight to your adversaries. A strong offense is still the best defense—provided it is not too offensive.

Follow-up Vigorously on Answers

But interrogatories are futile if they are not pursued—followed-up. Post the date the answers are due. Follow-up with a stock letter the day they are overdue. Here is an illustration:

Gentlemen:

Our records show that answers to plaintiff's interrogatories served on you in the above captioned case are now overdue.

It will be appreciated if you will see that these answers are properly completed and furnished to us without further delay.

We do not wish to ask the Court to impose sanctions for your delay, but we may be compelled to do so unless these answers are furnished forthwith.

Yours respectfully,

Demand Responsive Answers Under
Threat of Court Sanctions

When the answers to your interrogatories do come in, study them promptly. Do not accept such unresponsive answers as "improper"; "immaterial"; "irrelevant"; "incompetent"; "see Complaint"; etc., etc. If the replies are not directly responsive, serve a demand on your adversary by letter that these answers are to be supplemented at once, under penalty of sanctions. We regularly use a letter such as this:

Gentlemen:

We are this date in receipt of answers to plaintiff's interrogatories furnished to us by your office.

In reviewing them we find that answers to Interrogatories 1, 8, 11, 17 and 26 are not responsive.

We must, therefore, respectfully request that you furnish more responsive answers to these interrogatories at once.

Unless we receive these within 10 days, we shall bring the matter on for formal hearing before the Court on Motion to compel you to furnish more responsive answers.

May we hear from you promptly as to your intentions?

Yours respectfully,

The point is to pin the defendants down to prompt, complete, responsive answers to your interrogatories. Otherwise, the entire procedure can be futile and pretrial discovery can become a travesty or a farce. The courts recognize this fact and will help you to compel your adversaries to abide by the rules. Moreover, always remember two things viz: first, you will need these answers to guide you in your depositions which are to follow. Proper, responsive answers to your interrogatories can shorten and render every deposition you take less expensive. Without these answers you will be compelled to waste not only your valuable time, but your money as well on unnecessary exploratory or *pro forma* matters which could have been answered with simple yes and no answers in the interrogatories.

Second, remember that when, and if, you are in the middle of the trial of this case, those Answers to Interrogatories can be very beneficial in assisting you in establishing some specific point in your proofs. This in turn may very well save you the delay, inconvenience and expense of producing a separate witness to prove some essential point. Sometimes a single point can actually win a case for you, or protect your record in the event of an appeal by either side.

Depositions—The Important Key to Preparation and Settlement

Without question the most important tools in preparing a case for trial or settlement are the Depositions. We usually attempt to serve the notice of taking such depositions on our adversary first. This affords us the opportunity of selecting the date, time and place. Delay in doing this can force you and your parties to travel 20, 30 or even 50 miles to a strange office at a date, time and place which do not fit into your own schedule.

Moreover, your clients will feel more comfortable in their own hometown and in an office which they have been accustomed to visiting. Where, however, our opponents get the jump on us and do serve their notice first, we invariably respond by serving a counter-notice to take our own depositions. We usually specify the same time, date and place, and with the same Official Reporter as a matter of efficiency. We have found that unless you are dealing with clients who have difficulty with the language, the transcripts are 99 percent accurate. Hence, we waive the reading and signing of same by the witnesses as a matter of course and as a mutual concession to our adversaries.

Method, Manner and Extent of Depositions
Mark Your Strength as Adversary

The extent, manner and methods you employ in conducting your depositions are a further sign to your opponents (and the carrier he represents), of the type of adversary they are dealing with. Your opponents can usually tell if they are dealing with a neophyte or a veteran—a tough adversary or a pushover.

Hence, we welcome this contest as a challenge. The job of taking depositions is not assigned to a young immature attorney who is getting on-the-job training. Such attorneys are permitted to sit in and observe, but not to participate. Some attorneys have the idea that these depositions should be limited to the parties only. Not so. If there are key witnesses it may be more important to examine these witnesses on depositions than the parties themselves.

It will be necessary to subpoena those called who are not parties. Moreover, you cannot use the testimony of these witnesses as plenary evidence. But you can pin them down, limit their proofs or neutralize or destroy their testimony entirely. If the defendant calls them, you may use their recorded testimony to affect their credibility or impeach or destroy them by confronting them with this recorded testimony at the trial. And don't forget to make every notice and every subpoena served a Subpoena *Duces Tecum* so that they will be compelled to bring with them and produce their records and testify with respect to same.

Use Office, Courtroom or Convention Room if Necessary

Sometimes an impasse between or among the attorneys arises as to where and when depositions should be held. This may be due to the number of witnesses to be deposed. Sometimes the issue in dispute is the convenience of the larger number of witnesses. Thus, in a malpractice case the conference room of a hospital may be agreed upon as the place for taking them. If a governmental agency is a defendant in the suit, the county administration building might be the most logical site. Perhaps a conference room in the county courthouse may be made available for this purpose. If the number of witnesses is unusually large, a suite of rooms or even a convention room in a local hotel may be utilized.

We have used them all effectively. These depositions have run anywhere from a few hours, a few days, to a month. But they have all paid off. I once observed to a judge that "we seemed to be spending much more time on depositions than in trying cases." His response was immediate and unequivocal. "Excellent! Wonderful! Isn't that precisely what the Discovery Rules were intended to accomplish?"

Remember the Opponent's Summary of the Depositions— His Conclusions and Recommendations

Always bear in mind that at the conclusion of each deposition, the attorney for the defendant carrier usually dictates, privately and confidentally, a summary of the deposition. These summaries usually set forth the highlights of same and the attorney's impression of its significance if the case goes to trial. The Claims Manager of the carrier company frequently relies more on this synopsis and the recommendations set forth than he does on the depositions themselves. The volume of depositions he handles in the course of an average day makes it next to impossible for the claims manager to read them all.

The Burnt Hands Case

We once had a case where a client was engaged in the steel drum reclamation business. The drums had originally contained a substance which could become explosive and inflammable under certain conditions. They had been packed in the South and shipped to a Midwest consumer. When the drums were empty, there remained a slight residue in them which made them hazardous to use, difficult to salvage and sometimes a drug on the market, as well as a potential nuisance. The only safe salvage operation would have been to decapitate the drum with special equipment (which our client did not have) and to conduct the operation in an isolated place under a properly obtained variance (which our client had not yet obtained). One day a fire broke out among the stored drums. The plaintiff in seeking to extinguish the fire was severely burned about the hands and face when a second drum exploded near him.

Use of All Tools Fixes Liability and Assures Recovery

As usual, we sued the original manufacturer of the material; the customer who used it; the shipper who trucked the drums to our client's yards, etc. Originally the case seemed hopeless. The elements of contributory negligence and assumption of the risk seemed obvious. The case had been rejected by several prominent law firms. We nevertheless took the case. Our preliminary investigation indicated liability against someone. Our task was to ascertain who the culprit was and pin the liability on him.

The investigation and preparation of the case were extensive, intensive and, I might say, expensive, as well. Before we were through we had established, through demands for admissions; production of documents; inspections; interrogatories and depositions, all of the essential ingredients of liability at least against the manufacturer. The original customer and the trucker eventually escaped liability but solely because we were unable to establish proximate cause. The manufacturer of the product paid substantial damages to the injured claimant—and earned our office an equally substantial fee.

Use Qualified Technical Experts

Next to depositions in the order of importance is the retaining of qualified, eminent, outstanding experts in the special fields to cover the question of liability. We are never satisfied with one such expert. He may get sick, die, retire, move out of the jurisdiction or be otherwise unavailable at the time of trial. Hence, we usually locate and use at least two or three such experts. Their reports must be clear, concise, complete and answer the direct question: ''In your opinion as an expert in this field, were there such clear-cut violations of or deviations from recognized standards as to present reasonably foreseeable consequences which were the proximate cause of this accident?'' Armed with two or three such reports, the average defendant is going to think twice before risking a jury trial on the questions involved.

The Typical Technical Expert's Report

The following is a typical report from an expert in building construction:

''My comments on the above accident are as follows:

1. <u>Scaffold Planks</u>
    a. Since planks have to sustain the weight of both men and materials, their use and application are specified in the Construction Safety Code of New Jersey, as well as building standards.
    b. The platform ramp involved in the accident was known as a horse scaffold. The planks of the scaffolds, which were on 10'-0" centers, failed at time of the accident.

2. <u>Violation of Construction Safety Code of State of New Jersey by General Contractor.</u>

   a. This standard was adopted in July 1, 1968, and is enforced by the Department of Labor and Industry, Bureau of Engineering and Safety.

   b. The project had a General Contractor who is responsible for the overall project safety, including safety inspections, as described in "Section 3.14 and 3.15" of this Code. These sections were violated.

   c. The General Contractor failed to provide safe load-carrying equipment, as required by "Section 4.2, 4.36 and 4.37" of this Code.

   d. "Section 15" of this Code refers to scaffolds. Provisions of this chapter, as applicable to scaffold planks, was violated.

3. <u>Other Standards</u>

   a. The National Safety Council requires all scaffold planks to be inspected, tested, and checked for visible or audible damage, and if obvious deflections remain after the test load is removed, the plank is not to be utilized.

   b. The American National Standard A10.8-1969, entitled "Safety Requirements for Scaffolding," indicates that spans of 10'-0" should not be utilized with dressed lumber. This requirement was violated.

   c. The Scaffolding and Shoring Institute require planking on construction to be of "scaffold grade" lumber. The lumber of this planking was not certified for scaffold use."

The Uncertified Nondescript Scaffold Plank that Broke

The report covers a case where a laborer fell and injured himself severely on a construction job. A Dumpster had been backed up to a platform to receive the clean-up debris from all subcontractors. Since there was a 3' or 4' differential in the levels of the top of the platform and the floor of the Dumpster, a wooden horse and three 2" × 10" × 12' planks served as a ramp out to the middle of the Dumpster. One of these planks broke while the plaintiff was carrying out an armful of debris, and he fell striking his head on the metal floor and sides of the Dumpster.

As usual we sued several parties including the general contractor and the owner of the Dumpster. We knew that the owner of the premises could not be held in because it was a turn-key job with the general contractor in full charge of everything.

The usual intensive investigation and preparation disclosed: (a) that the plank was set up by a sub-contractor with the knowledge of the general contractor; (b) that the superintendent's office was in actual sight of the operation; (c) that the planks used were nondescript ones, the origin and ownership of which could not be ascertained; (d) that they were not tested or certified for such use; (e) that the usual markings to indicate such certification was missing; (f) that the size, position and mode of use were in violation of a Code established and promulgated by the State Department of Labor, etc.

When this set of facts was presented to a jury, a favorable verdict was obtained on behalf of the injured workman. The task was not easy. Perhaps the most telling point in all the testimony presented was that of the expert establishing deviations from recognized standards of safety. The favorable verdict assured our office of an adequate fee commensurate with the amount of the award.

Start Exploring Possibility of a Settlement Early

Somewhere along the line between the filing of the suit and the date the case is reached for trial we begin to explore the possibility of a settlement. This becomes more aggressive as soon as pretrial Discovery is complete and the end results of the injuries have been ascertained. We have found that at this point a properly-prepared settlement brochure can be helpful. This can be as simple or as elaborate as the facts and the size of the case warrant. We have used everything from a few paged unbound summaries to an elaborate leather bound loose-leaf plastic-window unit which we reserved for the particularly important cases in which our demand is large.

Can Use Settlement Brochure for Trial Guide

Incidentally, these Settlement Brochures sometimes prove ineffective. Sometimes our demand is rejected as excessive. In other instances the counter offer submitted is considered inadequate. In such instances we don't consider the time and effort spent on preparing the Settlement Brochure as wasted. We found that on the contrary it serves as an excellent guide in the actual trial of the case.

I have personally used such brochures many times with good results. When the trial is opened and we begin presenting our direct evidence, I start at the beginning and work my way methodically through the brochure. As each item is introduced in evidence, and each witness is called, I strip this material from the brochure. When I get to the last item ''Request to Charge'' I am confident that the case has been ''put in'' in the way it should have been to command an adequate verdict.

Typical Settlement Brochure

The following is a typical list of the Table of Contents only, of an elaborate Settlement Brochure indicating what its contents should be. We conceal nothing. We believe that there is strength in disclosure—particularly when it is all favorable to you:

TABLE OF CONTENTS

1. Short letter of transmittal and amount of demand.
2. Claimant's statement summarizing accident and effects.
3. Copy of police report.
4. Survey of premises involved.
5. Photo of premises involved.
6. List (only) of factual witnesses to be called.
7. List of technical expert witnesses to be called.
8. List of medical expert witnesses to be called.
9. Copy of reports of technical experts.
10. Copy of reports of medical experts.
11. Copy of hospital reports.
12. Copies of all bills for medical, surgical and hospital fees.
13. Photos of plaintiff showing all scars or other deformities.
14. Copy of life expectancy table with plaintiff's life expectancy circled for easy reference.
15. Summary of injuries and special damages (our form).
16. Detailed letter analyzing case; elements of damage, etc., showing how damages claimed were arrived at, followed by a restatement of the demand, ''expressly without prejudice.''

Form of Summary of Injuries and Out-of-Pocket Expenses

The following is a form we have designed and which we use regularly for the purpose of summarizing the injuries and special damages. It has been referred to as Item 15 in the preceding Table of Contents.

JOSEPH T. WHITE, COUNSELOR AT LAW,
61 MAIN STREET, ANYVILLE, N.J.

SUMMARY OF INJURIES AND OUT-OF-POCKET EXPENSES

Name of claimant _____ Age_____

Address _____ Phone _____

Date of accident_____ Place of Accident_____

Brief Description of Injuries:

(a)_____   (d)_____

(b)_____   (e)_____

(c)_____   (f)_____

Confined to_____Hospital, from_____to_____

Confined to bed from_____to_____Total_____Weeks
_____Days

Confined to home from_____ to_____Total_____Weeks
_____Days

Names and addresses of doctors, and bills to date:

_____ $_____

_____ $_____

_____ $_____

_____ $_____

_____ $_____

Total doctor bills $_____

Total hospital bills to date_____197____ $_____

X-rays taken at_____ Hospital $_____

X-rays taken at office of Dr. _____. $_____

Total medical bills $_____

Time lost from employment at_____

_____Days

from_____ to_____ _____Weeks © $_____ $_____

Itemize all other losses or expenses:

_____ $ _____
_____ $ _____

(Confidentially, if this case can be settled out of court, what is the minimum gross amount you would accept?)

$ _____

REMARKS:

Dated: _____ SIGNED _____

Detailed Letter Analyzing Elements of Damage

The following is a typical illustration of the form of letter analyzing liability and damages which we frequently use. This has been referred to in the preceding Table of Contents as Item 16.

October 23, 1975

Norton and Norton, Esqs.
180 Highway 35
Trenton, New Jersey

Morgan, Monaghan, & McQuaid, Esqs.
300 South Livingston Avenue
Camden, New Jersey

Kenneth J. Laws, Jr., Esq.
228 West State Street
Freehold, New Jersey

Re: Filpin vs. Flannel Associates, et als

Gentlemen:

We have reviewed the above case and analyzed the various elements of damages for the purpose of evaluating the injuries and submitting a formal demand as the basis for a possible settlement before trial.

The records show that this accident occurred on April 18, 197 , at the Flannel Companies Store in the Brunswick Shopping Center, New Brunswick, New Jersey. Our investigation indicates that the store had only been opened for a few weeks; that the shelves were still being stocked with heavy hand-trucks using the aisles as roadways; that the entire flooring had nevertheless been waxed and burnished to a high state of slipperiness; that much of the metal stock was covered with plastic and that scraps of this plastic had been permitted to be torn off and lie on the floor.

Moreover, it appears that Mrs. Filpin, while on a shopping tour with 3 of her women friends, and while about in the center of the store and as she had turned from a vertical aisle to a horizontal aisle, slipped and fell heavily on her hip because of a combination of the newness of the tile floor, the excessive wax and burnishing, and the fact that a piece of plastic had been caught under her heel, thus intensifying the excessive slipperiness of the floor.

Incidentally, independent witnesses verify the presence of the plastic on the floor and that its condition was such to indicate that it had been there for some time and had been walked over frequently since they called the attention of one of the store employees to its presence at or near the plaintiff's heel immediately after the accident, and suggested that it be removed so that no one else would suffer a similar fate.

Within a very brief period of time, an expert was brought to the scene who made extensive tests to establish the co-efficient of friction of the floor in the area and definitely established that even without the presence of the scrap of plastic the floor failed to meet minimum standards and that with the introduction of the plastic the extent of the slipperiness shot up drastically. Copy of this report has been furnished to you.

It is also interesting to note that witnesses established the fact that immediately approaching the site of the accident was a row of steel cabinets covered with plastic, some of which drooped down onto the aisle and that there was merchandise on the shelf which was covered with similar plastic.

As a result of the fall, the female plaintiff suffered a fracture of the head of the femur as a result of which she lost the head of the femur and it had to be replaced with a plastic one. She was confined to St. Mark's General Hospital continuously from the date of the accident on April 18, 197 , to May 6, 197 , when she was released to her home, where she has continued to be more or less totally confined up to the present time, or an approximate total of one (1) year.

The case is now approaching trial with 3 defendants still held in, namely, the owners of the premises, Flannel Associates, t/a New Brunswick Shopping Center, the lessee of the particular store in question, Flannel Companies, and the subcontractor, Met Maintenance, Inc., who was in charge of the cleaning and waxing of the floor in question. It is our belief that all 3 of these defendants are jointly and severally liable and will be found to be equally guilty by a jury, and that hence they should all join in a settlement.

It is generally recognized that damages fall into 4 categories. For the purpose of our discussing a possible settlement we have analyzed them under these respective headings, viz:—

I. MEDICAL SPECIALS

In the instant case the medical specials are considered the smallest part of the claim and may be roughly summarized as follows:

1. Bills covering Drs. Feinberg, Johnson and Felcau are approximately.................................$ 740.00
2. St. Mark's General Hospital bill 795.00
3. 3 follow-up x-rays, Morrigan Radiology Group 30.00
4. Cane and bed-pan 10.49
5. Bolster for Bed..   11.51
6. Medication (estimate) 100.00

Total $1,687.00

II. TEMPORARY DISABILITY

In this particular case, we see no point in discussing temporary disability, since plaintiff has been more or less totally disabled since the date of the accident. While initially she was totally disabled for the 2-1/2 weeks in St. Marks Hospital, and thereafter showed some sign of temporary recovery which permitted her to be transported by car to doctors and to get out into the yard occasionally, as a matter of fact from the approximate date she was taken to be examined by one of the defendant's doctors, she had a set-back and complete relapse into total disability and hence we must calculate her damages on the basis of total and permanent disability.

III. PERMANENT DISABILITY

While the plaintiff was 78 years old at the time of the accident, she theoretically had a life expectancy of 8.23 years. However, since that time, a year and a month has gone by and she still has a life expectancy of approximately 7.70 years. It is to be borne in mind that these are only estimates or averages, and with plaintiff's family genealogy it is quite likely that her life expectancy would have been substantially longer had it not been for this grievous accident. Hence there must be a correlation of the permanent and total disabilities to this life expectancy under 2 separate categories:

1. The monetary value of the aforesaid permanent injury which adversely affected the plaintiff's ability to perform her normal house-

hold functions in lieu of regular employment for the rest of her life; and

2. In addition to the foregoing, the monetary value of the aforesaid total and permanent disabilities which adversely affect the plaintiff and impair her normal enjoyment of life and the normal pursuits of various recreations and other social outlets which a person of her age and social status would normally enjoy.

It has been estimated that a person's day can be segregated into three 8-hour periods: one devoted to normal employment, one devoted to rest or recreational pursuits, and the third to sleep and rest. It is difficult to assess which of these 3 is the most important so far as any given person's life is concerned, but it may safely be assumed that all of them are extremely important and particularly to a person approaching the sunset years of her life when under the normal course of events she would be entitled to look forward to years of rest, recreation, freedom from pain and suffering, happiness and contentment. Suffice it to say that this woman because of the accident has lost all of these.

IV. PAIN AND SUFFERING COVERING THE ENTIRE PERIOD FROM THE DATE OF THE ACCIDENT TO THE TERMINATION OF PLAINTIFF'S LIFE EXPECTANCY

There is an old saying that when you have good health you have everything—when you have lost it you have nothing. It has also been said that no one can possibly visualize, understand or evaluate, the nature, degree and extent of another person's pain or the monetary value of same.

Philosophers through the ages have expressed the view that it is better to be a poor cobbler in good health than a wealthy king in poor health. Others with a gift of more lurid description have said that some type of pain can be likened to a "peep-hole into hell."

It is not difficult to visualize the excruciating nature of the pain of a fractured hip of and by itself. The area in question is extremely sensitive to pain by all medical standards. When you have superimposed upon this the actual breaking off of the head of the femur, all of this pain is thereby intensified. To have introduced into this sensitive area of disability an artificial head only tends to further exacerbate the agony and misery and indescribable pain to which the patient is thereby subjected under a normal period of recuperation and recovery.

However, when it is realized that even with the benefit of all of the advantages of advanced science, the healing process and recuperative powers of the body of this woman broke down, as a result of which she became totally disabled and was forced back to her bed of pain, it is safe to say that it will be difficult for any jury to possibly evaluate and place a proper award or compensation for the hours, days, weeks, months and years of pain, suffering and anguish which this poor, unfortunate woman is surely suffering and will continue to suffer in increased degree and severity up until the time that death relieves her of this burden.

While it may be argued that her life expectancy does not justify a very substantial recovery it must be borne in mind that recently the American Trial Lawyers Association published a somewhat analogous case in its law reports. An 88-year old woman lost her forearm through the malfunction of an automatic laundry mechanism. Although her specials were only $2,400.00 and her suffering and total disability much less than the plaintiff in this case, a jury awarded her $383,000.00, which was sustained on appeal as not excessive. It is our belief that the New Jersey Courts would act similarly on any verdict rendered in the instant case in light of plaintiff's much more extended pain, suffering and disability.

In the light of the foregoing facts, we believe this case has a minimum settlement value at this time of $200,000.00, and that is the demand which is hereby submitted without prejudice.

In the event that we cannot reach an amicable settlement before trial, you may consider this offer as automatically withdrawn and it will not be resubmitted.

We will appreciate your early advice as to whether or not you are interested in sitting down and discussing a possible settlement.

Very truly yours,

White, Brown & Black, P.A.

By

Alan J. Black

AJB:nh
Enc.

"Specials" Not Proper Guide to Settlement Value

Don't be bashful or backward about analyzing your client's losses and demanding appropriate damages for them. This is precisely what you are aiming at, i.e., converting damages into dollars. We have always taken the position that the rule of thumb between "specials" and the amount of the demand or the verdict is an unsound one.

If the "specials" are $5,000 there is no sound reason why the verdict or settlement should be limited to $20,000 or $25,000. To accept this theory is to tacitly ignore some of the most important elements of damages—particularly as to permanent disability (no matter to what extent) and its impact on earned income over the period of working life expectancy.

Even more important still it ignores the fact that a human being is not a robot—a mere working machine. It is generally conceded that the average person's life is made up of three daily sectors. He works eight hours, he sleeps eight hours and he lives eight hours. The most important part of his life is the eight-hour period when he actually lives, i.e., he does not sleep or work. If his ability to enjoy life and live out these hours fully and completely is diminished because of the injuries suffered, this element of damage must always be paid for—fully and adequately.

On one occasion when we submitted our detailed letter analyzing the elements of damages and tabulating how our demand was arrived at, an attorney for one of the defendant carriers facetiously remarked, ''I always wanted to know how a plaintiff arrived at these astronomical demands.'' We replied in kind ''Well now you know—and the jury will too, if you don't pay us before we go to trial.''

We are not unmindful of the famous *Botta* case in New Jersey—which has been approved and followed in many other jurisdictions—and the limitation it placed upon proof of damages. However, the basic ruling of that case was merely that an attorney may not arbitrarily place a price tag on pain and suffering at so much per hour, per day, etc. and then ask a jury to use this figure in calculating its verdict. The Court pointed out that in any event the damages to be awarded for pain and suffering should be *in a lump sum,* and not on a per-diem or per-annum basis.

However, this did not mean that a case had to be tried in a vacuum and that no reference could be made to the time elements involved in determining what would be an adequate award for either pain and suffering or actual disability. Obviously the *time element* involved is probably the single most important factor in placing a value on pain or disability, next to the severity of the pain and the extent of the disability! Moreover, in cases of permanency the life expectancy of the plaintiff should be used to the hilt.

When the Firm Offer Is Finally Secured

When you do finally get a final firm offer you now have the task of ''selling'' it to your client. This is not always easy. Without any help or encouragement from us, all too frequently a client may have astronomical figures in mind. If he does, you may be thwarted by your own client in reaching a settlement. Hence, it may require a softening-up process to bring your client in line so the parties may eventually get together and the case may be settled.

Five Tested Steps to Persuade a Client to Accept

To accomplish this we usually advance these five arguments to him gently but firmly: (1) your case is *not* the strongest case in the world on liability; (2) your medical proofs leave much to be desired in proving any permanent disability; (3) jurors are highly unpredictable; (4) if you win, the verdict may be smaller than the settlement; and (5) if you win and the verdict is substantially higher than the settlement, they will appeal.

Five More Softening-up Steps in a Tough Case

If these points fail to soften-up the plaintiff, we throw in a few more. Here they are: (6) we think the settlement is adequate; (7) your retainer gave us the right to make this decision—even though we do not want to; (8) you are not only jeopardizing your own recovery of damages you are jeopardizing our fees as well, which we have worked so hard and so long to earn.

If all of the foregoing persuasion still leaves the client unpersuaded, there is always the possibility of: (9) threatening to withdraw from the suit and substitute other counsel; (10) refusing to substitute another attorney unless the fees we have already earned are fully protected in the stipulation substituting other counsel. Somewhere along the line the client usually capitulates. If he does not, we go back and deliver an ultimatum to our opponents, i.e., pay more or try the case—we are ready.

**Try for Settlement Until the Bell Sounds—
Then Go in There Fighting**

Always bear in mind that efforts at settling a case are no sign of weakness. The other side are at least as interested as you are. Perhaps they are more interested since they have a larger case load to carry. The mere fact that initial overtures looking toward a settlement have not been productive should not deter you in the least.

Start the negotiations early. Continue them from time to time. Renew them at the end of each deposition. Renew them again at the pretrial conference. When the case is called on the trial list, mark it ready for trial, but suggest to the Court that a settlement conference might be productive. Even after the jury is drawn give your adversaries one final chance to settle—on your terms. If they refuse to settle, go ahead and try the case. You have prepared it superbly. Hence, you are ready, willing and able to try it. Now let the Court and jury see *how effective adequate trial preparation can really be*.

Chapter 8

HOW ESTATE PLANNING CAN HELP

BUILD A LAW PRACTICE

Estates Offer Fertile Field . . . "I Want My Will Made." . . . Does U.S. Court Decision Outlaw All Minimum Fee Schedules? . . . Fixing Fee on Drafting Wills Requires Skill and Diplomacy . . . Reasonable Fee Loses Estate . . . Drawing Will vs. Planning Estate . . . Not How to Plan an Estate, but How to Get One . . . Banks Can Advertise, but Not Attorneys . . . What Constitutes the Unauthorized Practice of Law? . . . Access to All Large Depositors Is Helpful . . . Direct Mail Campaign . . . How the Selection of Attorneys Is Controlled . . . How Banks Are Able to Control Attorneys . . . How to Meet This Type of Competition . . . Service as Deputy Surrogate . . . A $40,000 Legal Fee . . . Educational Talks Before Groups . . . Use of Wills and Estate Manuals . . . Estate Planning Mandatory in All Substantial Estates . . . Estate Plan Only as Good as Data Relied Upon . . . Only Legitimate Sources of Estate Work Are Through Your Clients . . . Every Unusual Occurrence Raises Question of Need for Will . . . Attorney's Duty to Warn Clients of Potential Tax Consequences . . . Where Failure to Plan Estate Caused $90,000 in Taxes . . . Where Timely Tax Planning Saved $75,000 in Taxes . . . Lawyer's Four Tools for Tax Savings in Estates . . . The Two-Trust Method . . . The Politician's Last Trick Is His Last Will

Estates Offer Fertile Field

There are relatively few fields of law that have universal appeal and interest. Estate Planning is one of them. Practically everyone has some kind of an estate which must be disposed of at the time of death. Hence this can be a fertile field for building up a law practice, if handled properly. Most average people are unaware of the great distinction between "having my will drawn" and "having my estate planned." There is a world of difference between the two, not only in the work involved but in the legal fees to be earned as well. The problem is to educate the public to this distinction and thus pave the way for conditioning them to appreciate the distinction and to be willing to pay the larger fees.

"I Want My Will Made"

Most clients will merely say "I want you to draw my will." In the old days the lawyer would make a few discreet inquiries as to the respective names of the spouses, the names and ages of the children, a few brief questions as to what the prospective testator owns and how he wants it divided. The will would then be drafted, signed by the testator in the lawyer's office, and the original will would thereupon be delivered to the client in a fancy parchment envelope with the words "WILL" engraved upon it. The fee would then be quoted and promptly paid in cash. Thereafter both the lawyer and the client would forget about it until the client died. This is definitely *not* the way to handle a will or an estate today. And yet great care must be exercised not to antagonize the client or frighten him off and into another law office by visions of excessive fees for either planning the estate or recommending that it be planned.

Does U.S. Court Decision Outlaw
All Minimum Fee Schedules?

For many years the members of local County Bar Associations established a so called Schedule of Minimum Fees to be charged. The fee for drafting a will moved up slowly from $25 for a simple will to $50 in many areas. Seldom, if ever, was there ever any mention made, much less suggestion of, an appropriate fee for drafting a complex or involved will or for "Planning an Estate." This more or less left to the lawyer the problem of fixing a legitimate fee for this type of service. Now, since the recent U.S. Supreme Court Decision, striking out minimum fee schedules in Virginia covering the examination and certification of Real Estate Titles as violations of the anti trust statutes or agreements in restraint of trade, the lawyer can rely no longer on even the schedules provided him.

Fixing Fee on Drafting Wills Requires Skill and Diplomacy

I learned a long time ago that setting the fees charged on wills and estates required the utmost skill and diplomacy. I recall one such instance very vividly. An elderly widow owned two combination residences and stores on Main Street which were built on the same large plot. She also had two sons who were then in their 40's or 50's. Her instructions were clear and terse: "I want Charlie to get #109 Main Street and Frank to get #111 Main Street." That was all.

Reasonable Fee Loses Estate

If I had advised her (as I should have) that she should have a survey made so that these commercial properties could be divided properly, I suspect she would have canceled out the will and have gone to some other competing attorney who would draw the will for her without a survey for a nominal fee. So I did the best I could. I personally paced off the plot, double-checked to ascertain how the plot would have to be divided to make sure that each son would have an adequate driveway. Then I drew the will, summoned her to the office to sign it and submitted my bill for $50. This was the minimum fee suggested at that time for a simple will.

The woman was outraged. She pointed out how Mr. Dave Davis, a local Notary Public and Commissioner of Deeds (who was also a retired surveyor) would have drawn it for $25 and probably made a more accurate division. Needless to say, I lost her and the two sons as clients. A short time later she died, and I then found out that indeed she was so incensed at my fee that she had another lawyer draw a new will the same day, probably at one-half the fee. (Incidentally, he adopted and used my division of the property in his will.) Naturally he represented the two sons as Executor, handled the estate and made a substantial fee for the work. In addition, the two sons generated additional legal work for my competitor since one of them later sought a divorce, while the other was seriously injured at work. This experience taught me a lesson I profited from greatly, i.e., don't worry so much about collecting a fair and legitimate fee for drawing a will, just make sure you are retained to handle the estate.

Incidentally, it is more important to cultivate the continued friendship of the executors rather than the testator or testatrix since it is the surviving executors who will retain the attorney to handle the estate. I recall that I was very friendly with a prominent business man who was the owner of a very successful wholesale plumbing supply business. In fact, I had luncheon with him occasionally. However, I neglected to cultivate the friendship of his wife, whom I had met on only one occasion. I was therefore shocked when, upon his death, the widow, instead of retaining me as the person who had drafted the will, retained another attorney of her own personal selection to handle the estate.

Drawing Will vs. Planning Estate

In more recent years, we found ourselves with our position reversed from that involving the widow and her two sons. An elderly doctor who was a widower and quite wealthy went to his lawyer "to have his will drawn." His lawyer correctly perceived that this was a matter that called for estate planning of the highest order. After numerous conferences with his client, considerable research and the drafting and submission of several alternate plans, the doctor selected the one having the largest tax savings potential. The will was drafted accordingly, duly executed by the doctor, and the bill of $1500 submitted to him to cover "Estate Planning and Drafting and Supervision of Proper Execution of Will."

The good doctor almost had a heart attack. He characterized the bill as exorbitant and refused to pay it. Some time later, he retained our office to defend him in the matter. We were finally able to persuade him that the fee was indeed legitimate by pointing out the tax savings to be effected by the estate plan proposed. However, he still protested vehemently and asked me, "What good will that do me—I will be dead?" When the bill was finally paid, I was surprised when the doctor advised me that he wanted a new will drawn at once. When I asked what changes he wanted made, he said, "None, I just want two new witnesses." We complied and he remained a client of this office until he died.

Not How to Plan an Estate, but How to Get One

I made a practice of attending a number of seminars on Estate Planning throughout the years. One of the overworked witticisms came from the attorney who stood up during the question-and-answer period and asked, "I think I know how to plan an estate—but tell us how to get one?" The answer usually was, "If the testator was your father's roommate at college, it helps." But the question is a serious one and deserves serious consideration. There certainly should be some legitimate and ethical method for the younger, ambitious lawyer to attract this kind of desirable practice. Some have found the answer in joining the Country Club, taking up golfing as a serious recreation, etc. These pursuits all have something to recommend them. The difficulty is that the prime prospective clients, who are somewhat elderly and wealthy, usually pair off with relatives and friends of their own age. This still leaves only the informality and camaraderie of the locker room for establishing these desirable contacts and friendships, and they sometimes pay off—but not often.

Banks Can Advertise, but Not Attorneys

The real problem in many sections of the country, particularly for the younger or middle-aged attorneys is the fact that while it is clearly unethical for them to openly or frankly seek this particularly lucrative law practice, no such restrictions are imposed upon the state or federal banks. The more they proliferate with their huge parent corporation and the numerous branches, the more aggressive they appear to become in seeking out and acquiring the executorship of every large or medium-size estate owned by their depositors.

As a result, many persons with substantial means now seem to prefer to have a bank preside over the administration and distribution of their total assets upon their death. These institutions will vigorously protest that there is always an attorney for the estate who passes on all of the legal aspects which may arise. Technically and on the record, this may appear to be true. But the question still arises as to what methods were used to select the attorney and how the attorneys are kept in line if they seek to exercise their legitimate authority and obligations in the supervision of the handling of their clients large estates.

Access to all large depositors is helpful. Some banks and particularly those with large and aggressive trust departments vigorously seek to line up and control this profitable estate work on two separate fronts. In the first place, they have access to the private and confidential information as to the size and worth of the actual deposits made by their customers in their institutions. As soon as these "prime prospects" are identified, they are usually marked for special notice and solicitude by the bank personnel and particularly the trust officers. This continues until their will is drawn and the bank is named as Executors and Trustees of their estates.

At least quarterly or perhaps monthly, or as often as the facts and circumstances seem to warrant it, many of these affluent large depositors are sent a series of attractively printed notes, memoranda, pamphlets, booklets, brochures, etc. with this single sales pitch, "You *need* this wonderful bank and its outstanding trust department as your Executor and Trustee." Many times this practice seems to be clearly within the area of specific legal advice, since some of them include quotations from the I.R.C. and the I.R.S. regulations, reported decisions by the Tax Courts, etc., etc.

The Selection of Attorneys

These banks will in many cases protect themselves from any charges of the unauthorized practice of law, by saying in effect, "You are always allowed or permitted to select and use your own attorney to work with the bank in administering the estate." But when the unwary depositor finally does sit down with the trust officers to discuss the making of his will, he is casually asked, "By the way, who is your *regular* attorney?" Being a peace-loving, non-litigious citizen, his first reaction is to answer, "I don't need any regular attorney—I never get into any trouble where I would need one." This may serve in many cases as the cue for the bank's representative to suggest gently, "Well, we could let you use the lawyer the bank always uses in cases of this kind, If you want us to contact him for you." About this time in the conference, it would be propitious, if not fortuitous, if the President of the Bank or the Chairman of the Board were to drop in accidently at the conference to greet the depositor warmly and assure him that he is doing the right thing and that he is in good hands. The depositor, surrounded by this great solicitude for his welfare, succumbs to these blandishments. The "Bank's usual attorney" is then called and since his office is, fortunately for him and the bank, nearby, he appears and joins the conference. The necessary information is secured and in due time the will is drawn and signed, making the bank the sole Executor and Trustee. Thus this new lawyer has acquired a new client out of the blue, and the bank a desirable estate. Substantially, this very scenario has happened to me on a number of occasions through the years, as a result of which some other attorney winds up handling the estate of persons you have known and worked intimately with for many years.

If by any chance the depositor falls upon hard times and upon his death his estate is diminished below the line upon which the bank can handle it profitably, the bank has no hesitancy to renounce its Executorship promptly and to advise the heirs at law and next of kin to retain the services of some other attorney.

Incidentally, if the estate is still substantial when the testator dies, the attorney recommended by the bank acts as the attorney for the estate—but in fact the bank does all of the work, makes all of the decisions and the attorney in effect becomes little more than a "yes" man. If the attorney attempts to assert himself or disagree with the bank on any matter except those which are strictly legal in nature, he may be politely reminded that the bank selected him and can also remove him with equal ease. The lawyer may, and usually does, get the point at once and may show his appreciation by reducing the legal fees he would normally charge so that there will be no complaint by the heirs if the bank charges and collects the full statutory fee to which it is entitled.

How to Meet This Type of Competition

What can the average lawyer do to protect himself from having his clients or potential clients diverted from his office in matters of Estate Planning? Obviously, he is prohibited from advertising his availability. Other effective and ethical methods may be available to him. I have yet to find the full or complete answer in my many years of practice—but I am still seeking it. There are some effective techniques available to the lawyers, but they fail to use them in many instances.

Services as Deputy Surrogate

Back in the mid-30's when I was a very young lawyer, I had the "Great Depression" to contend with in addition to all the other usual problems confronting the neophyte lawyer. I solved the problem of income, at least temporarily, by accepting appointment as Deputy Surrogate of my own county on a part-time basis. Actually, I was Counsel to the Surrogate since he was a layman with no legal training at all, although his salary was approximately twice the size of mine.

In addition to probating wills, appointing General Administrators, Trustees, Guardians, etc., I was given the responsibility of auditing all of the accountings filed by fiduciaries and reporting them personally in open court. The attorney for the estate and usually the trust officer of the bank, acting as Executor, would apply not only for approval of their accounting, but for allowances by the court of commissions and counsel fees.

A $40,000 Legal Fee

All went along routinely for a few years as the Depression droned on and on. However, on one Motion Day in particular, the court allowed one of the larger banks in the county a commission of approximately $40,000 and a prominent law firm handling the estate an additional $40,000 in counsel fees. The allowances, of course, were proper and routine on estates of this size, but this time, it started me thinking. Here was a firm of lawyers who were being awarded legal fees which equaled my salary as Deputy Surrogate for about ten years! Shortly thereafter, I handed in my resignation and decided that any profession which could award its practitioners that much compensation in a single matter deserved my full time and full attention. I have never regretted this decision.

Educational Talks Before Groups

During the years of service as Deputy Surrogate, I had met most, if not all, of the Trust Officers of the banks in the 25 municipalities embraced in the county. I had also met all or most of the practicing attorneys who handled estate work. I had also acted as guest speaker at innumerable luncheons, dinners and other public affairs sponsored by service clubs, Chambers of Commerce, political and church groups and every other type of organization imaginable, explaining the functions of the Surrogate's Office. I also wrote a weekly educational column on Wills and Estates which was later published and sold under the title of "Steps in the Administration of an Estate."

Hence, I had become rather well known throughout the county as a person possessing more than average skill and experience in the field of Wills and Estates. I thought that with this background all I had to do was to wait in my office and that attractive estate work would come flocking to my door. But nothing of this sort happened. It is true that occasionally I was brought into an estate by other counsel but these were usually the toughest kinds of matters to handle, i.e., Caveats against Wills, Will Contests, Exceptions to Accountings, etc. But after a short time, even this type of practice declined substantially.

Use of Wills and Estate Manuals

The average lawyer, no matter how gifted or well known he may be can not expect very many, if any, million-dollar estates to come to his office. In the first place, there are just not that many millionaires. By degrees it becomes evident that potential estates available fall logically into the usual categories, viz:

small, medium and large. Each law office may have set up a specific routine for each of these types. To illustrate, I know of a number of law offices which have prepared a ''Wills and Estates Office Manual'' and distribute a copy not only to every lawyer in the office but to each law secretary as well.

Thus instead of dictating each new will, the attorney in charge will give the secretary a brief memo with the basic facts of names, addresses, executors, beneficiaries, etc. and will indicate the various sections of the ''Manual'' to use to complete the will. This usually suffices for the small and many of the medium-size estates. However, all the larger ones are custom designed to make certain there are no slip-ups.

One of the difficulties in using the ''Manual'' in preparing wills for even a small estate is that in many instances such a will may end up by reciting a full page more or less devoted exclusively to listing the wide powers granted the executor. In smaller estates, this is of course frequently unnecessary, and in fact may only serve to confuse the client. Over the years we have found that wills for all of the small estates and many of the medium-size ones can be accurately and effectively handled by the use of a simple form designed by us entitled ''Data Sheet for Preparation of Wills,'' a copy of which follows this chapter. The form can be taken home by the client and discussed with the spouse and then filled in and returned to the office, or it may be filled in directly at the office, as you interview the client. A competent and trained para-legal secretary may also obtain the information from the client in the event the attorney is in court or is otherwise unavailable. Incidentally, the wills which may be handled in this manner are usually the routine ones requiring little, if any, estate planning.

Estate Planning Mandatory in All Substantial Estates

Some of the medium-size estates and *all* of the large estates should be preceded by careful Estate Planning before the will is prepared. This will require one or more extended office conferences with either one or both spouses; a careful analysis of the tax consequences of each devise or bequest; and at least a preliminary, confidential ''Estate Planning Inventory.''

The client should be advised that not only is good planning absolutely essential now, but that the facts and details set forth in this confidential inventory should be reviewed by the attorney and the client regularly every few years, or as often as may be deemed necessary in the light of any substantial or significant changes in the family size and expenses; the personal objectives of the testator; changes in the investment climate; changes in the tax laws under I.R.C., etc. It should be stressed to the client that not only the will itself should be reviewed regularly, but that all of the collateral matters upon which the estate was planned should also be reviewed regularly. These would include such items as insurance, investments, pension funds, family needs, tax consequences, etc.

Estate Plan Only as Good as Data Relied Upon

It should also be pointed out to the client that any Estate Plan is only as good as the accuracy of all the facts upon which it is based. Thus a properly prepared inventory which includes not only the assets of the client but all of the other factors listed above, will not only be imperative but if properly presented, will actually point up the need for the plan itself and the amount of good such estate planning will accomplish.

Incidentally, a "Preliminary Confidential Inventory for Estate Planning" has been developed and published by the Institute for Business Planning, Inc. and is available either singly or in quantities at a very modest price. When completed properly, forms of this kind will give both the client and the attorney a comprehensive and accurate list of practically all of the problems to be provided for in the Estate Planning. Moreover, it will actually point up the logical solutions for meeting these problems as well.

When the will is finally drafted, based on such data, this Inventory Booklet may be submitted to the client with the draft of the will annexed, much as an insurance planner would present a brochure covering the insurance coverage proposed for a family. Thus the client may review the entire matter with his spouse and his accountant, if necessary, before giving his final approval to the attorney. Incidentally, if the lawyer is not quite certain as to where he should include his estimated fees for legal services, they may be included under the general caption of "Administration Expenses." A list of the chapter heads in the booklet published by the Institute for Business Planning, Inc. is included for review at the end of this chapter.

Only Legitimate Sources of Estate Work
Are Through Your Clients

But the question still remains, "How can a lawyer attract desirable estate work into his office in a proper and ethical manner?" The answer is both obvious and simple. You can only attract it ethically through your existing clients. Did you ever stop to analyze or consider the fact that every existing client is a logical candidate for future estate work? If you enjoy the confidence and respect of a client sufficiently for him to have retained you for other legal services, why should not this apply with equal or even greater force to the handling of his estate?

Few new clients will come to your office in the first place expressly to have their wills drawn. They are likely to come in on any one of a dozen other matters. They may have been involved in an auto accident; or making a real estate purchase; or securing a mortgage loan; or they may be involved in a civil suit or claim against them; a divorce; a criminal or quasi-criminal matter; or to apply for Letters Testamentary or Letters of Administration on the estate of one of their parents who has just died. Yet every one of these clients is a potential estate client, if the matter is handled or approached in a dignified and professional manner.

Every Unusual Occurrence Raises
Question of Need for Will

Almost every unusual occurrence in the life of a family gives rise to the question of whether its members have executed wills to protect their family in the event of their untimely or sudden death. For example, in an automobile negligence case, the injured client might very well have been killed. If so, would there have been a will in existence to smooth the handling of the decedent's estate? Or in the case of a newly-married couple who are about to take upon themselves the mutual and reciprocal burdens they owe to each other; or the birth of a child adding to their responsibility; or in purchasing their homes; shouldn't they, and each of them, have a will and thus avoid unnecessary complications in a time of stress and sorrow? Or in the case of divorce, shouldn't they have individual wills to help solve the many problems which this new status in society will present to them? Thus it can be seen that there is no end to the variety of situations in which a lawyer not only has the ethical right and privilege of inquiring as to their will status, but a professional obligation to recommend that his clients think seriously of making their wills.

Attorneys Duty to Warn Clients of
Potential Tax Consequences

The banks may enjoy an almost exclusive contact and friendship with their large depositors—but the practicing lawyer has a very special entry to his own clients. He would be wise to use it. This is about the only way an attorney can hope to meet and overcome the banks' efforts to secure control of every sizable or desirable estate. I do not see any legitimate question of ethics or disciplinary rules involved. In fact, I have known of many cases where it would have been little less than legal malpractice not to warn existing clients of the legal and tax pitfalls which lie ahead unless these problems are anticipated and provided for by adequate Estate Planning.

Where Failure to Plan Estate Caused $90,000 in Taxes

One case comes vividly to mind. A middle-aged couple had an only child, a son. They both executed mutual and reciprocal wills while the son was only an infant. The man died prematurely while still in his 40's. The widow inherited a modest estate including a variety of stocks listed on both the New York Stock Exchange and the American Stock Exchange, which were then of a modest value. The widow moved to another state and we lost contact with her. However, when she died some 30 years later, it was learned that the only will she had ever made was the one we had drawn more than 30 years earlier. Meanwhile, a number of the blocks of stock she originally had, had split, not once, but several times in the intervening period. The effect of this was to increase the value of the estate to $500,000 or more. The son had grown up and had three children of his own. Paying a substantial estate tax was painful enough, but when he paid almost $90,000 in Federal Estate Taxes, it was even more painful. Most of these taxes could have been avoided by proper Estate Planning. You will note that I use the word "avoided" and not "evaded." There is of course a world of difference between the two.

Where Timely Tax Planning Saved $75,000 in Taxes

But sometimes fate intervenes to help rather than hurt a client. I had a close friend and associate who was a C.P.A. I dealt with him on almost a daily basis. We never discussed wills or Estate Planning. Then he suddenly suffered a slight heart attack. This shocked me into being very frank with him. I asked him bluntly if he had a will? Yes, he had one drawn many years ago when he was poor and struggling to support his wife and family. I persuaded him that we should both sit down together and just for the "kick of it," see how much death taxes we could have saved him and didn't, if the heart attack had been fatal.

We finally came up with a plan involving an Inter Vivos Trust to be substantially funded at once, plus the wills for him and his wife, providing for the usual split trusts. He was a little embarrassed to disclose his actual worth to me. We solved that easily by providing the Schedule of Assets for the Inter Vivos Trust on a separate sheet, to be prepared by himself confidentially. In this case we used a prominent bank with a strong Trust Department (since he was an officer and director). He died about six months later. In an estate approximating the one-half million mark the accountant estimated that we had saved the estate approximately $75,000 in taxes.

Lawyer's Four Tools for Tax Savings in Estates

I believe it is now generally known by most attorneys, and certainly by those who do any substantial amount of estate work, that there are four primary legal tools which can be used in Estate Planning to reduce the tax impact at the time of death, where the gross estate exceeds $60,000. These are (1) the once-in a lifetime gift of $30,000 ($60,000 where husband and wife); (2) $3,000 gifts per annum to any number of donees; (3) the use of the marital deduction amounting approximately to 50 percent of the adjusted gross estate; (4) the division of the residue in the will into two separate trusts. Under items 1 and 2, the client can progressively divest himself of a substantial part of his estate through tax-exempt gifts to various members of his family before he dies, such as to children, grand-children, etc. Items 3 and 4, as above set forth, come into play at the time of the client's death.

The Two-Trust Method

Through the use of the two testamentary trusts (or provision for two trusts in the Inter Vivos Trust), the client can permit his widow to receive the approximate 50 percent covered by the marital deduction and the benefits of the remaining approximate 50 percent covered by conventional trusts. In this way, the widow can receive the entire income from both trusts during her lifetime—with the right to invade the principal as well, if necessary, and the right to exercise a ''Power of Attorney'' upon her death as to the marital deduction trust. The explanation given to the client as to the necessity for this procedure is relatively simple. For instance, if the husband gave his entire estate to his wife, a tax would be imposed on the whole estate (exclusive of the exemption, of course) and then when the wife dies a few years later (as is usually the case), a tax would again be imposed on the whole estate for a second time. When these explanations are given to a client, they usually understand the need for Estate Planning—but even then, they are still averse to paying an adequate fee. However, this can be compensated for in some measure at least if the lawyer handles the estate, which is usually the case.

The Politician's Last Trick Is His Last Will

Finally, before closing this chapter, there is one incident which I must recount since it still amuses me (after the first shock wore off). One of our clients was a prominent politician. He came to the office to have his will drawn. We followed the usual system we have for many years. The will was finally drafted, we mailed a *carbon copy* to the client's home, advising him in the accompanying letter that we were doing this to afford him ample opportunity to study it and advise us if any amendments or corrections were required. Moreover, we further advised him that if the will was satisfactory as drawn, he should come to the office at any time which suited his convenience to sign the *original,* which we had retained for that purpose. Months and months went by and by some oversight, we did not follow through on this matter. When the politician died, about a year later, we learned for the first time that the wily old codger had carefully and legally executed the *carbon copy* with two neighbors serving as witnesses. When the son lodged the *Will* with the Surrogate for probate, that official demanded production of the *original,* but the son assured him that this "copy" was in effect the only "original" one in existence, since the actual original still lay in our office unsigned. The Surrogate conceded that under the circumstances, he had no other choice but to admit the signed copy to probate. Thus we not only did not handle the estate, but we were not even paid for drafting the will. I am sure that somewhere, beyond the "Great Divide" or across the "River Styx," there is an ex-politician who is quite satisfied with himself at the success of the last trick he played on a trusting attorney before he crossed into the "Great Beyond." Incidentally, we still mail out the *carbon copy* of the wills, but when indicated, we take the precaution of tearing off the portion where the signature would normally appear, or rubber stamp the body conspicuously as a "copy".

DATA SHEET FOR PREPARATION OF WILLS

Testator _____

Name of Testatrix _____

Address _____

FIRST CLAUSE: Usual clause directing executor to pay debts, funeral expenses, etc.

SECOND CLAUSE: List names and amounts of any special legacies.

Name of Legatee	Relationship	Legacy
_____	_____	_____
_____	_____	_____
_____	_____	_____
_____	_____	_____

THIRD CLAUSE: If spouse survives, do you wish entire residue, real, personal and mixed, to be left to spouse outright?

_____Yes   _____No

Full name of Spouse

Do you wish spouse to be named sole executor or co-executor?

_____Yes   _____No

Name of Executor (s)_____

FOURTH CLAUSE: In the event your spouse predeceases you, or you die simultaneously or as the result of a common disaster, or before title passes or within 6 months of your death from any cause, list the contingent beneficiaries and amount they are to receive.

Contingent Beneficiary	Relationship	Proportion of Estate
_____	_____	_____
_____	_____	_____
_____	_____	_____
_____	_____	_____

FIFTH CLAUSE: If spouse predeceases, etc. whom do you wish to appoint as contingent executor or executors?

Name of Contingent Executor (s)_____

Do you wish said contingent executors to also be named as trustees of your minor children during their minority?

_____Yes   _____No

Do you wish a trust created in your Will for any purpose? If so, explain. _____

_____

_____

SIXTH CLAUSE: Do you wish a clause inserted to provide for afterborn children? _____Yes   _____No

SEVENTH CLAUSE: Do you wish a clause inserted revoking all previous Wills? _____ Yes   _____ No

REMARKS:

Please set forth any additional remarks which will help in the drafting of your Will. _____

_____

_____

GENERAL NOTES:

1. Does your spouse want a Will drawn similar to yours? _____Yes _____No

2. List any Special Changes in Spouse's Will.

_____

_____

_____

3. Name of Contingent Executor (s) for Spouse's Will.

(Signed)_____

(Signed)_____

ESTATE PLANNING INVENTORY*

(Preliminary Inventory Questionnaire)

An estate plan should be carefully and regularly reviewed in the light of constantly developing changes in the client's financial situation, family size and expenses, personal and family objectives, changes in the tax structure and in the investment climate.

One's will, insurance, the ownership of family assets, investment policy, the benefits derived from employment, trust arrangements—all of these and many other aspects of the estate plan may be in need of rearrangement. They are certainly in need of a regular review. The most basic, and sometimes the most difficult, requirement of developing an estate plan (or reviewing and bringing up to date a previously developed plan) is nailing down the facts as to what the client has and as to the existing arrangements for its growth and ultimate disposition.

This "inventory"—originally developed by the Institute for Business Planning, Inc.—is designed to give you an accurate and complete picture of assets, what you and the client have previously done, and objectives. It marshalls the facts which permit an informed judgment as to whether one's estate plan is still sound and whether additional steps can be developed to utilize assets and income to realize financial objectives more effectively. With the facts called for by this form, it is possible to project the probable growth of the estate, determine how tax liabilities against it may be minimized, estimate how much income it can be expected to produce in retirement or for the family after death, measure future needs and propose methods of bridging any gaps between future income and future needs.

Remember: *An estate plan is no better than the facts on which it is based.*

---

*Copyright © Fourth Edition 1976 Institute for Business Planning, Inc.—IBP Plaza, Englewood Cliffs, N.J. 07632

123

PRELIMINARY INVENTORY QUESTIONNAIRE

FAMILY DATA

1. <u>Name</u>   Date of Birth   Health   Insurable
      Husband
      Wife

2. <u>Residence</u>
      Home address
      Business address
      Present main residence -- State
      Period of residence in present State
      If less than 10 years, list prior residences:

      Any other residence or place which may be considered a residence or domicile, such as apartment or house maintained elsewhere, including summer house, voting address, church membership, club membership, etc., in other state?

3. <u>Citizenship</u>
      Husband: USA ( )   Other ( )
      Wife: USA ( )   Other ( )

4. <u>Children and grandchildren</u>
      <u>Name</u>   <u>Date of Birth</u>   <u>Married</u>   <u>Number of Children</u>   <u>Occupation*</u>

      *Source of livelihood of married daughter, occupation of husband.

5. <u>Other dependents</u>
      <u>Name</u>   <u>Date of Birth</u>   <u>Relationship</u>

6. <u>Special family problems</u>
      Previous marriages and commitments therefrom (copy of decree and settlement papers)

      Prospective inheritances

ASSETS

Estimate the value of each of the following items of property owned by · you and your wife (if any) and indicate if jointly owned.

	OWNED BY		
	Husband	Wife	Jointly
A. Cash and accounts	$	$	$
B. Notes, accounts receivable, mortgages			
C. Bonds			
D. Stock			
E. Real estate:			
F. Employee benefits (bring in last statement and descriptive booklets)			
G. Stock options:			
Number of shares			
Option price			
Current value			
H. Insurance (bring policies)			
I. Personal effects			
J. Miscellaneous property (patents, trademarks, copyrights, royalties, etc.)			
K. Business interests (bring in last balance sheet and P & L statement, tax returns, buy-sell agreements, etc.)			

LIABILITIES

A. Real estate mortgages			
B. Notes to banks			
C. Loans on insurance policies			
D. Accounts to others			
E. Pledges to churches and charities			
F. Taxes			

<table>
<tr><td colspan="2">

CHECKLIST OF DOCUMENTS AND OTHER INFORMATION NEEDED

</td></tr>
</table>

		Delivered	Returned
1) Birth certificate -- yours, spouse's, children's	1		
2) Social Security No. . . . . Marriage certificate	2		
3) Deeds to realty	3		
4) Leases on property on which you are the lessor or lessee	4		
5) Partnership agreements	5		
6) Business agreement between yourself and associates	6		
7) Purchase & sale contracts	7		
8) Close corporation charters, by-laws & minute books	8		
9) Balance sheets & profit & loss statements for last 5 years, in all businesses in which you have a proprietary interest	9		
10) Personal balance sheets and income statements for last 5 years, if any were made	10		
11) Divorce decrees	11		
12) Property settlements with spouse antenuptial agreements	12		
13) Trust instruments	13		
14) Your will			
Spouse's will			
Will of other members of family, if pertinent	14		
15) Instruments creating power of appointment of which you are donee or donor	15		
16) Life insurance policies & dividend data	16		
17) General insurance policies	17		
18) Copies of employment contracts, pension benefits, etc.	18		
19) Other legal documents evidencing possible or actual rights and/or liabilities	19		
20) Income tax returns, federal & state, for past five years	20		
21) Gift tax returns and copies of revenue agent's reports if any	21		
22) Veterans service records	22		

ADVISORS

	Name	Address	Phone No.
Attorney	. . . .	. . . .	. . . .
Accountant	. . . .	. . . .	. . . .
Trust Officer	. . . .	. . . .	. . . .
Other bank officer	. . . .	. . . .	. . . .
Life Insurance Underwriter	. . . . . .	. . . .	. . . .
Investment Advisor	. . . .	. . . .	. . . .
Stock Broker utilized by client	. . . .	. . . .	. . . .
Tax Advisor	. . . .	. . . .	. . . .
General Insurance Broker	. . . .	. . . .	. . . .
Others	. . . .	. . . .	. . . .

COMPREHENSIVE INVENTORY QUESTIONNAIRE

Schedule A

CASH AND BANK BALANCES

	Bank	Average Balance			
		Self	Wife	Joint	Total
Cash		$	$	$	$
Checking Accounts					
Savings Accounts					
Total:		$	$	$	$

Schedule B

NOTES, ACCOUNTS RECEIVABLE, MORTGAGES

Debtor	Nature of Debt	Security	Maturity	Yield	Face Amount	Present Value
1.					$	$
2.						
3.						
Total:					$	$

Schedule C

BOND HOLDINGS

Description of Bonds	Ownership	Number of Units	Face Value	Cost	Annual Yield	Current Value
			$	$		$
Government Bonds	Ownership	Maturity	Annual Yield		Death Beneficiary	Face Value
Total Bond Value:						$

Schedule D

STOCKS HELD

Description	Ownership	Number of Shares	Cost	Annual Yield	Current Value
			$	$	$
Total:			$	$	$

Schedule E

REAL ESTATE

	Property #1	Property #2	Property #3	Property #4
Description				
Location				
Residence?				
Income Producing?				
Owned in Names of:				
Form of Ownership				
% of Cost Contributed by Joint Owners				
Date of Acquisition				
Year Joint Ownership Created				
How Acquired (Gift, Purchase, etc.)				
Cost Basis				
Names & Addresses of mortgagees, lienors, etc.				
Encumbrances: Amount				
Monthly Payments				
Annual Income (gross)				
Average Annual Interest				
Annual Depreciation				
Annual Costs (Maintenance, etc.)				
Annual Taxes				
Annual Net Income				
Present Taxable Value				

Schedule F

EMPLOYEE BENEFITS

Employer's Name and Address ....

Type of Plan (Obtain copies of Plans)	Check if Applicable·	Retirement Benefits	Amount Vested	Death Benefits
Pension		$	$	$
Profit-Sharing				
Savings				
Deferred Compensation				
Total:		$	$	$

	Company	Benefits	Beneficiary
Group Insurance			
Accident & Health			
Medical			
Surgical			
Hospital			

Stock Options: Number of shares now (........); later (........) list conditions of additional

options becoming exercisable ....

Give: Option price $ .... ; Current Value $ ....

Unrealized Appreciation $ _____

Schedule G

MISCELLANEOUS ASSETS

A. **Personal Effects**   Current Value

    Home furnishings $ ....

    Automobiles   ....

    Jewels & furs   ....

    Collections (art, etc.)   ....

    Miscellaneous personal effects   ....

B. **Intellectual Property**   Annual Income   Expiration   Current Value

    Patents $ .... $ ....

    Trade-marks   ....

    Copyrights   ....

C. **Other Contract Rights**: Give details of prospective profits, liabilities and values involved

....

                Total Value of Miscellaneous Assets $ ....

Schedule H

BUSINESS INTERESTS

Co. Name . . . . Address . . . .

Corp. . . . . Part. . . . . Sole Prop. . . . . State Inc. or Law . . . .

Partners or Stockholders Name	Age	Stock P'f'd. Com.	% Part- ner Int.	Title	Notes

Is There a Business Agreement? (give details or secure copy)

Is Partner Financially Responsible?

Type: Criss Cross ☐   Date Last Reviewed

    Partnership Entity ☐   How Funded?

    Stock Retirement ☐   Amount of Funding   Corporate Trustee

How Is Value Determined?   Any § 303 IRC Stock Redemption Planned?

Is Life Insurance Carried	Insured	Amount	Owner	Beneficiary
Purpose		$		

Capitalization:	Par Value	Div. or Interest Rate	Total Authorized	Total Issued	Callable
Common Stock	$				
Preferred					
Debentures, etc.					

Owner's estimate of value   Liquidation value

Book value as of

Is good will included in book value?

Average net earnings (after taxes), last 3 to 5 years

(Secure balance sheets and earning statements)

Checklist of Business Information

(1) List names, ages, and duties of "key men"

(2) In event of your death, or of any "key man," would there be difficulty in (a) continuing to receive credit? (b) continuing franchise?

(3) In event of your death would it be more desirable to conserve the business or to liquidate the business?

    (a) Does your family have the ability to continue it?

(4) Which associates or employees might like to purchase your interest at your death or retirement (even if they are not in a financial position to do so)?

    (a) Are you grooming replacements for yourself and other key men?

(5) Would you like to dispose of your business during your lifetime -- e.g., near the retirement age?

(6) Do you have any benefit, security, or incentive plans for your employees?

Have you considered such plans?

(7) Have you a business agreement which governs the disposition of the interest of any associate who dies?

Schedule I

PERSONAL LIABILITIES

Bills and accounts payable	$	Installment contrácts	$ . . . .
Loans and Notes		Joint notes	. . . .
Bank	. . . .	Notes endorsed	. . . .
Insurance	. . . .	Accounts guaranteed	. . . .
Brokers	. . . .	Realty taxes	. . . .
To others	. . . .	Personal property taxes	. . . .
Mortgages	. . . .	Disputed or past due taxes	. . . .
Current income tax-estimates		Unsettled damage claims	. . . .
Rent on unexpired leases	. . . .	Miscellaneous	. . . .
Total			$ . . . .

Schedule J

INCOME DATA

	Self	Wife	Others
Income sources	$	$	$
Salary			
Bonuses			
Commissions			
Dividends			
Interest			
Net Rents			
Royalties			
Business profits.			
Annuities			
Trusts			
Other			
Total:	$	$	$

For Last 5 Years	1	2	3	4	5
Total family income	$	$	$	$	$
Total tax.					
Living expenses					
Insurance premiums					
Available for other savings . .					
Top income tax bracket	%	%	%	%	%

Notes: 1. Obtain copy of income tax returns.
2. Identify all items of community property income if you live in a community property state.

WILLS, GIFTS, TRUSTS

WILLS

Get copies of wills of all family members. Review pertinent data on present and future will plans including the following: Specific Bequests; Specific Devised; Disposition of Residuary Estate; Tax Apportionment; Marital Deduction Provisions; Survivorship Presumptions Created; Trusts; Nomination of Executors, Guardians & Successors; Authority of Executor to Continue Business.

GIFTS

Obtain pertinent data on gifts previously made including the following information: Date; Donated Property; Donee; Value of Time of Gift; Present Value; Donor's Cost Basis; Has a Gift Tax Return Been Filed?; Have Tax Authorities Examined Returns?; Circumstances & Reason for Gift; Has Donor Retained Control?; Remaining Unused Lifetime Exemptions Under Federal & State Laws; Are Further Gifts Under Consideration? (Obtain copies of gift tax returns and any Revenue Agent's Reports.)

TRUSTS

For EACH trust, obtain copy and pertinent data including: Trustee; Date Created; Purpose; Revocable or Not (if revocable, how?); Nature of Corpus; Value of Corpus; Corpus Income; Beneficiaries; Gift Over; How are Income & Principal to be Distributed; Term of Trust.

POWER OF APPOINTMENT

If any member of the family group has the right to dispose of property not owned by him or her, be such right during lifetime or by will, details should be given and copies of instruments creating such right should be attached and the approximate value of the property given.

INTEREST IN ESTATE

Obtain copies of any instruments and pertinent data including: Is estate owner beneficiary of outright will? Trust? Does he have a life interest? A contingent interest? Value of interest $........... Estimated income $......... Disposition if he dies before receipt? Is he a grantee of a power to appoint outside of expected class? Right of withdrawal? Portion of amount? When? Restricted? Value of property subject to right $........? Year grantor deceased? Trust created before 10/21/42?

OBJECTIVES

I.   Death or Disability:

    a)   What are your spouse's minimum income requirements?

    b)   What income would you want her to have if possible?

    c)   What is the minimum income required for your family until all the children are no longer dependent?

    d)   Will any child be dependent after attaining maturity?   Give details.

    e)   To what degree is wife capable of managing financial affairs?

    f)   Will wife continue to live in present home?

    g)   Should mortgage be paid off?

    h)   Social Security status?

    i)   Should she be protected against: 1--possible senility,   2--possible second husband,
                                                 3--her caprices,   4--anything else?

II.   Retirement:

    a)   At what age do you wish to retire?

    b)   What is the _minimum_ income you need for retirement?

    c)   What income would you consider _ample_ during retirement?

    d)   Do you want excess of income over your minimum needs to go to your children, or to you?

    e)   What are your investment objectives?   Growth?   Income?   Safety?

III.   Children:

    a)   What are your hopes for your children and what are their capabilities?

    b)   Shall your children be permitted to consume capital or only income?

    c)   When and how should capital be distributed?

    d)   Should any special problems be considered and special allowances made,
        as for example, for physical defects, personality, ability, etc.?

    e)   What educational and business opportunities do you wish them to be provided for, if possible?

Schedule K

EDUCATIONAL FUNDS

Children	Preparatory		College		Professional	
	Date	Amount	Date	Amount	Date	Amount
		$		$		$
Total:		$		$		$

IV.   Gifts:

    1)   Do you have any plans for gifts to your relatives or others during your lifetime?
        If so, give details.

V.   Charity:

    1)   To which charities do you contribute regularly and how much per annum?

    2)   Which charities would you like to provide for, how much, and in what manner?

NOTES ON OBJECTIVES

Schedule **M**

ASSETS

	CLIENT			SPOUSE		
		Check Box If Jointly Owned			Check Box If Jointly Owned	
		w/SPS	w/Other		w/Clt.	w/Other
A. Cash and accounts:						
1. Cash in banks regular checking	$ _____	☐	☐	$ _____	☐	☐
2. Deposits in banks savings and others	_____	☐	☐	_____	☐	☐
B. Stocks:						
1. Stocks, liquid	_____	☐	☐	_____	☐	☐
2. Stocks, illiquid	_____	☐	☐	_____	☐	☐
C. Bonds:						
1. U.S. Govt. Bonds.	_____	☐	☐	_____	☐	☐
2. Other bonds.	_____	☐	☐	_____	☐	☐
D. Real estate:						
1. Residential	_____	☐	☐	_____	☐	☐
2. Unimproved.	_____	☐	☐	_____	☐	☐
3. Income producing	_____	☐	☐	_____	☐	☐
E. Receivables:						
1. Notes.	_____	☐	☐	_____	☐	☐
2. Mortgages.	_____	☐	☐	_____	☐	☐
F. Personalty:						
1. Autos, boats, etc.	_____	☐	☐	_____	☐	☐
2. Jewelry and furs	_____	☐	☐	_____	☐	☐
3. Objects of art	_____	☐	☐	_____	☐	☐
4. Furniture and household effects	_____	☐	☐	_____	☐	☐
5. Apparel and personal effects	_____	☐	☐	_____	☐	☐
G. Business interests:						
1. Proprietorships	_____	☐	☐	_____	☐	☐
2. Copartnerships	_____	☐	☐	_____	☐	☐
3. Close corporations	_____	☐	☐	_____	☐	☐
H. Shares in trust funds:	_____	☐	☐	_____	☐	☐
Total	$ _____			$ _____		

Schedule M (cont'd)   **CLIENT**   **SPOUSE**

Total Carried Forward: $ _____   Check Box of $ _____   Check Box of
                                        Beneficiary   Beneficiary

			SPS	Est.	Other		SPS	Est.	Other
I.	Insurance and annuities:								
	1. Ordinary life	_____	☐	☐	☐	_____	☐	☐	☐
	2. Group life	_____	☐	☐	☐	_____	☐	☐	☐
	3. Endowment	_____	☐	☐	☐	_____	☐	☐	☐
	4. Annuities	_____	☐	☐	☐	_____	☐	☐	☐
J.	Corporate benefits:								
	1. Pension	_____	☐	☐	☐	_____	☐	☐	☐
	2. Profit Sharing	_____	☐	☐	☐	_____	☐	☐	☐
	3. Deferred Comp	_____	☐	☐	☐	_____	☐	☐	☐
	4. Stock Bonus	_____	☐	☐	☐	_____	☐	☐	☐
	TOTAL ASSETS (owned).	$ _____				$ _____			
		_____				_____			

┌─────────────────────┐
│   LIABILITIES   │
└─────────────────────┘

			Check Box If Jointly Owned			Check Box If Jointly Owned	
			w/SPS	w/Other		w/Clt.	w/Other
A.	Real Estate Mortgages	$ _____	☐	☐	$ _____	☐	☐
B.	Notes to Banks.	_____	☐	☐	_____	☐	☐
C.	Loans on Insurance Policies. .	_____	☐	☐	_____	☐	☐
D.	Accounts to Others	_____	☐	☐	_____	☐	☐
E.	Pledges to Churches and Charities.	_____	☐	☐	_____	☐	☐
F.	Taxes.	_____	☐	☐	_____	☐	☐
	TOTAL LIABILITIES (owned).	$ _____			$ _____		

┌─────────────────────┐
│   SUMMARY   │
└─────────────────────┘

Total Client's Assets . . . . $ _____
    Less Liabilities. . . . .   _____
        Net Estate. . . . . $ _____

Total Spouse's Assets. . . . . $ _____
    Less Liabilities. . . . .   _____
        Net Estate. . . . . $ _____

Schedule N

ESTATE INVENTORY SUMMARY

Assets & Liabilities of: _____

Item	Present Value	Amount Taxable	Availability for Liquidity	Cost Basis
Bank Accounts:				
Checking				
Saving				
Bonds:				
Stock:				
Unrealized Stock Option Appreciation:				
Real Estate:				
Residence				
Other:				
_____				
Profit Sharing Plan:				
Life Insurance:				
Permanent				
Group				
Cash value of insur. on: _____				
Personal and Household:				
Gross Estate Inventory				
Less Debts:				
Net Estate Inventory				

Schedule N

ESTATE INVENTORY SUMMARY

Assets & Liabilities of: _____

Item	Present Value	Amount Taxable	Availability for Liquidity	Cost Basis
Bank Accounts:				
Checking				
Saving				
Bonds:				
Stock:				
Unrealized Stock Option Appreciation:				
Real Estate:				
Residence				
Other:				
_____				
Profit Sharing Plan:				
Life Insurance:				
Permanent				
Group				
Cash value of insur. on: _____				
Personal and Household:				
Gross Estate Inventory				
Less Debts:				
Net Estate Inventory				

Schedule O

SUMMARY OF DISTRIBUTION OF PROPERTY

A. Your Property

    (1) Passing by Will

    (2) Passing by Operation of Law

    (3) Passing by Contract

B. Mrs. _____ Property

    (1) Passing by Will

    (2) Passing by Operation of Law

    (3) Passing by Contract

<u>Schedule P</u>

+-------------------------------------+
| **LIFE INSURANCE SUMMARY** |
+-------------------------------------+

Insurance on: _____   Owned by: _____

Present Age: _____   Health: _____   Present Agent: _____

	Policy	# _____	# _____	# _____	# _____	Totals
1.	Company					
2.	Age at Issue					
3.	Type of Policy					
4.	Face Value					
5.	Dividend Additions or Accumulations					
6.	Terms Riders					
7.	Total Death Value					
8.	Net Premium					
9.	Cash Value					
10.	Policy Loans					
11.	Primary Beneficiary					
12.	Settlement Option					
13.	Remainderman					
14.	Secondary Beneficiary					
15.	Settlement Option					
16.	Remainderman					
17.	Amount Qualified for Marital Deduction					
18.	Notes					

Schedule **Q**

ESTATE TAXES AND EXPENSES

Assuming that _____ dies _____

Gross Estate (per Schedule N) .... $

Less Expenses and Debts:

    Accrued income tax .... $

    Debts

    Funeral expenses & last illness

    Administration expenses

        Total (3 cols) .... $ _____ $ _____ $

Adjusted Gross Estate .... $

    Less:

    Specific exemption .... $ 60,000

    Marital deduction

    Charitable deduction

        Total (2 cols) .... $ _____ $

Taxable Estate: .... $

Computation of Tax:*

    First bracket .... $

    Tax on balance

        Total .... $

Less State Tax Credit

    Fed. tax (2 cols) .... $ _____ $

Estimated State Tax* .... $

TOTAL TAXES AND EXPENSES .... $

_____

*Rounded to nearest hundred.

Schedule Q

ESTATE TAXES AND EXPENSES

Assuming that _____ dies _____

Gross Estate (per Schedule N)		$	
Less Expenses and Debts:			
Accrued income tax	$		
Debts			
Funeral expenses & last illness			
Administration expenses			
Total (3 cols)	$	$	$
Adjusted Gross Estate		$	
Less:			
Specific exemption	$ 60, 000		
Marital deduction			
Charitable deduction			
Total (2 cols)	$	$	
Taxable Estate:		$	
Computation of Tax:*			
First bracket	$		
Tax on balance			
Total	$		
Less State Tax Credit			
Fed. tax (2 cols)	$		$
Estimated State Tax*			$
TOTAL TAXES AND EXPENSES			$

---

*Rounded to nearest hundred.

Schedule **Q**

ESTATE TAXES AND EXPENSES

Assuming that _____ dies _____

Gross Estate (per Schedule N) $

Less Expenses and Debts:

    Accrued income tax $

    Debts

    Funeral expenses & last illness

    Administration expenses

        Total (3 cols) $ _____ $ _____ $

Adjusted Gross Estate $

  Less:

    Specific exemption $ 60,000

    Marital deduction

    Charitable deduction

        Total (2 cols) $ _____ $ _____

Taxable Estate: $ _____

Computation of Tax:*

    First bracket $

    Tax on balance

        Total $ _____

Less State Tax Credit

    Fed. tax (2 cols) $ _____ $

Estimated State Tax* $ _____

TOTAL TAXES AND EXPENSES $ _____

---

*Rounded to nearest hundred.

Schedule **Q**

```
┌─────────────────────────────────────────────┐
│         ESTATE TAXES AND EXPENSES            │
└─────────────────────────────────────────────┘
```

Assuming that _____ dies _____

Gross Estate (per Schedule N) $

Less Expenses and Debts:

    Accrued income tax $

    Debts

    Funeral expenses & last illness

    Administration expenses

       Total (3 cols) $ _____ $ _____ $

Adjusted Gross Estate $ _____

  Less:

    Specific exemption $ 60, 000

    Marital deduction

    Charitable deduction

       Total (2 cols) $ _____ $

Taxable Estate: $

Computation of Tax:*

    First bracket $

    Tax on balance

       Total $

Less State Tax Credit

    Fed. tax (2 cols) $ _____ $

Estimated State Tax* $

TOTAL TAXES AND EXPENSES $

_____

*Rounded to nearest hundred.

Schedule R

LIQUIDITY CALCULATION

Assuming that _____ dies _____

Cash Requirements:

Expenses $

Debts

Federal taxes

State taxes

Cash bequests

Exercise stock options

Capital gain on profit sharing plan

Other: _____

$ _____ $

Cash Available:

Government bonds $

Bank accounts

Insurance

Listed stock

Stock redemptions

Other: _____

$ _____

Shortage $ _____

<u>Schedule R</u>

$$\boxed{\textbf{LIQUIDITY CALCULATION}}$$

Assuming that _____ dies _____

<u>Cash Requirements:</u>

    Expenses $

    Debts

    Federal taxes

    State taxes

    Cash bequests

    Exercise stock options

    Capital gain on profit sharing plan

    Other: _____

                                                       $ _____ $

<u>Cash Available:</u>

    Government bonds $

    Bank accounts

    Insurance

    Listed stock

    Stock redemptions

    Other: _____

                                                        $ _____

<u>Shortage</u> $ _____

Schedule R

LIQUIDITY CALCULATION

Assuming that _____ dies _____

Cash Requirements:

Expenses $

Debts

Federal taxes

State taxes

Cash bequests

Exercise stock options

Capital gain on profit sharing plan

Other: _____

                                                        $ $

Cash Available:

Government bonds $

Bank accounts

Insurance

Listed stock

Stock redemptions

Other: _____

                                                        $

Shortage $

Schedule R

LIQUIDITY CALCULATION

Assuming that _____ dies _____

Cash Requirements:

Expenses $

Debts

Federal taxes

State taxes

Cash bequests

Exercise stock options

Capital gain on profit sharing plan

Other: _____
                                                    _____
                                                $ _____ $

Cash Available:

Government bonds $

Bank accounts

Insurance

Listed stock

Stock redemptions

Other: _____
                                                    _____
                                                $ _____

Shortage $ _____
                                                                   ==========

Schedule S.

NET DISTRIBUTION SUMMARY

Assuming that _____ _____ dies _____

Transfers by ▶	Will	Operation of Law	Contract	Less Exps., Debts, Taxes	Total
Outright to:					
_____					
_____					
_____					
_____					
_____					
_____					
In Trust # for:					
_____					
_____					
_____					
In Trust # for:					
_____					
_____					
_____					
In Trust # for:					
_____					
_____					
_____					
Other Death Transfers to:					
_____					
_____					
_____					

Schedule S

NET DISTRIBUTION SUMMARY

Assuming that _____ dies _____

Transfers by ▶	Will	Operation of Law	Contract	Less Exps., Debts, Taxes	Total
Outright to:					
_____					
_____					
_____					
_____					
_____					
_____					
In Trust # for:					
_____					
_____					
_____					
In Trust # for:					
_____					
_____					
_____					
In Trust # for:					
_____					
_____					
_____					
Other Death Transfers to:					
_____					
_____					
_____					

Schedule S

NET DISTRIBUTION SUMMARY

Assuming that _____ dies _____

Transfers by ▶	Will	Operation of Law	Contract	Less Exps., Debts, Taxes	Total
Outright to:					
_____					
_____					
_____					
_____					
_____					
In Trust # for:					
_____					
_____					
_____					
In Trust # for:					
_____					
_____					
_____					
In Trust # for:					
_____					
_____					
_____					
Other Death Transfers to:					
_____					
_____					
_____					

Schedule S

NET DISTRIBUTION SUMMARY

Assuming that _____ dies _____

Transfers by ▶	Will	Operation of Law	Contract	Less Exps., Debts, Taxes	Total
Outright to:					
_____					
_____					
_____					
_____					
_____					
_____					
In Trust # for:					
_____					
_____					
In Trust # for:					
_____					
_____					
In Trust # for:					
_____					
_____					
Other Death Transfers to:					
_____					
_____					
_____					

Schedule T

NET INCOME SUMMARY

For: _____

Income on Invested Capital

    Savings accounts $

    Bonds

    Stock

    Real estate

    Annuities

    Other: _____

    _____

        Total $ _____ $

Pensions

Deferred compensation

Social security

Wages

Other: _____

      Total income $

Less income tax

    Net _____ income $

Schedule T

NET INCOME SUMMARY

For: _____

Income on Invested Capital

    Savings accounts $

    Bonds

    Stock

    Real estate

    Annuities

    Other: _____

    _____

        Total $ $

Pensions

Deferred compensation

Social security

Wages

Other: _____

      Total income $

Less income tax

     Net _____ income $

Schedule U

SECTION 303 STOCK REDEMPTION ANALYSIS

For: _____

A.   Qualification by 35% Test

    1.   Total value of client's stock $ _____

    2.   Gross estate $ _____

    3.   Dividing 1 by 2, above, we obtain: %

B.   Qualification by 50% Test

    1.   Total value of client's stock $ _____

    2.   Net taxable estate $ _____

    3.   Dividing 1 by 2, above, we obtain: %

C. Effect of Redemption on Control	Value	No. Shares
1. Amount of client's stock	$ _____	
2. Maximum amount redeemable (taxes and costs)	_____	_____
3. Amount left in the estate	$ _____	
4. Total stock outstanding before redemption		
5. Client's percent of control (divide 1 by 4)		=======
6. Total stock outstanding after redemption		
7. Percent of control left to client's estate (divide 3 by 6)		=======

Control will be reduced by . . . . .   [%   ]

Schedule U

SECTION 303 STOCK REDEMPTION ANALYSIS

For: _____

A. Qualification by 35% Test

   1.   Total value of client's stock $ _____

   2.   Gross estate $ _____

   3.   Dividing 1 by 2, above, we obtain: ____ %

B. Qualification by 50% Test

   1.   Total value of client's stock $ _____

   2.   Net taxable estate $ _____

   3.   Dividing 1 by 2, above, we obtain: ____ %

C. Effect of Redemption on Control   Value   No. Shares

   1.   Amount of client's stock $ _____

   2.   Maximum amount redeemable   _____   _____
      (taxes and costs)

   3.   Amount left in the estate $ _____

   4.   Total stock outstanding before redemption

   5.   Client's percent of control (divide 1 by 4)   _____

   6.   Total stock outstanding after redemption

   7.   Percent of control left to client's estate
      (divide 3 by 6)   _____

   Control will be reduced by . . . . . | _____ % |

Schedule V

ANALYSIS OF INSTALLMENT PAYMENT
OF ESTATE TAX UNDER § 6166

For: _____

A. Qualification by 35% Test

    1.   Total value of client's interest $ _____

    2.   Gross estate $ _____

    3.   Dividing 1 by 2, above, we obtain: ___%

B. Qualification by 50% Test

    1.   Total value of client's interest $ _____

    2.   Net taxable estate $ _____

    3.   Dividing 1 by 2, above, we obtain: ___%

C. Amount Payable in Installments

    1.   Total value of client's interest $ _____

    2.   Gross estate $ _____

    3.   Federal estate tax $ _____

        Less credits*   _____

        Net federal estate tax $ _____

    4.   Installment amount equals the A3 percent
        times C3 net tax $ _____

---

*Credits for state death taxes, gift taxes on incomplete transfers, tax on prior transfers, and foreign death taxes.

Schedule V

ANALYSIS OF INSTALLMENT PAYMENT
OF ESTATE TAX UNDER § 6166

For: _____

A. Qualification by 35% Test

    1.   Total value of client's interest $ _____

    2.   Gross estate $ _____

    3.   Dividing 1 by 2, above, we obtain: __%

B. Qualification by 50% Test

    1.   Total value of client's interest $ _____

    2.   Net taxable estate $ _____

    3.   Dividing 1 by 2, above, we obtain: __%

C. Amount Payable in Installments

    1.   Total value of client's interest $ _____

    2.   Gross estate $ _____

    3.   Federal estate tax $ _____
         Less credits*   _____
         Net federal estate tax $ _____

    4.   Installment amount equals the A3 percent
        times C3 net tax $ _____

---

*Credits for state death taxes, gift taxes on incomplete transfers, tax on prior transfers, and foreign death taxes.

Schedule W

RECAPITULATION OF ESTATE DATA

Name .... Date ....

Address .... Phone ....

-- ASSETS --

Form of Asset	See Schedule	Owned by Self			Owned by Others in Family		
		Original Cost	Present Value	Annual Income	Original Cost	Present Value	Annual Income
Cash & bank balances	A	$	$	$	$	$	$
Notes, accounts rec., mortgages	B						
Bonds	C						
Stocks	D						
Real estate	E						
Life insurance	P						
Employee benefits (vested)	F						
Business interests	H						
Miscellaneous assets	G						
Total Family Assets		$	$	$	$	$	$

-- LIABILITIES --

	Self	Others in Family
Total -- See Schedule I	$	$

Present Net Worth $ .... $ ....

FUTURE INCREMENTS

	Self	Others in Family
Difference between cash and face value of life insurance	$	$ ....
Prospective gifts and legacies	....	....
Death benefits under employee benefit plans	....	....
Total:	$	$ ....
Probable Estate	$	$ ....
	Self	Others in Family

Schedule W (cont'd)

INCOME AND EXPENSE ANALYSIS

	Self	Others in Family
Income:		
Annual earned income	$	$ . . . .
Annual investment income	. . . .	. . . .
Total Income:	$	$ . . . .
Expenses:		
Annual living expenses	$	$ . . . .
Income taxes	. . . .	. . . .
Insurance premiums	. . . .	. . . .
Total Expenses:	$	$ . . . .
Balance:		
Available for other savings or investments:	$	$

FUTURE INCOME

Annuity and insurance income	$ . . . .
Other investment income (per year)	. . . .
Social Security (per year)	. . . .
Company pension plan (per year)	. . . .
Other employee benefits (per year)	. . . .
Total Future Income:	$ . . . .

FUTURE INCOME REQUIREMENTS

At retirement age (per year)	$ . . . .
For family after death (per year)	. . . .

CAPITAL NEEDED AT DEATH

Clean-up fund (see Schedule Q	$ . . . .
Education capital (see Schedule K)	. . . .
Capital needed to meet income deficit, if any	. . . .

Schedule **X**

```
┌─────────────────────────────────────────────────┐
│        CHECKLIST OF TENTATIVE SUGGESTIONS         │
└─────────────────────────────────────────────────┘
```

For: _____

		Client	Spouse
A.	**Major Suggestions**		
	Gifts to children....................................	☐	☐
	Gifts to trust (short-term).........................	☐	☐
	Gifts to trust (irrevocable)........................	☐	☐
	Insurance (offset tax; provide liquidity)...........	☐	☐
	Life gift to charity; remainder to children........	☐	☐
	Term gift to charity; remainder to children........	☐	☐
	Private annuity....................................	☐	☐
	Section 303 redemption.............................	☐	☐
	Two-part will.....................................	☐	☐
	Wasting marital deduction trust....................	☐	☐
	Split marital deduction trust......................	☐	☐
	Recapitalization of company.......................	☐	☐
B.	**Income**		
	Current income inadequate.........................	☐	☐
	Retirement income inadequate......................	☐	☐
	Dependent parent(s)...............................	☐	☐
	Dependent inlaw(s)................................	☐	☐
	Dependent relative(s).............................	☐	☐
	Wife's income inadequate..........................	☐	☐
	Wife has separate income (high bracket)..........	☐	☐
	Post-mortem income inadequate....................	☐	☐
C.	**Insurance**		
	Insurance payable to estate.......................	☐	☐
	Change beneficiary...............................	☐	☐
	Incidents of ownership owned......................	☐	☐
	Incidents have been assigned.....................	☐	☐
	Change ownership................................	☐	☐
	Reversionary interest exceeding 5%...............	☐	☐
	Premiums paid by insured.........................	☐	☐
	Premiums paid with donations by insured..........	☐	☐

Schedule X (cont'd)

	Client	Spouse
D. Jointly Owned Property		
Property in joint tenancy...	☐	☐
Joint bank accounts	☐	☐
Tenancy by entirety	☐	☐
Community property problems	☐	☐
E. Trusts		
Income reserved	☐	☐
Right to change beneficiaries	☐	☐
Reservation of reversion..	☐	☐
Taxable power of appointment......................................	☐	☐
Partial release	☐	☐
Complete release..	☐	☐
Effect of release on liquidity	☐	☐
Insurance trust	☐	☐
F. Liquidity Problems		
Mortgage	☐	☐
Insurance bank loans	☐	☐
Bank and personal loans	☐	☐
Margin accounts..	☐	☐
Widow's allowance..	☐	☐
Cash bequests	☐	☐
Contingent liabilities...	☐	☐
Adequacy of business agreement funding...........................	☐	☐
Liquid assets passing by contract	☐	☐
Liquid assets passing by operation/law	☐	☐
Insurance for liquidity..	☐	☐
G. Close Corporation		
Sell or retain -- weak management	☐	☐
Sell or retain -- inadequate capital	☐	☐
Sell or retain -- problems of distribution.......................	☐	☐
Sell or retain -- problems of fiduciary investments	☐	☐
Sell or retain -- volatile earnings..............................	☐	☐
Sell or retain -- vulnerable to competition	☐	☐
Sale to employees..	☐	☐

Schedule X (cont'd)

	Client	Spouse
H. Partnerships		
Liability for debts of firm	☐	☐
Estate requirements of liquidation agreements	☐	☐
Option agreements	☐	☐
Cross-purchase agreements.	☐	☐
Advantage of incorporation.	☐	☐
Subchapter S	☐	☐
I. Gifts		
Gift of cash.	☐	☐
Gift of matured endowments, etc.	☐	☐
Gift of proprietorship	☐	☐
Gift of listed or unlisted securities	☐	☐
Gift of notes receivable	☐	☐
Gift of realty	☐	☐
Gift of close corporation stock	☐	☐
Gift of partnership interest	☐	☐
Outright gifts.	☐	☐
Gifts by trusts	☐	☐
Outright gift -- donee creates trust.	☐	☐
Gift tax.	☐	☐
Remainder gift to charity.	☐	☐
Joint tenancy into tenancy in common.	☐	☐
Reorganization of corporation.	☐	☐
J. Wills and Intestacy		
Testamentary trusts.	☐	☐
Right of withdrawal.	☐	☐
Life income to wife and remainder to charity	☐	☐
Charitable bequests	☐	☐
Spendthrift clauses.	☐	☐
Intestacy -- division into shares	☐	☐
Intestacy -- probable refusal of heirs to take in kind	☐	☐
Intestacy -- minor heirs	☐	☐
Simple will	☐	☐
Pour-over.	☐	☐

Chapter 9

HOW TO BILL CLIENTS
SO THEY WILL UNDERSTAND
AND APPRECIATE YOUR WORTH

Not All the Traffic Will Bear . . . Results Count Primarily–Rather Than Effort . . . ABA Canons on Fees Widely Used . . . New Jersey Supreme Court Adopts ABA Canon on Fees–and Adds to It . . . The Time–Novelty–Difficulty and Skill Involved . . . A Real Novel Case . . . How to Win a ''Hopeless'' Case . . . Will It Preclude Other Employment? . . . How a $30.00 Fee Precluded $3,000 or $30,000 . . . Fees Customarily Charged in the Locality . . . The Amount Involved and Results Obtained . . . What Do You Charge for Recovering $100,000 Damages? . . . Charging Fees for the ''Rush Job'' . . . Is He a Regular or Transitory Client . . . The Experience, Reputation and Ability of Counsel . . . Is the Fee Certain or Contingent? . . . Is 33-1/3 Percent a Fair Contingent Fee? . . . Court Regulates Contingent Fees in Some States . . . Never Bill a Layman on the Basis of $50 to $100 an Hour! . . . Attorneys Usually Only Retain 25 Percent of Fee Collected . . . Courts, Agencies and Corporations May Be Billed on an Hourly Basis . . . Times Change, Prices Change–but Not Human Nature . . . Recent Public Reaction to Lawyers' Hourly Fee . . . Should Minimum Fee Schedules Be Abolished? . . . How Lack of a Guide Cost Me 90 Percent of a Fair Fee . . . Always Consult All Available Data and Statistics in Fixing a Fee . . . Can Every Lawyer be a Time-Keeper? . . . Some Basic Psychological Rules for Billing . . . A Simple One-

Shot Method of Furnishing an Itemized Bill . . . A Lawyer's
Combination Diary and Manual Can Prove Very Helpful . . .
Simplest Method of Time Keeping . . . Wealth of Data Before the
Diary . . . Wealth of Data After the Diary . . . Includes Daily
Time Charts Also . . . If Your State Does Not Have One, It
Should

Not All the Traffic Will Bear

In the final analysis we have to face up to the simple fact that as lawyers we adopted the profession of law in order to earn our livelihood. To state it more simply, we have more than a passing interest in the fees we will charge and collect. Reducing the proposition further and to its most practical form, we expect to be paid for our services—*adequately* and *promptly*. The problem is how to do this as effectively and painlessly as possible. Unfortunately I have seen occasionally, as perhaps some of the readers also have, the practitioner who says, at least to himself: "This is a one-shot proposition. I will never see this client again. I am going to charge him all that the traffic will bear."

This philosophy is shortsighted to say the least, not to mention the fact that it is also unethical and possibly illegal. If we are to treat the fixing and collection of fees in this callous manner, it will do substantial harm not only to the individual lawyer himself but to the profession as a whole. Bills for any service, professional or otherwise, must always be fair and reasonable and, indeed, itemized and documented in some cases if we are to retain our own self-respect and the respect of our fellow practitioners and of the community or city in which we practice. However, we can take some solace in the fact that there are a whole series of intangibles as well as tangibles which may be used in the computation of our fees.

I recently attended a seminar at a State Bar Convention in one of our Eastern states where the speakers undertook to establish that "effort" was the prime ingredient which a lawyer's bill for fees should reflect. One speaker after another developed the theme that if you exerted a great amount of effort on behalf of the client—even if you lose—he would gladly pay you what your services were reasonably worth. Not so! I felt so strongly about the matter that I later wrote an article on the subject, published in a state bar journal, disputing this thesis.

Results Count Primarily—Rather Than Effort

I have found from years of practical experience that what really persuades a client to pay you your fees willingly is the beneficial and satisfactory results which you achieve for him. This is simple ordinary common sense. No doubt the client appreciates all the efforts made on his behalf but the real acid test of your worth is how much good were you able to accomplish for him? The Canons of Ethics promulgated by the American Bar Association many years ago, and particularly those dealing with fees, clearly recognized that the *amount involved and the results obtained* were an important element in determining the reasonableness of the fee charged.

ABA Canons on Fees Widely Used

Since we have mentioned the ABA Canons on Fees, we may as well develop this point further at this time. These Canons on Ethics have been widely adopted by some, if not all, of the various Bar Associations throughout the 50 states. Some of the states have seen fit to supplement or amend these Canons, but in the main they still form the basis of what is considered ethical and proper when it comes to the question of how to evaluate what constitutes a fair and reasonable fee for services rendered.

New Jersey Supreme Court Adopts ABA Canon on Fees—and Adds to It

The Supreme Court of my own State of New Jersey not only adopted all of the elements originally set forth in the ABA Canon on fees but supplemented and amended them slightly in an effort to further improve and refine them as you will observe from the following list:

DR 2-106 Fees for Legal Services.

(A) A Lawyer should charge no more than a reasonable fee. A fee is excessive when, after a review of the facts, a lawyer of ordinary prudence would be left with a definite and firm conviction that the fee is in excess of a reasonable fee. Factors to be considered as guides in determining the reasonableness of a fee include the following:

(1) The time and labor required, the novelty and difficulty of the questions involved, and the skill requisite to perform the legal service properly.

(2) The likelihood, if apparent to the client, that the acceptance of the particular employment will preclude other employment by the lawyer.

(3) The fee customarily charged in the locality for similar legal services.

(4) The amount involved and the results obtained.

(5) The time limitations imposed by the client or by the circumstances.

(6) The nature and length of the professional relationship with the client.

(7) The experience, reputation, and ability of the lawyer or lawyers performing the services.

(8) Whether the fee is fixed or contingent.

(B) At the request of a client, a lawyer shall submit a fee dispute to the local ethics committee for resolution.

(C) A lawyer shall not enter into an arrangement for, charge, or collect a fee for representing a defendant in a criminal case which is substantially contingent upon the result.

(D) A lawyer shall be disciplined if he shall enter into an agreement for, charge, or collect a fee so excessive as to evidence an intent to overreach his client.

No alert lawyer can review this list of the elements which go into the makeup of a fair and reasonable fee and not be entirely satisfied, delighted in fact, to be afforded such a wide range for his resourcefulness and imagination. Let us briefly analyze these elements to appreciate fully their breadth, depth and scope and, likewise, their fairness to both lawyer and client.

The Time—Novelty—Difficulty and Skill Involved

As to item No. 1: Obviously the purpose or object of this one was to separate the wheat from the chaff—the simple, ordinary, mundane item of practice from the novel, complex and difficult one that requires not only time and talent but perhaps a touch of genius to handle successfully. This element of charging fees is one that makes the practice of law and particularly the handling of difficult cases so fascinating.

A Real Novel Case

By way of illustration—a man in his middle forties once came into this office. He was an only son and his mother had died in childbirth. His father had remarried promptly but the second marriage had not worked out so well. Returning home one evening he discovered his wife in what was then euphemistically described as "in flagrante delicto." She frankly admitted that she did not love her husband. The next day she left the matrimonial abode and openly took up residence with her paramour in a nearby community where she was still living some 20 years later when her husband died.

I questioned the son as to the size and nature of the estate, whether his father left a will, etc. It developed that most of the estate was in improved real estate, title to which the father had placed in the joint names of himself and his second wife. He had indeed left a will in which he gave all of his estate which "he was legally able to" to his son. He confirmed his intention to make his son his sole beneficiary and to expressly disinherit his wife by saying in effect "I leave my wife absolutely nothing except such interest in my estate as the law allows her."

Obviously the problem was threefold: (a) the real estate consisted of several fairly valuable pieces of improved realty; (b) the form of the deeds meant that the surviving spouse took full legal title upon her husband's death as tenant by the entirety or joint tenant in most states; (c) the drafting of the will in the fashion indicated, instead of helping the testator and his son, actually injured them both by literally and in actual effect, confirming the legal devolution of the title to the wife.

How to Win a "Hopeless" Case

Probably the ordinary practitioner would have thrown in the sponge immediately, considered the case hopeless and withdrawn promptly and collected a nominal fee for advice. Not so with our office. The facts intrigued me. How could a rank injustice such as this be permitted within the law? How could a loyal and dutiful son receive nothing of his father's estate while a faithless wife living in open adultery with another man became the principal, if not the exclusive, beneficiary of the estate of her husband she had deserted many years ago. We did some research and some reasoning and applied some common sense. Then we filed a suit against the widow. We set up a half dozen or more causes of action as I recall it. These included (1) that adultery barred jointure; (2) that there was a de facto divorce; (3) that there was a de facto remarriage to the paramour; (4) that the wife was guilty of fraud and deceit in contracting the original marriage; (5) that the placing of title in two names was a mutual mistake of fact; (6) that a court of equity should grant a recision or at least a reformation of the deeds; (7) that a court of equity should not permit such an unjust enrichment in favor of the wife in the face of her perfidy and infidelity, etc.

There were probably more counts but this will give you some idea of the *time . . . labor . . . skill . . . difficulty,* etc. involved in handling this litigation. When the case was reached for trial it was settled with the son receiving about 70 percent of the estate and the widow gladly accepting 30 percent. When you handle an involved case in this manner and snatch a substantial victory from what initially seemed like a sure defeat, there is no difficulty in justifying a substantial fee and the client is usually glad to pay it.

The Trial Judge asked: "Why have you set up seven or eight Causes of Action in this case when all you need is *one sound one*?" We replied: "Your Honor, we just weren't entirely certain as to which one *you* would consider sound." The Judge recommended the settlement. Apparently he wasn't entirely certain either.

Will It Preclude Other Employment?

2. The second item is intended to compensate the lawyer, in some measure at least, for the loss he may suffer through alienating other potential clients. There is no question but that this element may be a very substantial one and yet it may be difficult to pinpoint or evaluate. It is difficult to understand why anyone inserted the clause "if apparent to the client." This would seem to make the client the final judge of how adversely it would affect the lawyer if he accepted the proffered retainer. I would not worry about this aspect of the matter at this time.

How a $30 Fee Precluded $3,000 or $30,000

I recall very vividly one such instance in my own career when I was just starting the practice of law. In the average medium-size town or community, the leading citizens are frequently the small shop owners such as the grocer, butcher, hardware store proprietor or tavern owner. When an attorney can count among his clients a distributor or wholesaler or an industry, he is usually considered as having "arrived." In this case, I represented a grocer and butcher. I had represented him when he purchased the business as well as representing him in a small estate and some other miscellaneous matters. Hence, when he insisted that I also handle his collection cases, I did not have the courage, foresight or will power to refuse. Among the claims was a small overdue grocery bill for $95 owed by a Frank Duvrill. With my usual diligence I collected it—and incidentally earned a fee of $20 or $30—plus the permanent enmity of the debtor naturally. What I did not know was that poor Mr. Duvrill was to originate more legal business in the next few years than any other individual in the community. He was successively (a) arrested on a criminal charge; (b) injured in a rather serious auto accident; (c) had a minor child also injured; and (d) was sued for divorce, all within a year or so, and the legal fees would have easily reached from $3,000 to $30,000. Although we had been friendly before I handled the collection suit, he steered clear of my law office thereafter, whenever misfortune befell him and he needed legal services. This is a classic illustration of the application of item 2.

Fees Customarily Charged in the Locality

As to item 3: This requires little discussion. Each county bar association usually formulates and publicizes to its members its recommended minimum fee schedule, (which is now under attack). Most attorneys accept and adopt these schedules as prima facie evidence of the "fee customarily charged in the locality for similar services." However, it has to be borne in mind that this is only one of the criteria—and that all eight tests should be taken into consideration in the ultimate determination of the fee. Incidentally, the U.S. Supreme Court has recently declared some sections of this minimum fee schedule unconstitutional.

The Amount Involved and Results Obtained

As to item 4: This is probably the most significant and important of all the criteria, i.e., "the amount involved and the results obtained." Your attention is invited to the fact that these two points are consolidated in the one item and for good reasons. The amount involved standing by itself has little significance to either the lawyer or the client unless the attorney wins the case or is able to reduce substantially the loss or exposure to the client. Hence the two are indivisible, interrelated and interdependent.

Thus, if a man is sued and the exposure is only $5,000 and you win the case, obviously the bill you submit must bear some reasonable and legitimate relationship to the amount involved—even if it costs you or your office $6,000 in time and effort to win it. Any fee in excess of one-third or one-half of the amount you had saved your client would be considered excessive. A fee of 25 percent would be more reasonable and a fee of 20 percent would probably be the average.

What Do You Charge For Recovering $100,000 Damages?

On the other hand if you represent a female plaintiff in a slip-and-fall case who has suffered a fractured hip or vertebra and you obtain a verdict of $100,000 for her, one-third of the recovery would seem to be fair and reasonable. This would be true even if your actual time and out-of-pocket expenses did not come anywhere near approaching this sum. This reasoning is sound not only because of the amount involved and the results obtained, but because you have given due consideration to the remaining seven factors also involved in fixing the fee.

Charging Fees for the "Rush Job"

As to Item 5: This is more or less self-explanatory. I do not recall this rule being included in the original list as first promulgated by the American Bar Association. It is obviously a product of our modern times, when time itself is at such a premium and clients are willing to pay to have preferential or expeditious treatment of their cases.

By way of illustration, if a client comes into the office Friday afternoon at 4:00 p.m. with an emergent matter and wants an injunction obtained the following morning, you have many problems to contend with. There are pleadings to be drawn, witnesses to be interviewed, affidavits to be drawn and executed, a judge to be located (who is available and willing to hear you), orders to be drawn and served, etc., etc. Incidentally the office staff is on a five-day week and does not work on Saturdays. If you want to take this work on this basis, irrespective of the outcome, the fee would have to be two or three times what it would normally be. The client would probably expect to pay the premium fees. However, I recommend that you take no chances—tell him so before you undertake the assignment. Better still, have him make out a check for the fees while he is so determined and enthusiastic about pressing the litigation.

Is He a Regular or Transitory Client

As to item 6: This is relatively simple and easy of application. If your relationship with the client has been long and cordial and profitable, you may want to, and in fact should, take these factors into consideration in fixing your fees. On the other hand if your client is a transitory one who vacillates from one law office to another; who comes to you infrequently or irregularly, there is no reason why he should not pay top dollar for the services he wants—particularly in the type of emergent matter described under item 5.

Then, of course, there is the occasional corporate client whose corporation is in an excess-profit tax bracket and who says to you—"Don't worry about the fees, they are 100 percent tax deductible." That client is an angel. Give him good service—he deserves it.

The Experience, Reputation and Ability of Counsel

As to Item 7: This is almost as flexible as items 1 and 4 and can be equally productive of substantial fees. *Experience, reputation and ability* can command a high price in the market place. They should not be sold short. The old adages apply in law as in every other walk of life viz: You can always reduce the price by cutting the quality; if you buy shoddy merchandise you can get it cheaper; you usually get only what you pay for, etc., etc.

Is the Fee Certain or Contingent?

Item 8 is the one which is probably the subject of most discussion, most condemnation and most abuse. I personally feel that contingent fees are wholly justified and that they have had a salutary effect upon the administration of justice. Backed by great wealth and an array of skilled and well-paid defense counsel, large corporations, steamship lines, railroad and utility companies, insurance carriers, etc. would be practically *immune* from suits by the average man and woman unless there were trained, skilled, qualified personal-injury lawyers available to handle their cases for them on a contingency-fee basis.

The difficulty arises when the attorney overestimates the value of his services and raises the contingent fee charged to the point where the injured litigant begins to wonder whose case it is—and who was actually injured, he or the lawyer.

Is 33-1/3 Percent a Fair Contingent Fee?

33-1/3 percent has been recognized for many years as a fair and reasonable contingency fee in difficult and substantial cases. Where one appeal is involved the fee could be 40 percent. If two successive appeals are involved it could go as high as 45 percent. Beyond these percentages, an attorney is trespassing pretty close to what might be considered unreasonable. I have personally handled many cases on the bases indicated and the net profit ultimately realized has confirmed my belief that such fees are justified—and that any lesser fee would have resulted in a loss or inadequate compensation. It is a well-known fact among trial lawyers that where the recovery is relatively small, such as $5,000 or under, that such cases are usually handled at a loss to the office. Yet someone must handle them unless the injured party is to be deprived of his legal rights. Moreover, you must handle them or the prospects are that you will not be afforded the opportunity of handling the larger ones.

A Court Regulates Contingent Fees in Some States

However, in recent years the courts of some of our states have deemed it necessary to intervene and to exercise controls to prevent any over-reaching in the matter of contingent fees by a few over-enthusiastic attorneys. Thus, in New Jersey the maximum contingent fee that we charge a minor is now 25 percent rather than 33-1/3 percent. On the other hand, even 33-1/3 percent is now keyed to the size of the verdict or settlement recovered and gets gradually smaller as the amount increases. These rates became effective recently and now require the attorney to file signed copies of his retainer and closing statements with the Administrative Director of the Courts to confirm the amount of the contingent fee collected. The present fee schedule in New Jersey is as follows: Maximum Limits for Contingency Fees on Net Sum Recovered

(1)   50 percent on the first $1,000.000 recovered.

(2)   40 percent on the next $2,000.00 recovered.

(3)   33-1/3 percent on the next $47,000.00 recovered.

(4)   20 percent on the next $50,000.00 recovered.

(5)   10 percent on any amount recovered over $100,000.00.

(6)   Where the recovery is for the benefit of an infant or incompe-
tent, by settlement without trial, the foregoing limits shall apply, except that the fees for any amount recovered up to $50,000.00 shall be 25 percent.

All of this seems fair and reasonable to the courts and to the laymen naturally. But the asserted power of the court to inject itself into matters of this kind and thus regulate and control the contractual relationship between an attorney and his client seems like a dangerous precedent to many attorneys. As a result the power of the court to control these fees was tested in the United States federal courts as being in violation of the constitutional rights of the parties. But the attorneys lost!

Never Bill a Layman on the Basis of $50 to $100 an Hour!

To get back to the subject of non-contingent fees, there is one thing that I am absolutely certain about. No lawyer outside the large firms should disclose either in the statement to his lay clients or in the press or other public forum that the value of his services is predicated upon $50 per hour or $75 per hour or $100 per hour. This kind of an explanation is bound to wreak havoc with the legal profession generally and the lawyer involved in particular. Quotation of such fees outside the large cities not only has been known to create hostility but actual physical violence on the part of some clients. Occasional disputes between attorney and client in which the attorney is assaulted have been found in some instances to be directly traceable to the quotation of fees of this kind. This natural resentment is understandable when the client is in the low-income bracket where he cannot command hourly wages of 10 percent of the rate of compensation quoted by the attorney—and in some instances cannot even find employment.

Attorneys Usually Only Retain 25 Percent of Fee Collected

We as attorneys, of course, recognize the fact that $50 or even $100 per hour is not excessive in view of the overhead involved. The difficulty is that some attorneys live in ivory towers and have lost touch with some of their fellow men and are oblivious to the need of establishing a more realistic communication with their clients. Rather than quote a per-hour evaluation on my fee when it is substantial, I frequently explain to a client that 50 percent of the fee goes to overhead and of the remaining 50 percent another 50 percent goes to pay my income taxes to the U.S. Internal Revenue Service which leaves me only 25¢ on the dollar of any fee collected.

Hence, in my judgment the best method of pursuing any billing of a client is to absolutely avoid any price tag per hour, basically because it is an unrealistic method of calculating fees. It does not tell the whole story. It puts the attorney on the defensive. All this can be avoided if the attorney will just stick to the eight criteria already discussed and itemize the work actually performed. Keep your time charts by all means, but use them for calculating your profit or loss on a case.

**Courts, Agencies and Corporations
May Be Billed on an Hourly Basis**

In certain cases, the attorney may be forced to bill on an hourly basis. Probate, Bankruptcy and Equity or Chancery Courts frequently insist that an affidavit be furnished specifying the approximate time expended by the attorney. Many federal agencies such as HEW (Health Education and Welfare), covering work on Social Security appeals, etc., likewise insist on verified statements as to time expended. We recently had such a matter where the fee asked for was a nominal one of $1,300. The official hearing the matter rejected the application until we furnished a breakdown of the time involved. However, the hours only totaled about 26 hours more or less and hence the rate came out at about $50 per hour. In order to buttress this factor, we supplemented the bill with a detailed affidavit incorporating the ABA criteria and bore down heavily on item 4 covering the "amount involved and the results obtained." In the instant case the results meant to the appellants that they would receive approximately $30,000 additional payments during their life expectancy.

Times Change, Prices Change—but Not Human Nature

It may be safe to assume that in the case of the courts and administrative agencies and even in the case of corporations as a rule, they are usually aware of the overhead and tax problems involved in operating an office and realize that $50 or $75 per hour is never "net" to the attorneys. Years ago in my early practice, the pastor of the local church was building a new community house. He was not sufficiently knowledgeable to obtain a firm bid or a "turn-key" contract and hence it was being built on a "cost plus" basis with his paying for the labor and material as they were built. I can still hear the good pastor complaining from the pulpit:

"These building mechanics are charging me $8 per day—EIGHT DOLLARS A DAY. Now we all know that nobody could possibly do $8 worth of work a day."

And every parishioner obviously agreed with him. Yet today these same building mechanics are getting $8 or $12 *an hour* for the same work. It is true that times have changed. Prices have changed. Wages have changed. But human nature has not changed. The average man and woman today consciously or subconsciously says to himself:

"We all know that no lawyer can possibly do $50 or $100 worth of work in an hour."

Recent Public Reaction to Lawyers' Hourly Fee

This belief of mine was recently borne out. In a nearby state, a municipal attorney's fees were investigated by a crusading newspaper. When questioned as to the basis of his fees, he said he usually charged $50 per hour. Literally, as well as figuratively, all Hell broke loose. Editorials were written. Letters to the editor appeared. The local, county and state Bar Associations announced that they would look into the basis for charges for legal services. Some of the state legislators began drafting bills to introduce in the state legislature attempting to control legal fees, etc., etc.

Should Minimum Fee Schedules Be Abolished?

Also as a side reaction, the State Bar Association decided that the minimum fee schedules promulgated by the County Bar Association for specific services should be abolished as unfair ''price fixing'' and possibly a violation of the Federal Anti-Trust Laws. I have always believed and still believe that these minimum fee schedules are justified as guidelines. I believe that they serve a very useful and salutary purpose. Where, may I ask, is any attorney, whether neophyte or veteran, able to find adequate data as to what constitutes a fair and proper fee for performing a specific function?

Certainly the law schools do not touch upon it. The average lawyer certainly does not run the entire gamut of such services in a lifetime. In earlier times a young lawyer might have been assumed to have learned some of these fees during the service of his so-called clerkship. However, his preceptor would hardly discuss fees with a law clerk. Today clerkships are being abolished in some states in favor of a concentrated training in ''skills and methods courses.'' This leaves most lawyers in a quandary where they have to guess or speculate on what a specific service may be worth.

Such hit or miss methods could wreck a whole system, subject it to competitive bidding and cut-throat competition. It is difficult enough to have to wrestle with the question of fixing an appropriate fee in a unique case such as described in criterion No. 1 of the ABA and New Jersey Cannons on Fees. Unfortunately, the majority of cases fall into category No. 3, i.e., ''the fee customarily charged in the locality for the same service.'' From what source is the average attorney to ascertain this standard fee if not from published fee schedules? Surely not from hearsay or guesswork. I recommend that all lawyers retain a copy of such Minimum Fee Schedules as guidelines, to help them in fixing a fair fee.

How Lack of a Guide Cost Me 90 Percent of a Fair Fee

By way of illustration, I recall once where lack of information as to the appropriate elements involved in fixing a fee, such as items 1 and 4 above referred to, led me into a position where I was able to collect only 10 percent of the fee that

I should have charged and collected. I had been practicing only a short time. A wily brick and tile manufacturer asked me to appear in Washington to resist the National Recovery Administration (NRA) in formulating a code to regulate the entire industry throughout the then 48 states. I was naturally thrilled at the assignment. The Federal Statute was clearly worded so that theoretically only the large existing *trade organizations* could help formulate a "Code" which would be binding upon the entire industry.

The brick and tile industry had 4 large trade organizations all headquartered in the Midwest. Naturally we assumed that any Code would be slanted in favor of that area, with its freight differentials, etc.—and we were right. I explained to the local plant owner that only a trade organization could offer a Code of its own or hope to block any submitted. His reply was: "Then we will organize our own trade organization."

As a result he contacted some 10 or 12 New Jersey brick and tile manufacturers and in due course I incorporated them into a "trade organization" which was fully qualified to be heard or to formulate its own Code. We went to Washington. On the way he pointed out what he viewed as the unfairness and unsoundness of the proposed Code formulated and sponsored by the National Trade organizations. When the hearing opened in the morning I was ready. However, my sponsor stayed a discrete distance away from me. The hearing was scheduled to have as its presiding officer General "Ironpants" Johnson, but in his absence was chaired by Hon. Malcolm Muir. We were allowed to challenge any part of the Code except its constitutionality.

I literally took the Code apart; threw the proceedings into confusion with my opening statement that "this Code will wreck the brick industry in my state." The result was that the officers of the national organizations and the Code makers stayed up all night rewriting the Code to present to the assembled manufacturers from the 48 states, the next morning.

While it was being presented my doughty and indefatigable local plant manager was making marginal notes pointing out its alleged continuing defects and passing them on to me. I began the second day's hearing with the introductory statement that "this revised Code is worse than the first one. It will not only destroy the industry in my state but in half the remaining states in the nation." Suffice it to say that at the end of the second day the Code was still far from adoption. The hearings had to be adjourned without date because the Auto and Steel industries were scheduled for the next hearing, and Coal and Oil after that. The ultimate result was that before our hearing was rescheduled the Supreme Court had declared the act unconstitutional. Meanwhile the industry was permitted to continue unhampered by any Codes and probably saved a million dollars or more in New Jersey alone.

When it came time to bill the New Jersey Association for my fee I was at a loss to know how to evaluate my services. There was nothing similar to this on any of the minimum fee schedules. It was the depression. I lacked the foresight to discuss the value of these services with anyone. Had I done so, I probably would have learned that they had a minimum value of $5,000 even in those days and probably $50,000 today. However, being a modest young man and rather immature and sophomoric I submitted a bill for $500—or about 10¢ on the dollar of what the services were worth. My clients not only seemed unappreciative but also took 18 months to pay me.

Always Consult All Available Data and Statistics in Fixing a Fee

I think this is a classic illustration of how ignorance of what constitutes an adequate fee can be extremely costly. It taught me a lesson from which I have profited throughout my subsequent practice. I now weigh the value of my services not only based upon the criteria set up by the ABA Canons, but I also consult the standard fee schedules promulgated by the Bar Associations. By a process of evaluation and comparison with analogous matters I make certain that any bill submitted for services takes all these factors into consideration.

Moreover, it is to be borne in mind that fee schedules promulgated by the various Bar Associations are *minimum* ones only. They are merely intended to prevent competitive bidding and cut-throat competition. The attorney is given free rein to submit bills for higher fees than those listed provided he can justify them because of the unique character of the services rendered or the results obtained. In my judgment, if these schedules of fees were made "Advisory" instead of mandatory and carried no penalty for not adhering to them, they would be upheld by the courts as valid.

For reference and comparison only, there is included in this chapter a typical schedule of fees recommended by a typical County Bar Association. I am satisfied that a careful study of them will prove very helpful in assisting the average attorney to determine the approximate minimum value of services rendered.

Can Every Lawyer Be a Time-Keeper?

There are, of course, some attorneys who insist that the only proper method of fixing legal fees is by a careful maintenance of time charts on a quarter-hour basis throughout the day. This means that a written memorandum must be maintained either in a diary or on separate charge slips indicating to what client or to what case this particular time is to be charged. There are a variety of diaries, charge memos (usually in triplicate or quadruplicate) available for purchase today.

The difficulty with this method is that it takes up so much additional time of the attorney and of the office staff to properly compile same. Personally, I have always found that such record-keeping distracted me from more creative work and hence was costly in the long run. It also required additional office help; required extra billing and worst of all forced the attorney to expose the hourly rate at which he was charging his client. It may be that some attorneys have the requisite psychological and philosophical makeup to use this technique. However, I do not believe that the more dynamic and active attorneys will find this method suitable for use, unless they assign a secretary to maintain the actual time records. I say this notwithstanding the fact that many statistical studies show that this method of ''timekeeping'' increases the attorney's average annual income, by as much as 40 percent.

Some Basic Psychological Rules for Billing

There are, of course, some basic rules, both practical and psychological, for billing a client. In any event, the bills should be submitted promptly. I usually submit the bill within 24 hours or 48 hours at the latest after the work is completed. Follow-up statements are rendered regularly and promptly on the first of every month thereafter, until the bill is paid. Studies showed that the longer the delay in submitting the bill, the more dilatory the client is likely to be in paying it. Moreover, studies show that where the bills are substantial and yet are not itemized they create not only resistance to payment but resentment by the client as well. I have found that the more information the bill contains the more satisfied the client is with the work done and the results achieved. I have also found that it is a good practice to accompany an itemized bill with a letter which again summarizes briefly yet clearly and succinctly these three factors: (a) the amounts involved; (b) the effort expended; and (c) the results achieved.

A Simple One-Shot Method of Furnishing An Itemized Bill

I am including in this chapter three typical bills which I classify as poor, fair and good for your study. Obviously, they represent only my personal opinion.

I might say that through the years I have adopted a method of billing clients which has proved both satisfactory and effective to both attorney and client. Its virtue lies in the fact that it is itemized and detailed and presents a running narrative of the case; indicates the amounts involved; the efforts expended and the results achieved without specifying any hourly basis. What I usually do is call in a secretary, refer to the correspondence in the file which has been maintained in chronological order fastened to the back of the file with an Acco expanding clip. As each item of correspondence is examined it calls to mind, not only the work done in this communication, *but the conferences, communications, and activities* which preceded or followed the particular letter in question. I dictate the estimated time involved for each item in minimum multiples of 1/4 hour—for office use—but the actual time element is not disclosed to the client unless he demands it.

The approximate date or dates when each of these services was rendered is indicated in the left margin of the itemized bill. Thus, if the services extended over a period of months or years, this itemization might run anywhere from six pages of legal cap to 20 or more pages of legal cap.

A Lawyer's Combination Diary and Manual Can Prove Very Helpful

Thus far I am sure that the reader would have little difficulty in perceiving that I am not exactly enthusiastic about the much touted practice of maintaining accurate time records to increase receipts. I am sure that this attitude on my part is due primarily to my own individual characteristics. Frankly, in our state we have the benefit of a very excellent "Lawyer's Diary and Manual." It is published yearly in a bound volume of approximately 7-1/2″ × 10″. A separate, lined page is provided for each day of the year. The page, in turn, has 36 separate lines. Obviously, this is ideal not only for posting future appointments but also ideal for maintaining a bound record of all of the work performed by an individual attorney in a given day, in addition to the listed appointments.

I have attempted to maintain this diary on a daily basis and to indicate the amount of time spent on each individual case. Unfortunately, I lack the will power to maintain this procedure. However, my son, on the other hand, has no difficulty in entering his activities in the diary. I have seen his diary and have observed that he has listed as many as 40 or more individual telephone conferences a day. He tells me that this has been very effective and helpful to him in billing clients.

Simplest Method of Time-Keeping

I have also attempted to introduce into the office system other methods of time-keeping. These include a small printed pad, such as is used to record incoming telephone calls. We have had them made up in a distinct contrasting color. There are lines to indicate the name of the case, and a series of boxes to indicate the nature of the work performed, i.e., whether it is a personal interview or a conference, or an interview with a witness, or a telephone conference with a client personally, or with some other party connected with the case, or a matter of legal research, or a matter of dictation. There are also a series of boxes for the time element involved, with a minimum of one-quarter hour in all instances. These sheets can be easily filled in by merely jotting down the name of the case, checking off the type of work performed in the appropriate box, and checking off the time element involved in a separate box. These small, loose memo sheets can then be maintained in the proper file until the time for billing arrives. This type of pad is standard with most printing or stationery firms dealing in legal supplies.

You can, therefore, also perceive that I have recognized the intrinsic value of maintaining time records. I am satisfied that they can, and in fact do, increase a lawyer's receipts. My principal objection to them has been my own personal shortcoming in my ability to maintain such records properly. However, even when they are maintained either by the lawyer or a secretary, I still stand by my basic premise that the time element should not be used or even disclosed to a lay client, unless it is absolutely necessary or they demand it.

Wealth of Data Before the Diary

Incidentally, the Lawyer's Diary and Manual I referred to is one of the most comprehensive aids to a practicing lawyer that has ever been devised. In addition to the diary itself, it includes an index running into six pages and listing every conceivable data that a lawyer might require on instant notice. These include the name, address, telephone number of every department and agency of the State; the Rules of the U.S. District Court; the Federal Judiciary; the State Judiciary, embracing all the judges at every one of the five levels; the Trial Hearing and Motion Schedules for every court; specific rules covering the filing of Briefs, Orders and Memoranda in all courts; the membership of the Committee on Character and Fitness; the membership on the 21 County Ethics Committees; the Fees and Costs established by law or the rules of the court covering all Federal and State Courts; Sheriff's Mileage Fees in all counties; a List of the Municipal Courts with sound recording; all the Municipal Courts in the 565 municipalities; *60 compact pages containing a complete digest of the civil practice and procedure in the State;* Data on Enforcing Security under the UCC; Vital Statistic Sources throughout the United States; Court Schedule, Holiday and Tax Date Reminders. All these appear in the front of the book before the diary itself starts.

Wealth of Data After the Diary

In the back of the book a similar volume of data is furnished consisting of a complete address and telephone directory of every attorney practicing in the State, set off on paper of a contrasting color; a Bar Directory of the State, classified according to Cities and Counties; State Bar Association Officers throughout the U.S.; Bar Associations throughout the State of N.J.; Minimum Fee Schedules for every one of the 21 Counties; Addresses and telephone numbers of all Certified Shorthand Reporters; Directory of Names, Addresses and Telephone Numbers of all Title Abstracters within the State; Alphabetical list of every municipality in the State indicating their respective counties; Detailed list of all key municipal officials in all the municipalities throughout the State; Real Estate Tax Rates by county and municipalities throughout the State; Hospital Directory by municipality and county throughout the State; Medical Charts for attorneys' use covering all the bones and muscles in the body; composite from covering individual limbs; Workmen's Compensation Disability Schedule; Inheritance Tax Rates and Exemptions; Mortality Tables; Tables of Life Expectancy; Index of all the Marriage and Divorce Laws in the U.S.; List of all Insurance Companies and Claim Managers in the State; Index of the Names, Addresses and Telephone Numbers of all the County Officers in the 21 counties; a Table Showing Interest Approximations; Perpetual Calendar covering the year 1776 to the year 2000.

Includes Daily Time Charts Also

Incidentally, this book also contains a sufficient number of pages to be used as a time-calculation chart covering the time spent by the attorney on specific cases.

This was the primary reason that I mention this "Lawyer's Diary and Manual." However, I thought that while I was about it, I might just as well indicate how effective and efficient an attorney can be by maintaining a handbook constantly on his desk which provides *ready access to this tremendous volume of data,* which the active attorney needs and uses in the course of his everyday practice.

If Your State Does Not Have One, It Should

If your particular state does not have such a combination Lawyer's Diary and Manual, this affords you another opportunity of showing your leadership among the members of the Bar. Check out some first class publisher in your own state and have him compile and publish a similar volume for your own state.

This type of compilation is so unique that it can be copyrighted. Such a volume can produce a very attractive income on an annual basis. Every lawyer in the state is an automatic purchaser.

TYPICAL COUNTY BAR ASSOCIATION'S RECOMMENDED SCHEDULE OF MINIMUM FEES

1. SCHEDULE IS ADVISORY ONLY

Experience has indicated that the average time expended, computed at a minimum hourly rate, would result in the following suggested charges. All charges for legal services should be based on an hourly rate which takes into consideration the following criteria:

(1) The importance of the dispute or jeopardy as to which professional services were made necessary;

(2) The nature and extent of the jeopardy or risk involved or incurred.

(3) The nature, extent and difficulty of the services;

(4) The experience and legal knowledge required, and the skill, diligence, ability and judgment shown;

(5) The time necessarily spent by the attorney in the performance of his services;

(6) The results obtained;

(7) The benefits or advantages resulting and their importance;

(8) Any special circumstance, including the standing of the attorney for integrity and skill;

(9) The overhead expense to which the attorney has been put.

2. HOURLY SERVICES RATES

For all services not otherwise covered in this Schedule, including office conferences and telephone consultations, per hour ....$ 50.00
For any portion of an hour, not less than 10.00
Research and brief writing, per hour 60.00

3. ADMINISTRATIVE & MUNICIPAL PRACTICE

Appearances: (exclusive of preparation which shall be charged for at not less than the hourly services rates set forth in this Schedule)
State agencies, per session... 250.00
Municipal governing bodies, per session 200.00
Planning Board, per session . 200.00
Board of Adjustment, per session 200.00

County Tax Board Appeals
50% Percent of first year's tax Savings
Representation of governing bodies, school boards and other municipal agencies
Attendance at meeting of governing body or board, per session 150.00
or
Annual retainer providing for equivalent
Attendance at meetings of boards of adjustment, planning boards and boards

3. ADMINISTRATIVE & MUNICI-PAL PRACTICE *(Continued)*

of health, per session 150.00

or

Annual retainer providing for equivalent

4. CORPORATIONS AND PARTNERSHIPS

A. Domestic

Formation of simple
   corporation 350.00

Stockholders agreement or voting
   trust.......................... 125.00

Amending corporate charter . 125.00

Acting as registered agent ... 100.00

Acting as registered agent, filling reports and conducting
   meetings 150.00

Dissolution proceedings 350.00

Simple corporate resolution.. 25.00

Change of registered agent or
   office........................ 75.00

B. Foreign

Authority to do business in New
   Jersey 250.00

Acting as registered agent ... 125.00

Withdrawal from State 75.00

Change of registered agent or
   office........................ 75.00

C. Not for Profit

Formation 100.00

D. Partnerships

Drafting of Partnership
   agreement 300.00

Registration of trade name ... 50.00

Dissolution, including notices to creditors and agreements 250.00

5. BANKRUPTCY

Filing petition, appearance at first
   creditors meeting, appointment of
   trustee

(a) Business bankruptcy 600.00

(b) Individual bankruptcy 500.00

(c) Husband and wife,

additional 150.00

Each subsequent appearance. 200.00

Objecting to discharge

(a) Prepare and file objections 125.00

(b) Each appearance 200.00

Filing creditors proof of claim 50.00

6. COLLECTIONS, COMMERCIAL

Collections prior to suit

   On the first $750.00....... 20%

   On the excess of $750.00 15%

   Minimum fee 15.00

Collections after suit

   On the first $2,000 .... 25%

   On the excess of $2,000 to
      $5,000.................... 20%

   On the excess of $5,000.. 15%

   Non-contingent suit fees—
      add 25.00

Actual appearance or supplementary
   pro., add

   Home County District
      Court 50.00

   Other District Courts 75.00

   County and Superior
      Courts 100.00

7. DRAFTING DOCUMENTS AND LEGAL INSTRUMENTS

Simple Affidavit 25.00

Escrow Agreement 25.00

Assignment of Judgment..... 25.00

Assignment of Lease.......... 25.00

Assignment of Rent........... 15.00

Assignment of Stock
   Certificate 10.00

Bill of Sale, simple 50.00

Bill of Sale, with inventory . 75.00

Bill of sale, Bulk Sales Act . 125.00

Bond, collateral or indemnity 50.00

Bond and Mortgage........... 75.00

Building Contract............. 150.00

Contract for Sale of Real
   Estate....................... 75.00

7. DRAFTING DOCUMENTS AND LEGAL INSTRUMENTS

(Continued)

Deed conveying real estate ..	50.00
Discharge of Mechanics Lien	25.00
Cancellation of Mortgage	15.00
Discharge of Mortgage	20.00
Release from Part of Mortgaged Premises	50.00
Discharge of Mechanics Notice of Intention	25.00
Discharge of Stop Notice	25.00
Extension of Mortgage	35.00
General Release................	25.00
Lease	
Commercial	125.00
Residential	50.00
Prepare and file Mechanics Notice of Intention	25.00
Option to Purchase Real Estate........................	75.00
Warrant to Satisfy Judgment	25.00
Power of Attorney, simple...	25.00
Security Agreement	75.00
Financing Statement	25.00

8. CONTINGENT FEES

In cases where a client's claim for damages is based upon the alleged tortious conduct of another, the fees shall be as set forth in R.R. 1:21-7

9. COURT ACTION AND LITIGATION, OTHER THAN CONTINGENT OR COMMERCIAL

Superior and County Courts

Retainer depending upon nature of case.	
All pleadings up to pretrial, including interrogatories	300.00
Motions	
Uncontested.................	150.00
Contested	175.00
Depositions (in County), per session	150.00
Depositions (out of County), per session	200.00
Pretrial conference with memorandum	150.00
Trials, per day..............	350.00
Municipal Court Appeals	
Appeal on the record below	250.00
Appeal on trial de novo...	350.00

District Courts

In Defense

Appearance or answer and up to trial	150.00
Trial, per day..............	150.00
Tenancy	
Dispossess, non-payment of rent......................	100.00
Dispossess, all other.......	150.00

Municipal Courts

Disorderly persons offense...	200.00
Bastardy........................	250.00
Preliminary hearing—indictable offense	300.00
Motor vehicle violations	
Careless Driving	150.00
Reckless Driving...........	250.00
Leaving the scene of an accident	250.00
Drunken or Impaired Driving...................	500.00
Other moving violations ..	150.00
Prosecution of complaint, per session	150.00

Condemnations

Where condemning authority makes offer before property owner retains counsel: If complaint has not yet been filed, 20% of the difference between the amount of the offer and the total recovery, however, in no case less than the total of the hourly and per diem charges involved in the matter.

In matters where less than $5,000 is involved: For preparation and trial

9. COURT ACTION AND LITIGATION, OTHER THAN CONTINGENT OR COMMERCIAL

(Continued)

charges before the commissioners or appeal, fee should be based upon total hourly and per diem charges as set forth in this Schedule.

In matters involving a sum in excess of $5,000; One-third of the difference between the last firm offer made by the condemning authority prior to client retaining counsel and the total recovery.

10. DOMESTIC RELATIONS

Matrimonial Litigation—divorce, annulment and separate maintenance
Uncontested, resident
    defendant 600.00
Uncontested, non-resident
    defendant 650.00
Contested (either party) plus per
    diem 850.00
Uncontested, non-resident defendant,
    with special substituted service
    problems 700.00
Representing defendant, uncontested
    on all issues 400.00
Motions (See Section 8 of this Schedule)
Drafting property settlement
    agreement 300.00
Domestic and Juvenile Court appearances, per appearance 250.00

11. WILLS AND ESTATES

Drawing simple Will 50.00
Drawing Will with trust
    provisions 75.00
On estate valued at $60,000 or less, involving ordinary amount of work, 5% of total assets, but where the principal beneficiary is also the fiduciary 3%.
On estate valued at over $60,000 involv-

ing ordinary amount of work:
(a) First $100,000 .... 5%
(b) Excess of $100,000 to
    $1,000,000 .... 3½%

A fee should be charged for services rendered in connection with assets of estate not passing by way of Will but reported in the Federal Estate Tax Return on New Jersey Inheritance Tax Return.

Except as indicated above, counsel fees should not be less than the statutory commissions allowed the fiduciary.

12. FORECLOSURES

Mortgage-fee of $300 plus taxed costs,
    plus 1½% of amount due on mortgage
Tax Sale Certificate 400.00
Tax Sale Certificate (In Rem—per
    certificate) 125.00

13. REAL ESTATE & CONVEYANCES (COMPLETE REPRESENTATION OF CLIENT IN TRANSACTIONS UP TO $25,000)

Representation of Sellers 250.00
Representation of Purchasers
    without mortgaging financing. 300.00
Representation of Purchasers
    with conventional mortgage
    financing 350.00
Representation of Purchasers
    with F.H.A. or V.A. mortgage
    financing 400.00
Representation on refinancing
    lending institution mortgage . 250.00

(All transactions involving more than $25,000 consideration or requiring negotiations by attorney or extraordinary services shall be charged for by special arrangement with client)

14. MISCELLANEOUS SERVICES

Change of name.................... 200.00
Adoptions
    From an approved agency or by
       step-parent.................... 200.00
    By any other placement...... 300.00
    Contested........................ 350.00

15. EXPENSES AND DISBURSEMENTS

All fees listed in each Section of this Schedule shall be paid net to the attorney and are to be in addition to all filing fees, Realty Transfer Fees, recording fees, net cost of Title insurance premiums, searches, surveys, investigations, court costs, travel expenses, medical reports, long distance telephone tolls, photo-copying, expert testimony, appraisals and all other out-of-pocket expenses and disbursements.

16. COMPETITIVE BIDDING DISAPPROVED

Responding to invitation from any client, public or private to submit a competitive bid for legal service is disapproved.

EXAMPLES OF BILLINGS

"POOR"

WHITE, BLACK & BROWN, P.A.

A PROFESSIONAL CORPORATION

ATTORNEYS AT LAW
WHITE BUILDING-61-67 MAIN ST.
ANYVILLE, N.J. 08872

———

STATEMENT

Mr. Lawrence J. Sauerwein

PROFESSIONAL SERVICES RENDERED in connection with the handling of the Estate of Helen M. Sauerwein, dec'd. from probate of Will at Surrogate's Office in Freehold up to and including final settlement of same...	1,000.00

"FAIR"

WHITE, BLACK & BROWN, P.A.

A PROFESSIONAL CORPORATION

ATTORNEYS AT LAW
WHITE BUILDING-61-67 MAIN ST.
ANYVILLE, N.J. 08872

———

STATEMENT

Mr. Lawrence J. Sauerwein

PROFESSIONAL SERVICES RENDERED in connection with the handling to the Estate of Helen M. Sauerwein covering period Nov. 21, 1975 to Aug. 11, 1975 as follows: (a) All services in connection with probate of Will at Freehold, N.J.; (b) Conference with Executor and preparation of Transfer Inheritance Tax Return and attending to execution of same and filing with County Super.; (c) Collection of Assets, and paying legacies and debts; (d) Preparation of a Stipulated Informal Accounting and having same executed by all parties in interest; (e) Having appropriate Refunding Bonds and Release signed by all beneficiaries and distribution of net assets of estate..	$1,000.00

"GOOD"

WHITE, BLACK & BROWN, P.A.

A PROFESSIONAL CORPORATION

ATTORNEYS AT LAW
WHITE BUILDING-61-67 MAIN ST.
ANYVILLE, N.J. 08872

STATEMENT

Mr. Lawrence J. Sauerwein

PROFESSIONAL SERVICES RENDERED in connection with the handling of the Estate of Helen M. Sauerwein, dec'd. from probate of Will and Surrogate's Office in Freehold up to and including final settlement of same, as per itemized statement annexed hereto and made a part hereof...	$1,000.00

ITEMIZED STATEMENT

for PROFESSIONAL SERVICES RENDERED in connection with the handling of the Estate of Helen Sauerwein, Deceased, from the initial probate of the Will up to and covering the closing out of said estate, including but not being limited to the following:

Nov. 21, 197 —Received from Lawrence J. Sauerwein, copy of Will and Death Certificate covering Helen Sauerwein with request that we make arrangements for probate.

Dec. 2, 197 —Communication with Surrogate's Office and lodging Death Certificate and photo copy of Will and advice as to who would appear as attesting witness.

Dec. 2 to
Dec. 13, 197 —Arrangements for admission to Will for probate in Surrogate's Office in Freehold.

Jan. 14, 197 —Telephone advice as to steps to be taken to transfer title to your mother's automobile, and forwarding Certificate of Letters Testamentary and confirmation of same by letter enclosing Certificate of your appointment as Executor.

Jan. 27 to
Jan. 29, 197 —Office conference and review of assets of the estate

Jan. 28, 197 —Communication with Harris Upham & Co. to establish value of DuPont and Gen. Motors Stock as of Nov. 1, 1974

Jan. 29, 197 —Communication with General Motors and DuPont Co. to ascertain their requirements to effect transfer of stock

Jan. 29, 197 —Communication with South Amboy Trust Co. to verify amount of deposit, etc.

Feb. 17, 197 —Preparation of Affidavit establishing identity and transmittal to Mr. Sauerwein

Feb. 1 to
April 4, 197   —Legal Research on best methods of handling tax
                 impact on estate in view of several methods by
                 which the assets were held jointly with the
                 decedent and others.

April 4, 197   —Having memorandum of law prepared by Attorney
                 Baker covering these points.

April 4, 197 to
April 17, 197   —Preparation of N.J. Transfer Inheritance Tax
                 Return and having same properly executed at
                 the office.

April 17, 197   —Communication to Monmouth County District
                 Officer—Transfer Inheritance Tax Bureau for-
                 warding him original Transfer Inheritance Tax
                 Return with Supplemental Affidavit duly executed es-
                 tablishing origin of the funds making up the joint accounts.

April 17, 197   —Furnishing copies of above to Mr. Sauerwein for his
                 information

April 21, 197   —Communication with Monmouth County District Supervisor
                 furnishing him copy of inventory of opening of safety
                 deposit box.

April 22, 197   —Furnishing copy of above to Mr. Sauerwein for his records
                 and information.

June 12, 197   —Receipt from Trenton Office of Transfer Inheritance Tax
                 Bureau of transfer inheritance tax bill amounting to
                 $421.87.

June 12, 197   —Careful examination and study of bill together with
                 worksheet showing manner in which tax was arrived at and
                 discovering several errors which had to be corrected
                 so that a corrected and reduced tax bill would be issued
                 by the estate.

June 12, 197   —Extended communication to the Trenton Office of N.J.
                 Inheritance Tax Bureau outlining the errors and re-
                 questing their correction and issuance of a revised
                 tax bill

June 25, 197   —Receipt of revised tax bill from N.J. Inheritance Tax
Bureau at Trenton revising the original tax from $421.87
to $185.84, representing a reduction of $236.03.

June 25, 197   —Communication to Mr. Sauerwein verifying the above
reduction and requesting certified check for $185.84

July 8, 197   —Communication to N.J. Inheritance Tax Bureau forwarding
certified check for $185.84 to cover revised tax

July 16, 197   —Communication to Mr. Sauerwein forwarding the Gen.Motors
Stock Certificates with instructions to have same signed
by him and signature guaranteed by a commercial bank and
returned to this office.

July 17, 197   —Receipt from Mr. Sauerwein of stock certificates properly
endorsed for transfer and remailed same to transfer agent

July, 197   —Receipt from Mr. Sauerwein of written instructions as to
manner in which various joint accounts were to be
relisted

Aug., 197   —Preparation of separate letters of instruction for disposition of assets in three banks.

Aug., 197   —Receipt from General Motor transfer agent of new, reissued
stock certificate in the name of Lawrence J. Sauerwein

Chapter 10

HOW TO MAKE CONTINUING
YOUR LEGAL EDUCATION
PRODUCE CASH DIVIDENDS

*Continuing Education Essential to Survival . . . Use the Advance
Sheets and the Official Publication . . . The Most Pleasant and
Profitable Reading in Your Life . . . Reproduce, Tear Out and
File the Decisions with the Pending Cases They Apply to . . . Use
Your Current Decisions to Guide Your Current Trials . . . Wide
Variety of Publications Can Lead to New and More Profitable
Techniques . . . Use the Institute for Continuing Legal
Education . . . The Laborer Turned "Able Seaman" . . . Did the
Defendants Convert a Laborer into an Able Seaman? . . . The
Compensation Case Becomes an Admiralty Case . . . Listening to
a Cassette for a Few Hours or So Can Help You Become Some-
thing of an Expert . . . Many Special Problems Involved for Mal-
practice Cases . . . How Cassettes Can Simplify Research . . .
How An Investment of $10-$20 in Cassettes Helped Produce a
$10,000 Fee . . . Safaris to Far Away Countries Are for the
Affluent . . . How to Preserve the Results of Your Research . . .
A Dozen Reference Files Keep Essential Data at Your Finger Tips*

Continuing Education Essential to Survival

As in almost every field, law is subject to rapid changes in substance
and procedure. The old rule of *stare decisis* has been changed many times particu-

193

larly in recent years. As Mr. Dooley said in effect "Always the courts follow the elections." It has been estimated that some 50 percent to 80 percent of what is even presently being taught in some college courses will be obsolete in ten years. While the profession of law is notoriously conservative and slow to change, it is still imperative to keep abreast of all the latest decisions. This is particularly true as to the county or state in which you practice and in the specific fields toward which your practice gravitates. It is the only method I know of by which you can make your professional income keep pace with inflation.

Use the Advance Sheets and the Official Publication

Most states have some recognized weekly publication which is the authorized spokesman for the courts. It carries brief digests of recent decisions, amendments to the rules, court calendars, as well as general social news of Bar activities, including individuals, organizations, etc. These publications are usually sufficiently newsy to attract even the busiest lawyer to read them regularly. It is the official weekly reports of the various state courts on the Appellate level, usually referred to as the Advance Sheets, which are compulsory reading. These usually are issued in soft covers, of the proper page size and in numerical sequence for later publishing in hardback buckram bound permanent volumes. In New Jersey, these Advance Sheets cover the current decisions of the Supreme Court as well as the Appellate Division of the Superior Court, and are mandatory reading if an active lawyer wants to keep abreast of the latest developments in the law.

The Most Pleasant and Profitable
Reading in Your Life

If the lawyer adopts the correct attitude toward this compulsory reading, it will cease to be a bane and become a treat. After a while you will cease to consider this reading as a chore and look forward eagerly to receiving the new issue and to read it avidly. The secret is to look upon them in this triple aspect. In the first instance they are vivid, sometimes lurid accounts of some gripping drama in the otherwise drab life of some ordinary man or woman. Second, their reading is going to arm you with the necessary information and authority to keep you at the top of your profession. Finally, and perhaps most important of all, if you read these reports with an eye constantly cocked toward the question of how you can apply this newly-gained knowledge to the *cases presently pending in your office*, you will find that these reports are the most profitable reading, dollarwise, that you may ever do.

Reproduce, Tear Out and File the Decisions with the Pending Cases They Apply to

It is true that in a lawyer's busy schedule he may fall a half dozen or even a dozen weeks behind in this essential reading. If this happens, I suggest you set one evening aside to catch up. Pick out your favorite chair in your den at home, pile up the booklets on the floor on your left side. As you finish reading each one, tear off the upper right-hand corner of the cover to confirm this fact, and pile them on the floor on the right side of your chair for prompt return to the office. Make a game out of seeing how many of the current decisions you can apply to your own pending cases. If you are fortunate, you may sometimes hit the jackpot by finding a current case directly on "all fours." More often you will find some isolated point in the decision which will help you on some critical point of law. In any event they are all "grist for the mill," and extremely useful *and profitable* grist as well. If you are too busy to read every decision in full, at least scan all of them. If your practice excludes criminal work, you may omit these cases entirely if you must.

But when you find a case that helps you, underline the salient facts and finding of the court. Mark the margins as well as the cover to simplify finding it. When these Advance Sheets are returned to the office, a brief memo to a secretary will instruct her to photo-copy the marked sections and file in the appropriate pending files. Since these Advance Sheets are soon to be replaced by bound volumes (at least once or twice a year) there is no particular virtue in maintaining them intact. Do not hesitate to tear out the specific cases which may help you immediately. However, if you do this be sure to mark on the preceding page a reference to the file in which the torn sheets may be found if needed. In some cases I will put the entire Advance Sheets in the file, particularly if the case is scheduled for early argument or actual trial.

Use Your Current Decisions to Guide Your Current Trials

I can personally attest to the fact that in some of these reading sessions, particularly where the Advance Sheets have gotten 10 or 12 weeks ahead of me, it is not uncommon to find three, four or perhaps a half dozen cases, either directly in point or extremely helpful in the handling of pending litigation. That is why I say that reading them can be made not only enjoyable but profitable as well. In one instance I recall we had a slip-and-fall case pending in the office in which the injuries involved a fractured hip. The accident had occurred at the fresh produce counter of a self-service supermarket when the claimant slipped on a cabbage leaf. It was next to impossible to establish "notice" to the owner or operator as to how long this single cabbage leaf had been on the floor. We might have lost the case by an involuntary dismissal under the law at that time.

However, we discovered that in a recent case a Trial Court had permitted a case to go to the jury on the basis that the string bean upon which the claimant had fallen was so trampled upon that the jury could have drawn a legitimate inference from that fact alone that it had lain on the floor long enough to give the owner or operator at least constructive notice of its presence. It so happened that in our case the cabbage leaf was in substantially the same condition. It was black, brown, withered and beaten up—obviously trampled upon by many feet. The jury brought in a verdict of $42,500 based largely upon this evidence. While the law of notice has since been liberally expanded in many jurisdictions, this type of evidence can still be extremely helpful in the proper presentation of a case.

Wide Variety of Publications Can Lead to New and More Profitable Techniques

There are many other items of reading material which even the busiest lawyer must find time to peruse if he wants his income to reach the magic mark of $100,000 per annum. If you have a monthly State Bar Journal, be sure to read it regularly. There are frequently some lead articles which will help you to a more productive and profitable practice. I served as a member of the Editorial Board of the New Jersey State Bar Journal and contributed a series of two dozen or more of such articles over a span of 12 years. These ranged from *The Highest Role of the Lawyer* to *Slip-and-Fall Cases Can Be Handled Profitably*. The wide awake lawyer should be constantly on the alert for this type of article and should make a practice of clipping them and filing them for appropriate reference.

For those engaged in the field of personal injury cases, there are various publications which cover recent decisions throughout the United States in most fields. These include tort, admiralty, aviation, railroad and compensation fields. These too can be extremely productive. By checking recent decisions in these fields in other jurisdictions, you can obtain direct leads to identical or analogous decisions in your own state with a minimum of research. If you find none in your own state, cite the most recent cases in out-of-state jurisdictions. It will impress the court as well as your adversaries with your legal erudition. And the Trial or Appellate Court may even adopt the philosophy of their colleagues on the bench and follow their decision. A prominent Justice of the U. S. Supreme Court was recently quoted as saying: "I am not so much interested in finding a precedent, as I am in establishing one." Let us say *Amen* to this philosophy, provided always that the new precedent is a sound one which promotes the cause of justice.

Use the Institute for Continuing Legal Education

There is no question that continuing your legal education is actually essential to survival. That is precisely why the Practicing Law Institute has proven so popular although reportedly not so profitable. Sessions and seminars are held throughout the United States in larger cities several times a month throughout the year on a wide variety of subjects. Leading lawyers in the various fields lecture, conduct seminars, followed by question-and-answer periods, workshop demonstrations, etc. These are usually buttressed by printed texts of the program to follow while it is in progress, and complete transcripts at its completion. This is an excellent method of absorbing a distilled, highly-concentrated synthesis of the current state of the law in a given field. Attendance at some of these, particularly those in the area in which a major portion of your practice normally falls or in which you have a special case which is pending or anticipated, can prove highly profitable.

The Laborer Turned "Able Seaman"

I recall one particular case we had which involved a laborer who had been engaged to "trim" coal in barges moored to a nearby dock at South Amboy, New Jersey. As the barge was shifted under the coal hopper, it struck the dock throwing Charlie Pressler from the deck of the barge on to the dock and from thence into the water, breaking both legs. The insurance carrier covering the owners and operators was on the job the next day, actually taking taped interviews while Charlie was still in the hospital having his fractures set. They were equally prompt in issuing him weekly checks for some small pittance like $31.01 per week under the Longshoreman's and Harbor Workers Compensation Act. Our office almost fell into the trap.

Since our home city was not a port city, litigation involving navigable waters was infrequent. Frankly, we were not abreast of it. However, we took the normal procedure. We wrote the federal agency concerned, obtained the forms of claimant petition under the Act, prepared and filed them and waited for the formal hearing to be scheduled. Meanwhile, Charlie continued to receive his extremely modest weekly payments. I checked the statutes and noted that the maximum award he would probably receive at the end of his temporary disability, and based upon his estimated permanency, would be somewhere in the neighborhood of less than $20,000 at that time.

This idea distressed me. I could not get it out of my mind. This seemed like such a rank injustice to Charlie who was in his middle 50's and handicapped by two stiff legs which rendered him fairly close to 100 percent permanently disabled. There was something about this matter that just did not seem right in my book of what justice should be for an injured workman.

Here was a man who was hired as an ordinary laborer to level coal with a shovel as it was dumped from the coal cars into the hold of the barges under the hopper. Investigation disclosed that from three to six empty barges would be brought in by tug and moored to the nearby dock at the same time. As one barge was filled, it had to be moved away and an empty one moved up to replace it. 90 percent of the movement was accomplished by a power-operated winch on the dock. Wind, waves and the natural tide provided the balance of the motive power. Charle's job was merely to board the empty barge when the shifting operation began and to throw a hawser from the stern of the barge to a large cleat on the dock to hold the barge fast. A second laborer was performing a similar operation at the bow of the barge.

While I was mulling over Charlie's predicament I signed up to attend a tort seminar at Newark, sponsored by the American Trial Lawyers Association. One of the seminars included the subject of Admiralty. I attended this in order to brush up on this fascinating subject. One of the lecturers was a prominent Philadelphia attorney who was a partner in a law firm specializing in Admiralty. He was a most interesting speaker and I listened attentively, made copious notes, took down numerous citations and resolved to follow all of these items through when I got back to the office.

Did the Defendants Convert a Laborer into an Able Seaman?

That very evening the solution of Charlie's problem came to me in a flash. Indeed his employers had done Charlie wrong. He was just a laborer hired to shovel coal. What was he doing on an empty barge in navigable waters with a hawser in his hand, as the barge swung wide of her mooring in choppy waters on a windy day, as it struck the dock and knocked him off his feet seriously injuring him? I thereupon decided that his employers had arbitrarily converted this poor fellow, without his being fully aware of it from an ordinary laborer into an "able seaman" just as much as if a captain had ordered him to climb the mizzen mast of a four-masted schooner on the open seas.

The Compensation Case Becomes an Admiralty Case

We immediately canceled receipt of the small checks under the Federal Compensation Act and filed suit in Admiralty alleging unseaworthiness, negligence and various violations under the Jones Act. Figuratively we joined everybody as defendants including the railroad, the barge line, the land owner, the operator of the winch, the captain of the barge, etc. The case eventually came on for trial at Newark, New Jersey. The Trial Judge apparently considered our theory a little too fine spun for recognition and entered a judgment of no cause for action against the claimant. However, on appeal to the U.S. Circuit Court at Philadelphia the Trial Court was reversed by a closely-divided vote. When the case was rescheduled for trial, the defendants paid Charlie $100,000.

Thus a case which started out as a modest Federal Compensation case produced a substantial fee for the office. This is just one isolated illustration of how attendance at a single seminar triggered an idea which later developed into a sound theory of law and produced an excellent recovery which made both Charlie and our office well pleased with the results.

Listening to a Cassette for a Few Hours or So Can Help You Become Something of an Expert

In recent years, the problem of keeping abreast of current litigation has been made increasingly easier. Cassettes covering tapes of lectures on practically every conceivable subject are now available, singly, in sets and in series. We have subscribed to a number of them. With a battery-operated recorder these tapes can be played and replayed as you drive your car for any considerable distance. They usually run 30 minutes to a side. It takes but the flip of the wrist and the fingers to reverse the cassette for the second 30-minute play on side number 2. This can prove to be one of the most profitable hours of relaxed and pleasant listening you can ever engage in.

Many Special Problems Involved for Malpractice Cases

By way of illustration we had a malpractice case pending in the office. It involved a Bob Harrison who was stricken with severe abdominal pains early one morning around 2:00 a.m. He was taken to a nearby hospital where the diagnosis was a kidney stone lodged in his *right* ureter. The X-rays confirmed it. Follow-up X-rays covering the next two days, with consultations by roentgenologists and urologists, again confirmed the diagnosis. These X-rays even pinpointed the exact location of the stone.

Armed with this data the hospital staff wheeled Bob into the operating room, propped up the final X-ray plates in the shadow box but apparently *reversed* the plates so it showed the stone as if it was in the *left* ureter. An incision was made by the attending surgeon, the left ureter exposed and found to be clear of obstruction. Bob was sewed up and had to wait seven days more until a different set of surgeons could make a new incision on the right side and remove the stone.

How Cassettes Can Simplify Research

Once again we sued everybody who had anything to do with it. But malpractice claims against the doctor—and particularly against a prominent hospital with a good reputation are not the easiest task in the world. Hence, the case required extensive legal research to make certain that the case was bottomed soundly on the law. The facts certainly seemed clear enough. But more important still it required extensive study and research in the various techniques for the proper preparation and presentation of the essential, *competent*, *admissible* evidence before a court and jury. While the facts were relatively simple, we were met by a barrage of highly-technical defenses advanced by some of the best defense counsel in the state. One of them made a specialty of defending medical malpractice cases exclusively.

We began our preparation by reviewing all the books in our reference library on the subject. These were supplemented by purchasing the latest text books available. We next checked on all the seminars recently held on the subject, purchased all the transcripts available and reviewed them. Finally, we purchased a series of cassettes and listened to each of them. These tapes proved to be the simplest, most pleasant and most effective means of illustrating and demonstrating the best techniques for preparing and presenting a case of this type. On a single one-hour drive to my summer home at the Shore I could play both sides of a cassette. Each cassette was loaded down with valuable information which we proceeded to employ.

How an Investment of $10-$20 in Cassettes Helped Produce a $10,000 Fee

We compiled and served comprehensive sets of interrogatories on all defendants. These were followed up by depositions covering all the defendants including their servants, agents and employees. They were held in the conference room of the hospital to reduce the inconvenience to the doctors, nurses and members of the hospital staff to a minimum. The case was exhaustively investigated down to the last X-ray, the last report, and the last record of the hospital and its staff to pin down and point out where the responsibility lay for reversing the X-ray plates.

In the course of the depositions, when we got down to the final pin-down question submitted to each of the four nurses and three doctors present, i.e., "What did *you personally* and precisely do to make reasonably sure that the proper X-ray plate was properly set up in the operating room for the surgical team?"—counsel for one of the defendants instructed the witness not to answer! We transcribed the record and particularly the precise question, and moved for an order compelling an answer. At this stage the case was settled for $30,000.

Since the plaintiff was young and vigorous and in excellent health and made a full and uneventful recovery, it was difficult to establish any genuine permanent disability except for the unnecessary scarring and the additional week of intensive pain awaiting the second operation. We attribute much of our success in obtaining a satisfactory settlement in this case to the use of these cassettes. Sometimes an investment of $10 or $20 in items of this kind can assist in the collection of a $10,000 fee.

Safaris to Far Away Countries Are for the Affluent

In recent years, a practice has developed for some attorneys to take safaris by jets to far off countries to visit and observe at first hand the judicial processes of these countries. I applaud the underlying theory behind these junkets. I likewise applaud the fact that they are in most cases a tax-deductible item. Their practical utility, however, to the lawyer struggling to reach the $100,000 per annum income somehow escapes me. In my judgment, these trips are ideal for the affluent. I recommend that they be deferred by the struggling lawyer until he has reached the magic figure. In the meantime I suggest that it would seem much more effective and practical to invest the time and expense involved, in purchasing and using the text books, transcripts and cassettes I have previously discussed.

How to Preserve the Results of Your Research

When you have invested so much time and effort and energy and enterprise in your legal research, it would be little short of criminal not to make certain that it was properly protected and preserved and indexed for constant reference. This extends not only to the special items researched for your individual cases but to legal data generally. These special items can always be safely filled with the individual cases to which they apply. Transcripts, briefs, memorandum of law, citations of legal and medical texts will always be available for future reference should a similar or identical case arise. But I am now referring to printed data in these fields of law generally. The basic law, of course, is to be found in the digests of your own state and sister states, in Corpus Juris Secundum or A.L.R. or the wide variety of other digests and texts and law reports in the law libraries at every county seat.

A Dozen Reference Files Keep Essential
Data at Your Finger Tips

Initially, we maintained only a single file marked "Legal Books." Later, we added a second one captioned "Medico-Legal Books." These two files rapidly expanded to the piont where they became unmanageable. It took too long to find the specific book we were looking for. At this point we again sub-divided this reference data into an even dozen of separate files as follows: (1) Trial Tactics; (2) Personal Injuries (auto, products liability, aviation, etc.); (3) Medico-Legal Data; (4) Corporation Law; (5) Municipal Law; (6) Criminal Law and Procedure; (7) Estate Law; (8) Trust Law; (9) Real Estate—Developments, Condominiums; (10) Condemnation (eminent domain); (11) Taxes Generally; (12) Miscellaneous.

We now find that the average secretary can locate and order almost any item on any subject we need with a minimum of time and effort. We recommend that this wealth of data be kept available at all times. Frequently we have found that the purchase of a single book for $20 or $30 can produce dividends a thousand-fold.

Chapter 11

HOW TO RECOGNIZE AND UTILIZE
COLLATERAL INCOME OPPORTUNITIES

Law Opens Many Avenues of Income . . . Part-time Public Posts . . . Part-time Judge of Magistrate Court Offers Many Advantages . . . Municipal Attorney Post Can Lead to Substantial Fees . . . County and State Agencies Offer Many Part-time Positions . . . Serving as Officer or Director of Lending Institutions Can Be Lucrative . . . Savings and Loan Grow From $300,000 to $25 Million . . . Most Corporations Need Better Directors . . . Counsel for Tax Lien Claimant Leads to Court-Appointed Directorship . . . Every Day Offers Investment and Speculation Opportunity . . . Purchase of One Building Brings in Eight Times the Price in Rents and Quadruples Sales Price . . . Purchase of Dormant Developments and Empty Plots for Rapid Resales

Law Opens Many Avenues of Income

I do not know of any profession that opens the door to so wide a variety of sources of income as the law. It has been widely recognized for many years that legal training fits a man for a wide variety of pursuits. Thus far I have not referred to this advantage enjoyed by the average lawyer. Perhaps, however, it is this very advantage which enables him to see so many avenues of legitimate and proper profit for himself as he continues the regular practice of law. Let us just examine a few of them.

203

Part-time Public Posts

Today, positions in public life and connected directly or indirectly with public boards, bureaus and authorities are mushrooming as never before. In the state legislature many years ago, I made a speech on the floor of the House of the Assembly against the "evils of ever burgeoning boards, bureaus and agencies." The conditions at that time were moderate and mild compared to what it is today. Every branch of government is expanding. The public is constantly demanding more services at every level. The result is more boards, bureaus and agencies—and all of them, or at least most of them, need counsel. Therefore, one of the first steps I recommend (if you have the time and energy) is to accept a part-time post as attorney or counsel for some such public body. I do not mean a "no show" political plum—but a genuine, bona-fide legal post which will take only one or two evenings a week or a month, but one which will definitely supplement your income. There are positions of this kind available not only for the young lawyer—but the mature, hard-bitten practitioner as well.

Part-time Judge of Magistrate Court Offers Many Advantages

By way of illustration, when I started to practice law, I accepted appointment for a few years as a local magistrate. In those days, the post was called Recorder or Judge of the Police Court. The pay was not large, but the contacts were invaluable. Omitting the defendants and the complaining witnesses entirely, the daily contacts with many members of the police department were very helpful. Similar contacts can be valuable to any lawyer, and particularly those whose practise extends to the personal injury field.

I do not intend for a single moment to suggest that any police officer would engage in ambulance chasing or touting a particular attorney, even if he was a judge. What I refer to is the prestige which a position of this kind creates for the attorney; his exposure in the local press; the respect and deference which his conduct of the court can engender among the parties appearing before the court, among their attorneys, and the public as well. The officials responsible for the appointment of the judge usually take an interest and a justifiable pride in how he performs his duties. All of these factors cannot help but generate new and profitable practice for the attorney who is doing a good job, and eventually promotion to higher, more prestigious and more remunerative positions.

Municipal Attorney Post Can Lead to Substantial Fees

Next in order, I became the municipal or corporate counsel for the town. While the judge of the police court sat one night a week, corporate counsel attended two business meetings or conferences and two public meetings a month. All of these meetings were held at night. This left the entire day free for the normal practice of law. Night work is not exactly desirable, but to develop a profitable practice, and to do it in a hurry in your career, it is sometimes necessary.

A post of this kind is not easy to come by. The annual legal fees for counsel in a rapidly-growing community can help you reach the bench mark of $100,000 per annum. Naturally, these posts are sought after aggressively, but there are probably more than 30,000 of these positions available in the nation today. In addition, more legal positions are now proliferating as never before —even at the local municipal level. Many legislatures are insisting that so-called subordinate municipal bodies be independent and autonomous. It is now mandatory in many states that each of these boards and bodies has its own counsel. Gone are the days when a single municipal attorney served as counsel for the parent body and its subordinate boards and agencies. Instead, there are as many as three or four, or even more, separate attorneys serving these boards, bureaus and agencies, in the average-size community.

These can include the Planning Board; the Board of Adjustment; the Zoning Board; the Board of Health; the Board of Education. In the light of recent decisions of the U. S. Supreme Court, local prosecutors are now commonplace, as well as local public defenders. All of these positions pay respectable salaries. Some of them are based on annual retainers, with fees permitted for all extra work not considered routine.

County and State Agencies Offer Many
Part-time Positions

On the county and state level, the same situation prevails. The county counsel now has a half dozen part-time associates. The County Planning Board; the County Welfare Board; the Sheriff; the Surrogate; etc. all have their own counsel. All indigent defendants are entitled to be represented by counsel in all cases where imprisonment could be part of the punishment meted out. This court decision has expanded the horizon for defense lawyers tremendously.

Nor are these opportunities limited to the younger attorneys alone. The courts have held that defendants charged with serious crimes are entitled to mature, capable, experienced attorneys who can adequately and properly defend them. This has resulted in the setting up of Public Defender systems operating side by side with the Prosecutor's or District Attorney's Office and extending into practically every village and hamlet in the nation. So, if you have the time, the inclination, and the willingness to devote a few hours a day, a week, or a month, to a public or quasi-public post, the jobs are there for the asking. They will not only supplement your income substantially, but lead to bigger and better opportunities almost on a daily basis.

Serving as Officer or Director of Lending Institutions Can Be Lucrative

Next to part-time public positions, there are part-time private positions with corporations, banks, insurance companies and the like. Banks are also mushrooming all over the country. They all need counsel not only in their organization, but in their development and expansion as well. Valuable estate, mortgage, corporation and collection business flows from positions of this kind and can supplement your regular income greatly. Building and Loan Associations, Savings and Loan Associations, and similar home financing institutions are also expanding as never before. The rapid growth of the population; the constantly growing GNP; the inflationary economy; the ever-recurring need for young couples to find homes in an ever-expanding economy—all invite and encourage the creation and expansion of such thrift organizations.

Make it your business to become associated with such an organization early in your career. If you cannot become counsel, then accept a post as an "Assistant Counsel"—if it is offered to you. Take an active part in the work and expansion of the institution. Eventually you at least can hope to succeed to the highly coveted post of counsel.

To supplement my own income, I became a director in such a small association. The board was not particularly progressive. I inherited the job of chairman of the advertising and promotion committee by default. No one else wanted the job. At that time, the institution had assets of only $300,000. Even this meager capitalization was not certain. It had an old-fashioned sinking fund set up. Under it, members saved $1 a month on five or ten shares by payment on the monthly meeting date. Ten to 14 years later, each share matured at $200. However, after saving with us regularly for this long period, as soon as their shares matured and became worthwhile, they took the accumulated $1,000 or $2,000 out and transferred it to some "regular savings bank" which competed with us!

Savings and Loan Grow From $300,000 to $25 Million

Fortunately our state laws, and there are similar laws in most states, permitted us to become a full-time, fully-insured savings institution. This permitted us to abolish the sinking fund idea and to retain all accumulated savings as deposits and to continue to pay attractive dividends on them. With a little energy and imagination, I persuaded the Board to convert to this new operation; did all the legal work; and saw this small institution grow from $300,000 to $25,000,000 in a relatively few years.

All of its money had to be invested promptly to meet the dividends. The principal investment was in prime first mortgages on nearby homes. By degrees this work alone kept the office quite busy and helped carry the overhead at least—and it was all emanating from one single client! The moral of this story is that if you cannot find a struggling bank or a small savings and loan association which will retain you as counsel—consider starting one of your own. But if you do this, you will have to be ready for some hard work—and learn to love it, because it can be a grueling uphill fight.

Most Corporations Need Better Directors

Directorships in corporations can also supplement your income. I venture to say that there is hardly a corporation in the nation today—large or small —that has adequate, active membership on its board of directors. Lawyers have trained minds. Their background and training enables them to recognize a problem as it arises; to analyze it and to assist in its solution.

That is precisely why many wide-awake, progressive corporations welcome new blood on their boards and usually they are lawyers. The fees paid can supplement your professional income substantially. Fees paid for attending directors' meetings range from nominal sums to several hundred dollars a meeting. But these fees are minimal compared to the exposure you receive to a wide variety of other profitable investments and adventures.

Counsel for Tax Lien Claimant Leads to
Court-Appointed Directorship

I represented a municipality with a tax lien of almost $200,000. It was against a large corporation which was then going through reorganization. The corporation's plight was rather desperate. As it sold one small parcel after another, the court held the usual hearing on notice to all creditors. I was always the culprit. As a preferred creditor holding a tax lien, I invariably announced that my client demanded the entire proceeds of the sale.

I soon became the most unpopular counsel in the courtroom. After this had gone on for a year or so, I made a personal study of the company; its assets; its liabilities; its cash flow; its mode of operation; etc. Since I lived in the community and was in daily contact with the operation, I was probably in a much better position than any of the other attorneys to discover a potential means of getting the corporation back on its feet and out of court. The judge handling the matter was probably one of the greatest and most competent jurists on the bench at that time. I took the liberty of conveying my ideas to him, for raising the $200,000. He not only accepted them, but adopted them as well.

The single thing that had been preventing the reorganization of the company and its release from the court's jurisdiction was its inability to pay off the huge tax lien held by my client. The idea I proposed to the court permitted the company to raise the necessary funds and pay off its entire tax lien, including interest, down to the last dollar. This was done and the company went back into normal operation with a new board of directors. The court in recognition of my contribution to the survival and rehabilitation of this distressed corporation appointed me as one of the two court-appointed directors. I held the post for the next 20 years until the company was eventually acquired by a conglomerate and eventually liquidated its assets.

Every Day Offers Investment and
Speculation Opportunity

In the course of all of the various activities of the active practitioner, there is scarcely a day or a week goes by that something does not cross his desk or come to his attention which will serve to supplement his professional income substantially. Sometimes these opportunities presented are superior to regular or normal income. I say this because the additional income would be in the form of long-term capital gain, and hence not subject to the high tax bracket rates. In this manner, the attorney would be able to retain most of the profit realized instead of paying it out in taxes.

Purchase of One Building Brings in Eight Times Its Price
in Rents and Quadruples Sales Price

I could cite a dozen such opportunities. One or two of these will serve as illustrations. As I left my office in the Liberty Theater Building one evening, I noticed a sign in the doorway of a store and attached dwelling across the street on the corner of Main and Dane Streets. My trained eye told me it was a legal notice of some kind. This prompted me to cross the street and read the notice. It covered the usual foreclosure of mortgage procedure. The sheriff's sale was scheduled two weeks hence. The Execution recited the gross amount to be raised by the sale. The figure seemed a fairly modest price to pay for the building. However, the owners, who incidentally were not clients of mine, apparently could not meet it. Hence, I had no legal or moral restraints with respect to this opportunity.

Without inspecting the building premises (except for the outside), I contacted the financial institution to ascertain if they would sell this property to me in the event they bought it in at the foreclosure sale. I also checked up to find out if they would consider an 80 percent purchase money mortgage if I made a down payment of 20 percent. They tentatively agreed to these terms.

A few weeks later, I was the owner of the property, with only 20 percent paid down. Within a few months, I had increased the rent on the store by 50 percent. The chain store occupying it resisted, but eventually agreed. With the expenditure of a few thousand dollars, I converted the single-family attached dwelling to a two-family house. In this manner, I doubled the rent.

After holding this one investment for about 18 years, my records showed that in rents it had brought in more than eight times the purchase price paid for it. When it was sold, the price was approximately four times the purchase price. The capital gain realized was so substantial that the tax paid to IRS almost approximated the initial purchase price.

Purchase of Dormant Developments and Empty Plots for Rapid Resales

Illustrations of this kind can be multiplied many times over. Tax foreclosures of unimproved realty offer a fertile field for rich rewards with small investments. Sometimes a small development may die aborning. There may be nothing seriously wrong with the project except that it was underfinanced or improperly managed. While it is not wise for a lawyer to get into this type of project too deeply unless he has a special knack for handling them, they can sometimes be swung on very small investments. They may then be resold promptly to persons who know their business and have adequate financing. Among my own circle of friends in the legal profession, I know of one attorney who bought a development of some 100 completed homes. Another bought an office building in the city. Another bought a partially-completed development with additional acreage still to be subdivided. All of these purchases were at depressed prices. In each instance, the purchasers made handsome profits which greatly supplemented their normal income.

My grandfather had a yen for acquiring vacant plots. He could not resist purchasing isolated parcels of a few acres which he perceived were in the path of progress. I seem to have inherited some of these faculties. I, too, followed suit. Some of the values climbed almost astronomically.

In one such instance, I bought the remaining lots of a defunct or moribund development which lay behind my home. As I was closing the title, the attorney representing the seller asked "Confidentially—what are you going to do with this land? What are your plans?" I replied "Nothing in particular. I like lots of elbow room. While I am shaving in the morning I like to look out the rear window and see some trees and open spaces." He said "What? For 2,000 feet in each direction?" The investment paid off handsomely and greatly supplemented my income.

This chapter has only skimmed the surface of the opportunities open to the active, wide-awake attorney to supplement his professional income. These opportunities present themselves almost daily. The alert attorney will find as his day-to-day activities increase in tempo that his real task is in analyzing the opportunities and selecting the right ones. A sage once observed that it takes a wise man to distinguish between temptation and opportunity. This admonition is certainly appropriate for the attorney. He will be subjected to conflicting advice. There will be those who will tell him that he should follow the admonition that a "shoemaker should stick to his last"; that he can lose more by getting involved in fields in which he has no experience or particular aptitude. Other attorneys will solemnly advise him that whatever assets or estate they have managed to amass came from collateral investments producing long-term capital gains, etc.

My only advice to attorneys is that they would be well advised to analyze carefully every opportunity as it presents itself. As time goes on, they will develop a knack for spotting the genuine "money maker" and seizing the opportunity with alacrity. Their common sense and accurate judgment will enable them to shy away from the investments that are unsound or unproductive. Suffice it to say that a lawyer of average intelligence can certainly supplement his income greatly from sources unrelated to his law practice. In some instances, this collateral income may even *exceed the $100,000* per annum we have been discussing.

Chapter 12

HOW TO DEVELOP A FAVORABLE
"PR" WITHOUT VIOLATING
ETHICAL STANDARDS

Join a Church or Synagogue–and Participate . . . Don't Wait for the Invitation to "Move Up Higher" . . . Just to Show Which Side You Are On . . . Service Clubs Are Naturals for Contacts . . . Bringing in a $100-Million Industry to Home Town and More Millions of Taxes and Payrolls . . . Donate Your Services to the Red Cross, Salvation Army, Boy Scouts, etc. . . . The Boy Scout Organizational Plan that Lasted 20 Years . . . Check the Local Government for Waste and Extravagance . . . Speak Up for Better Government . . . The Public Will Eventually Applaud Your Crusading Efforts . . . Corporate Counsel Job Affords Great "PR" Opportunities . . . Good Government Brings Great Improvement and Low Taxes . . . Legal Fees Substantial –but Less than a Fraction of What They Saved . . . You Can Be Well-Paid for Promoting Civic Virtue . . . Try Giving a Little of Yourself Away–Even if It Is Only Advice . . . Your Clients Are the Nucleus of Your "PR" Staff . . . Furnish Clients with Copies of Communications . . . Furnish Clients with Copies of Depositions, Trial Records, Briefs, etc. . . . Publish Your Historical and Educational Speeches in Book Form . . . Essays by a Counsel to the Consul . . . A Speech on the Courts of New Jersey Leads to Publication . . . You Can't Advertise, but You Can Become a Public Figure

Join a Church or Synagogue—and Participate

The most logical place in the world for a lawyer to begin to improve his image is to join a church or synagogue and become active in it. He does not need to have the pomposity of a Clarence Day in "Life With Father" when he tells even the Deity how to run the church and the world, but simple membership is hardly enough. There are dozens of activities associated with every house of worship; innumerable societies to join; countless social gatherings and social events; drives of all kinds. Nor do you have to be carried away with the idea of any of these activities. Just a reasonable degree of participation in these events will suffice.

Gradually, the group will come to recognize you as an attorney, and as such, a leader in the professional life of the community. They will be proud to have a person of your prestige belong to their congregation. You will be assigned only to dignified positions; those thought to be prestigious. These may very well include such posts as: usher; trustee; legal advisor; honorary chairman of some drive for funds; principal speaker at some special annual celebration or the like.

Don't Wait for the Invitation to "Move Up Higher"

Don't be afraid to sit in a prominent seat near the front where you can be seen. Don't count on the Biblical injunction to take a lower seat on the prospect that someone will invite you to move up higher. They wouldn't dare do that. They would consider such an action as an intrusion on your personal prerogative to sit where you pleased—or where you felt most comfortable.

Just to Show Which Side You're On

If someone suggests that you are something of a hypocrite for sitting near the front, ignore that also. Tell him you don't pretend to be any paragon of virtue or better than the next fellow. Merely assure them that, as Holmes used to say, you too have within your heart a delicate plant of faith, hope and charity, which you believe needs to be nurtured and watered occasionally to survive. Or you may tell them that you go to the church or synagogue just to let the public know which side you're on.

Personally, I admire Woodrow Wilson's observation that it is better to have erected a temple in your heart to which you repair regularly than to attend public services weekly. Such religious or spiritual connections may be suitable for a college president or even the nation's president but they might be considered inappropriate for the aspiring attorney. Such an attitude, unless expressed regularly, might be misunderstood and misconstrued as a form of "Godlessness."

Service Clubs Are Naturals for Contacts

Any one of the various national and international service clubs is a natural for the lawyer, young or old. The members are usually the backbone of the community. Many may already be your clients. If not, this type of meeting affords a fine opportunity to meet and mix with them at social and fraternal levels as well as on a professional or business basis.

And do not hesitate to go through the chairs. In this manner, you will necessarily meet and come to know on an intimate basis, not only the members of your own group but those of many of your neighboring communities as well. If there is not a service club or a Chamber of Commerce or a "Business and Professional Men's Club" in your community—wonderful! Go out and organize one at once. You are a leader—prove it!

Bringing in a $100-Million Industry to Home Town and More Millions of Taxes and Payrolls

One of the first organizations I ever belonged to, after starting to practice law, was the local "Businessmen's Association." As a professional man, I was welcomed and respected. I sometimes think they actually deferred to me. They probably felt that I joined them only because the town was too small to have a "Professional Men's Association"—and they were probably right. I was made counsel as well as Chairman of the New Industry Committee. This gave me the right to use their stationery and use some initiative as well.

Quite by accident, I read in a weekly newspaper published in an adjacent community that the National Lead Co. was seeking a new plant site along the water front. I dropped everything and dispatched a telegram to the home office saying in effect, "Don't make any decision until you see what we have to offer you." The result was that eventually this huge, nationally known industry built a plant in our local community costing upwards of $100 million and brought to the community millions of additional dollars of taxes and payrolls, and this was all because of a single telegram! Such activities and results cannot help but automatically promote the image and public relations of the person responsible.

Donate Your Services to the Red Cross, Salvation Army, Boy Scouts, etc.

Next, take an active part in one or more national organizations such as Red Cross, Salvation Army, Boy Scouts, Cancer Crusades, Cerebral Palsy, March of Dimes, etc. Volunteer to do this work in all sincerity and with a generous heart. Please don't think that you always need to have a so-called "angle" or a selfish or personal interest. If you do, I am sure that some of those working with you will sense it; will detect it, and your activities and efforts may very well do you more harm than good. Every lawyer, sometime in the course of his career should act as local, county or even state chairman of the Red Cross drive, March of Dimes, the drive for the benefit of the brain-injured children, Christmas Cheer fund, Community Chest and the like.

I recall once that I was invited to head up a local Boy Scouts drive for funds. It was difficult to spare the time but I managed to do it. Having taken the job, I decided it had to be done properly. I laid out the town into 14 geographical districts; appointed 14 vice-chairmen; had them select or appoint 10 block-captains each. When this was done, I sent out a form letter for them all to meet at the city hall. We gave them the usual pep talk, distributed their paraphernalia and sent them out on their mission with vim, vigor and verve.

The Boy Scout Organizational Plan that Lasted 20 Years

The result was that we collected more that year than any preceding year. The pressure to accept the chairmanship again the following year was almost irresistible. However, I managed in some manner to excuse myself gracefully and diplomatically. But I am pleased to report that for the next 20 years they used the precise type and form of collecting organization I had introduced. For all I know, they may still be using it. As a result, a small town became a legend at the county and state headquarters of the organization. The only material reward that I can recall, was to be invited as principal speaker at some of the larger functions of the organization. However, I am certain that this experience helped my general reputation in the area, if nothing else.

Check the Local Government for Waste and Extravagance

Next, take an interest in your local, county and state government. All of these are crying for attention. All of these could stand improvement; fresh ideas, fresh enthusiasm, fresh dedication and devotion to the public welfare and probably some fresh blood, but not bloodshed. Attend the public meetings of your local government. Check up on the kind and quality of governmental service that is being rendered and the cost of same. Find out if there are any hidden or obvious drains on the local purse, such as "no show jobs," nepotism, excessive salaries, duplication of jobs and efforts. Waste and extravagance are usually rampant at every level of government, from the local city hall on up.

Speak Up for Better Government

It can be safely assumed that you will not be popular at first for this activity, particularly with the local politicians. However, it takes someone with a trained mind to do this type of missionary work. For too many years we have permitted our governments to operate practically by default. The results have been a lowering of the caliber of many men who seek public office. Too often, they are there solely for their own personal profit and agrandizement. Some even boast about it so callously as to suggest, "Give me one more two-year term, and I will be all set."

This type of callous disregard for the trust reposed in a public official deserves the attention of some courageous and conscientious citizen. I would like to nominate an aspiring and ambitious lawyer for this task. The public frequently criticizes lawyers for dominating public office, but I am confident that if it were not for the dedicated, zealous lawyer in public office today, our governments would be in very serious straits—much worse than they are in today!

The Public Will Eventually Applaud
Your Crusading Efforts

Eventually, the public will realize that you are carrying on the investigation, or crusade, or whatever you want to call it, on their behalf. Public relations of this type can be extremely helpful if handled properly. With his trained mind; his investigative propensities and his power of analysis, the attorney can usually detect anything unusual or improper that is going on in a public office. If he has reasonable grounds to believe this is the case, he can attend public meetings, ask pointed questions and in this manner alert the press or other media to what is transpiring.

If the facts warrant it, the attorney may also write articles or speak at various affairs as to what his investigations have disclosed. If he is lucky, the attorney may be retained by a group of public-spirited businessmen or interested citizens to carry on his work, or he may be asked to head up a reform movement if conditions are really bad enough to justify this action. Finally, if a reform group wins the election and comes into power, he is the logical man to be Counsel or head up the law division. Now he is in a position of power where he may very well wind up in the public eye, with favorable news stories, covering his recommendations for better government appearing in the local press on a regular basis.

Corporate Counsel Job Affords Great "PR" Opportunities

I served for more than 15 years as Corporate Counsel of my own community. Fortunately, I received the appointment directly from the elected officials on a voluntary basis. As I review my years of service, I find it difficult to realize the wonderful, tremendous opportunities this position afforded for *useful, worthwhile public service*. Initially the town was small, with a population of 10,000 which grew to 35,000 within the next two decades. There were numerous challenges for leadership, for service, and incidentally, favorable opportunities for publicity. By careful suggestions and guidance and the exercise of large quantities of tact, diffidence (and patience), I was able to lead the governing body into many worthwhile, constructive programs. I make no claim to the actual authorship of these projects other than the inspiration I may have given them. I am happy to say that by far the majority of the actions of this public body during my tenure were high-minded, public-spirited and accomplished in a sound, orderly, constructive manner. From a strictly legal standpoint, I hope that I played a modest part in these achievements.

Good Government Brings Great Improvement and Low Taxes

Parks and playgrounds were constructed in every section. Public utilities were extended to the outlying areas. Industry was encouraged to expand. Streets and roads were improved. Sanitary sewer disposal systems were enlarged and improved; police and fire departments were trained and expanded; the community acquired 500 acres for a well field and built its own water treatment plant. Moreover, one-half dozen new schools were contructed as well as a library and an athletic stadium, etc. Yet the town was able to maintain it's position among the 3 percent in the state whose homeowners paid the lowest taxes. In other words, 97 percent of all of the other homeowners in the state paid more taxes. I am reasonably certain that the excellent achievement could not have been achieved without sound legal guidance at every step.

Legal Fees Substantial—but Less than a Fraction of What They Saved

Moreover, no such substantial progress could ever have been achieved without a corresponding substantial expenditure for legal services. Every bond, every large improvement project, required extensive legal services. The governing body, as well as the public at large, recognized that these legal services were necessary and in fact essential, and were willing to pay for them. When an isolated critic appeared to protest such fees, I took the position that substantial as they may have seemed, such legal services saved the community ten times to 100 times the amount of the fees paid. In some instances the amounts saved represented 1,000 times or in one specific case 10,000 times the amount the community had actually paid in fees on such matter as tax reapportionments and similar matters, *And I could prove it.*

You Can Be Well-Paid for Promoting Civic Virtue

The beauty of it all was that I was able to go about, figuratively speaking, a knight in shining armor, riding a white horse, crusading for good government; applauding the good; condemning what I conceived to be bad; and being paid well for my legal services to boot. This is a fascinating occupation if you can achieve it. It's one which I guarantee to bring to you and the profession as a whole an improved image as well as a good "PR" which is both proper and ethical.

Somewhat later, after I had left public office a new administration took over. I did not like what I saw happening. Once again, I entered the lists, to restore good government. In the early days, one had to exercise great care, caution, and circumspection as to everything he said or wrote about another person, even if he was a politician or a candidate for public office. Not so today! Since the U.S. Supreme Court decision in *Sullivan vs The New York Times,* you can now tell the facts about a candidate for public office with inpunity. All that is required is that you use reasonable diligence to ascertain the accuracy of these facts and that you avoid malice. Hence, I have not hesitated to call candidates "unfit," "totally unqualified," "a menace to good government," and to express the opinion that their election would be a "disaster," etc. It was extremely effective!

Try Giving a Little of Yourself Away—
Even if It Is Only Advice

This time I was doing it purely *pro bono publico*. It is my considered judgment that every man owes a debt to society. Woodrow Wilson said that everyone "should advance society by at least the measure of a single generation's progress." I applaud this view. To see wrong and not condemn it is to condone it. Try to do something good just for the sheer pleasure of doing it. I recommend this even at the risk of being called a "sanctimonious so-and-so." In other words, try giving a little bit of yourself away to a worthy cause—even if it is only advice.

Sometimes I have even seen an unexpected reward come to such unusual or singular individuals. Perhaps it is only a street or lane which may be named in their memory. Or there might be a school or a library. These are the encomiums usually reserved for public-spirited persons who render some service to their community, county, state or nation, just a little bit above and beyond the call of duty.

Your Clients Are the Nucleus of Your "PR" Staff

There are literally countless avenues open to the lawyer to improve his public image right in his own office. He frequently overlooks the opportunity of building and consolidating his public image—beginning with his own clients. Here is the nucleus of the public relations staff. They have voluntarily selected you because of their faith and confidence in you. Why not utilize this headstart as a foundation? In the first place, most clients feel that attorneys are too reticent, too impersonal, that they never advise their clients as to where their case stands or what the attorney is doing for them. This is a condition which should be remedied promptly.

Furnish Clients with Copies of Communications

How simple it is merely to instruct your secretary to send a carbon copy of each letter involving a client, to the client for his personal records and information. In this manner, he will be kept fully apprised of every action taken—of every step in the progress of *his* case. He will appreciate your solicitude for him and this will reflect itself in the fees he will eventually pay you willingly. He is willing because he knows the work you have done for him. If you have a good duplicating machine (and no office should be without one) you may also make photocopies of each letter received by you concerning his case and mail them to your client also, with a personal note added. The little extra expense involved for stamps and envelopes is negligible in comparison to the good this service will do. Besides the client's home, his desk, or his dresser drawer will continue to bear evidence of the fact that your office represents him, and that you are his attorney. This perfectly legitimate public relations may very well serve to inform his relatives, his family and friends of the same fact.

Furnish Clients with Copies of Depositions, Trial Records, Briefs, etc.

This same rule applies when you have extra copies of client's depositions, an extra copy of the record of the case; (or appendix, as it is sometimes called); briefs on appeal, etc. They will read these avidly. Some will even make them prime exhibits on the end tables in their living rooms to impress their neighbors and friends. If you are talking about public relations, these items are "naturals."

Publish Your Historical and Educational Speeches in Book Form

There are always educational speeches to be made by lawyers and educational books and articles to be written by them. These certainly are legitimate activities for every lawyer and above the slightest criticism as to ethical propriety. The importance of speech-making is dealt with in a subsequent chapter, so I mention it here only in passing. As to articles and pamphlets on historical or on legal subjects there is no reason why they cannot be published in the same manner as briefs and circulated among your fellow attorneys. Occasionally, you may consider one of your educational speeches of such quality and importance that you fear it may be lost to posterity. If so, you may call it an essay and have it printed in modest quantities for circulation among your closest friends and clients and fellow lawyers on appropriate occasions.

Essays by a Counsel to the Consul

I once knew a very distinguished counselor who represented the Consul General of an important European country for many years. His own family had emigrated from their birthplace in that country some years before. He was proud of the social, political, cultural and historical background of his parents' native land. As a result, he was called upon to deliver addresses on numerous occasions at the celebration of various national holidays celebrated by the immigrants to this country.

These addresses were, in effect, essays and models of English and of erudition. He was so proud of them that he had each of them published, (with covers no less), and would present his friends and contemporaries and colleagues with a copy on the slightest suggestion that they were interested. All I know is that he had an extensive and extremely lucrative practice. Moreover, he stands out in my memory as one of the really distinguished members of the Bar I had had the pleasure of meeting through the years. I am certain that this procedure was quite ethical or he would never have entertained the thought of pursuing it. In addition, it added prestige to his stature as a public figure as well as a scholar and a gentleman.

A Speech on the Courts of New Jersey Leads to Publication

I recall that the first compilation of my speeches I ever published, happened quite by accident. Reverend Samuel Blair, Pastor of the First Methodist

Church of my hometown, had invited me to be guest speaker at a regular monthly meeting of the Parish Men's Club. I was busy at the time and at a loss to select a topic. I had no time for research or to prepare any material. The thought struck me, "Why not talk about something I know from A to Z—the court system of New Jersey." I covered the subject matter in less than an hour. The audience received it warmly.

The clergyman was obviously fascinated by it. He suggested that such a discourse deserved to be published; that if he had made it, he would want it published. Taking this cue, I began to assemble selected speeches from the preceding years and I included this talk as the first of several volumes of addresses I had published, covering both platform and legislative addresses. It never became a best seller but from that time on I was usually referred to in all introductions as "an author" as well as a member of the Bar. Some of my clients are still the proud possessors of this volume and maintain it in their home libraries.

You Can't Advertise, but You Can Become a Public Figure

Public Relations is admittedly a delicate subject in all of the professions. This is particularly true in the field of law. Direct advertising is strictly barred, as it properly should be. This is on the theory that if you have the essential qualifications to meet the high standards of your profession, the public will soon learn of it and presumably beat a path to your door. However, I have never found out how they were supposed to learn of your particular talents, but in some way, they apparently do.

A satisfied client is still the best advertisement any lawyer can hope for. You can multiply these satisfied clients utilizing some of the suggestions set forth above. If you do manage to achieve this objective, your PR problem will be solved *perfectly* and *permanently,* and this will reflect itself in your professional income.

In the meantime, the diplomatic, discreet and above all, the ethical employment of some of the ideas discussed above should prove of some help to the aspiring attorney seeking to reach the magic mark of a $100,000 practice per annum.

But the old axiom still remains that the single best advertisement any professional man can have is a *satisfied client.*

Chapter 13

THE PRACTICAL SIDE OF ETHICS

Public Focus Now on Ethics of All Lawyers . . . Only 18 Percent Of Public Have Confidence in Lawyers . . . Honesty Is the Only Policy . . . Clean as a Hound's Tooth . . . Avoid Even the Appearance of Impropriety . . . Ethics Should Be a Required Subject of Study . . . A.B.A. Updates Its Code of Professional Ethics . . . Every State Should Adopt and Enforce the A.B.A. Code . . . If in Doubt, Research the Subject . . . A.B.A. Sets Up Its Own Ethics Committee . . . Many Canons Designed to Protect the Dignity as Well as the Integrity of the Bar . . . The Inherent Ability to Distinguish Right from Wrong . . . Principal Violations Fall into Approximately Seven Categories . . . Improper Publicity to Attract Clients . . . Charging Improper Fees . . . Furnish Clients Quotes or Guidelines . . . Negligence or Incompetency in Handling a Case . . . Failure to Segregate Client's Funds or Assets and Maintain Books and Records to Prove It . . . Keep Client's Escrow Funds to a Minimum . . . Don't Keep Financial Records on Scraps of Paper . . . License Is Worth from $1,000,000 To $10,000,000 . . . Outright Conversion, Embezzlement or Larceny : . . The Client's Security Fund . . . Conflicts of Interest . . . Representing a Buyer and Seller . . . Advise Clients of Their Rights in Writing . . . Representing all Individual Partners or All Corporation Officials . . . Buying an Interest in Client's Cause of Action is Prohibited . . . Problems Peculiar to Public Officials . . . Three Suggested Tests . . . No Man Can Serve Two Masters . . . Offenses May Occur Outside the Practice of Law . . . Keep Clients Advised of Progress of Case

Public Focus Now on Ethics of All Lawyers

The best proof that the question of Ethics in the legal profession is something which concerns both laymen and lawyers alike is the frequency with which articles on this subject continue to appear in the public press—including many of our leading magazines with international, as well as national, circulation. Recently such a periodical published a question and answer article on the subject "Complaints against Lawyers—Are they Justified?" The person interviewed was Thomas Ehrlich, Dean of the Law School of Stanford University. He admitted that the public's opinion of lawyers has not been very high since the time of Shakespeare, and that Watergate merely intensified that situation.

Only 18 Percent of Public Have
Confidence in Lawyers

He pointed out that in a recent poll in California, only 18 percent of those interviewed had "a lot of confidence" in the legal profession. Shortly after the article covering Dean Ehrlich's views appeared, a news story from California seemed to justify the public's evaluation of lawyers in general. The California Committee of Bar Examiners reported that on the results of the first test candidates for admission to the Bar were required to submit to on the subject of Professional Responsibility over 44 percent of those taking the examination failed.

Meanwhile, clear across the country, when the State Bar of New York propounded a series of questions on Ethics to a number of lawyers, it was found that many of the lawyers queried could not answer half of the questions correctly. The only hopeful sign on the horizon is the fact that the American Bar Association has now adopted a rule requiring all law schools to include training in Professional Responsibility before they can win accreditation.

Honesty Is the Only Policy

"Honesty is the best policy" was once recognized as an honorable and respected statement of principle. But not for long, because to the ethical person, honesty is the *only* policy. To paraphrase this one might say that in the law profession acting ethically is the best policy. But once again, those with proper and acceptable concepts of morality would have to say also that acting ethically is the *only* policy. This is true because the attorney who seeks to build up a lucrative practice soon will find out that the only worthwhile and lasting practice must be based on an "ethical" practice. It is the only sure and certain way of winning the respect, admiration and *confidence* of your fellow attorneys, the courts and your clients. Thus, the aspiring lawyer has a double motive in acting ethically.

Clean as a Hound's Tooth

"He must be as clean as a hound's tooth" is an old-fashioned expression which President Eisenhower was fond of using to describe the high type of persons he sought to surround himself with. He knew that if he appointed men who were even suspected of being untrustworthy, the public would lose confidence in his administration. If the public *thinks* there is any question as to a lawyer's integrity, this factor alone may very well block his professional advancement and hence diminish proportionately his professional income.

Avoid Even the Appearance of Impropriety

And it does not matter if the lawyer is, in fact, the soul of integrity. If the public is led to believe otherwise by his conduct, the penalty will be the same. Thus, it is not only imperative for the lawyer to avoid any professional impropriety, but to avoid even the appearance of any such impropriety. This is one of the recognized canons of ethics included not only to protect the individual lawyer but the profession as a whole. Like Caesar's wife, the individual lawyer must so live as to be above suspicion not only in his professional life, but in his private life as well.

Ethics Should Be a Required Subject of Study

In the light of these facts and of their importance, it seems strange that relatively few law schools include "Ethics" as a required subject and a standard part of their curricula. Many older practitioners feel that it should be a mandatory subject. So, too, in states still providing for the service of "clerkships" or "internships," there are few opportunities for learning even the fundamentals of the subject. Few Bar Examiners of whom I am aware propound adequate questions on this subject. Hence, it is easy to understand why some of the older practitioners, as well as the younger ones, seem to obtain their knowledge of this subject empirically rather than going directly to a recognized source for proper guidance.

A.B.A. Updates Its Code of Professional Ethics

Many years ago, the A.B.A. promulgated its Canons of Professional Ethics running from Article 1 to Article 47. In recent years, the A.B.A., after extensive and intensive studies has superseded these articles, using a new set of "Disciplinary Rules of the Code of Professional Responsibility." These rules run from DR 1-101 to DR 9-102 with each article having a number of subsections. They were adopted only after prolonged and serious review of the subject matter to bring the rules or canons up to date, to clarify any possible ambiguity and to aid the attorney to follow the straight and narrow path of rectitude and moral worth in the pursuit of his profession. Some states valued these A.B.A. Disciplinary Rules so highly that they adopted them either *in toto* or with only minor revisions. The Supreme Court of New Jersey adopted them in their entirety with only a single exception, i.e., DR 6-101 "Failing to Act Competently." Apparently this was considered as inviting too much controversy as to what constituted competency in the practice of law.

Every State Should Adopt and Enforce the A.B.A. Code

It would therefore appear that every attorney today, irrespective of the state in which he practices, should familiarize himself with this set of detailed rules to insure that he observes them both in letter and in spirit at all times. To assist the attorneys in this respect, a complete set of the Rules are included at the end of this chapter.

Every attorney would be wise in ascertaining if his own state has adopted its own set of canons, and if so, to familiarize himself with them. If the canons in use in your own state appear to be inadequate, ambiguous or obsolete, this would afford the alert, ambitious attorney the opportunity to seize the initiative in having his own state adopt the A.B.A. set of rules as its own. This would certainly mark him as a leader among members of his profession and one who appreciates the importance of Ethics as an evidence of the profession's ability to police itself properly and of its intention to do so. Incidentally, the disclosures in the so-called "Watergate" affair in the nation's capital and the number of attorneys involved therein would seem to make it necessary to update every individual state's machinery for purifying and policing the legal profession *by its members*.

Otherwise, there may be a public outcry to have the profession policed by laymen rather than by lawyers themselves.

If in Doubt, Research the Subject

This volume would not be complete without at least some discussion of Ethics. And yet the subject is so broad, has so many facets and is so dependent upon the factual situation in each separate case, that no textbook of this size could ever cover it in detail or in depth. Hence, I can only hope to touch upon the highlights at best. It would be wise for the average practitioner to purchase Drinker's book on Ethics; to review the subject of Attorney and Client in *Corpus Juris Secundum* ALR, Am. Jur. or some other text enjoying a nationwide reputation, and to review the same subject in the Digest of his own state. Thus, he will be able to make his own personal judgment, based on at least this brief research, on any point in which he may have some doubts.

A.B.A. Sets Up Its Own Ethics Committee

The American Bar Association has also set up its own Advisory Committee on Ethics. It has already issued almost 1300 formal opinions. It is doing a magnificent job, and has been very helpful to lawyers across the country.

New Jersey, too, is fortunate in having a central advisory committee on Ethics appointed by the Supreme Court with state-wide jurisdiction, whose primary function is to hand down advisory opinions in advance of the matter actually coming into active controversy. This committee is also doing an excellent job. Finally, I might suggest also that as a last resort you get the opinion of some of the old-timers who have been practicing long enough to know the proper answer almost by instinct.

Many Canons Designed to Protect the Dignity
as Well as the Integrity of the Bar

Speaking of instinct, the average practitioner with a fairly well-developed sense of moral values and the ability to distinguish right from wrong, in most cases should not have too much difficulty in deciding whether a proposal or a program is ethical or unethical. In my judgment the rules or canons are intended to prohibit acts which are either *malum prohibitum* or *malum per se*. The first group of prohibitions has been made in order to protect the dignity and integrity of the profession or to avoid even the appearance of impropriety so that the high reputation of the profession may not be impugned or tarnished by acts which, although innocent in themselves, may raise doubts or suspicions in the public mind.

The Inherent Ability to Distinguish Right from Wrong

The second group—matters which in themselves are inherently bad —requires no extended discussion. If a lawyer violates these prohibitions, it would seem to raise serious doubts as to his fitness to practice law in the first place. Neither his fellow practitioners nor the courts are going to show him much sympathy if he seems oblivious to, or unable, to distinguish right from wrong.

Principal Violations Fall into
Approximately Seven Categories

Aside from the two general characteristics of Ethics I have referred to, it has been my observation that most of the complaints against attorneys, either by their fellow practitioners or by their clients, or the public, generally fall into approximately a half dozen or so of clearly defined categories. At least these seem to be the ones that the authors of the canons or Disciplinary Rules devoted much of their time and attention to.

They also appear to be the ones on which advisory opinions have been sought most often or the ones which the courts have had to rule upon most frequently. These would seem to include (1) Improper Publicity; (2) Negligence or Incompetence; (3) Fees Charged; (4) Proper Segregation of Client's Funds and Assets; (5) Maintaining Proper Books and Records; (6) Conflict of Interest; (7) Plain Outright Conversion, Embezzlement or Larceny of Client's Funds or Assets. To begin with, it is to be noted that the above classification of offenses has been listed in approximately the inverse order of their seriousness or importance. I cannot cite any authority for this statement so I must confess that it is at least my considered judgment, and I believe that I can support that judgment by substantial supportive evidence.

Improper Publicity to Attract Clients

Improper publicity as covered in five or more of the Disciplinary Rules are thus: Publicity generally; Professional signs, stationery, law lists, etc.; Recommendation or suggestion of need of legal services; Trial conduct; Trial publicity, etc. While none of these may be immoral in themselves, it is easily recognized that most, if not all of them, may demean the profession, lessen its dignity and hence lower the public's respect for, and confidence in, the Bar as a whole.

But frankly you must go a step farther to unearth and expose the basic evil or offense involved. Why would any lawyer be guilty of these violations? The only obvious reason would be an attempt on his part to attract laymen to his office as potential new clients who otherwise would not be attracted to his office.

Perhaps again there is nothing inherently or morally wrong in these acts, but they are obviously unprofessional and constitute improper advertising and solicitation of clients at least indirectly if not directly, and hence are unfair and unjust to fellow attorneys who rigidly and rigorously observe the Disciplinary Rules prohibiting this course of conduct. Habitual violators are certainly inviting reprimand or censure until they discontinue such violations of recognized professional conduct.

Charging Improper Fees

As to fees charged, this has always been a rather delicate subject to discuss much less to handle. The Disciplinary Rules have covered this subject very thoroughly. Elsewhere in this book, I have analyzed the various elements that may, and should, enter into the fixing of a legitimate and proper fee. I cannot understand why this field should give attorneys so much of a problem. I think that what the Ethics Committees and the courts having jurisdiction of the Bar are seeking and trying to ascertain is whether the fees charged are so unconscionable as to indicate clearly that the lawyer has over-reached his client. If he has, he is certainly inviting a disciplinary action against himself and the punishment will usually reflect the gravity of his offense.

Furnish Clients Quotes or Guidelines

The surest way to avoid any misunderstanding is to quote the client the fees in advance if it is at all possible. If this cannot be done then at least quote the client a maximum and a minimum and put it down in letter form or include it in the retainer itself. Always remember that contingent fees in criminal matters are always improper and absolutely prohibited; that contingent fees in tort cases are regulated by statute or the courts themselves in a number of states, including New York and New Jersey. It is also to be borne in mind that fees charged to minors and incompetents are subject to close scrutiny by the courts to make sure they are fair and reasonable. In my judgment if the fees charged have some reasonable relationship to the effort expended and the results obtained (as well as the other tests listed under DR 2-101), you should have no trouble sustaining the fees charged. However, it is always best to err on the side of charging *a little less* than the case is worth, than to charge even *a little more* than it is worth for the good of all concerned. Never—never seek to charge "all the traffic will bear" because this is not only unethical but counterproductive as well.

Incidentally, complaints by clients to County Ethics Committees regarding fees are reported to have increased as much as 500 percent in some areas during the current (or recent) recession.

Negligence or Incompetency in Handling a Case

As to the alleged negligence or incompetency in the handling of a case, these usually depend in large measure on the point of view of the parties involved. Incompetence is a rather harsh assessment of what may actually constitute ordinary negligence instead. Permitting the Statute of Limitations to outlaw a claim before suit is filed; dilatory conduct in drafting and having executed a new will or codicil for an ill or elderly person, as a result of which the testator's wishes and intentions are thwarted, are also other examples. Still another clear illustration is failing to have a key witness in court during a trial, as a result of which a client's case is lost. There are numerous examples of negligence which in effect are malpractice claims against the attorney. No conscious, moral culpability may be involved. The injuries suffered by the client may be subject to accurate, arithmetical computation. Hence the necessity for every lawyer to carry Professional Liability Insurance with a financially responsible company with adequate coverage.

With such coverage and the assurance that if the claim of negligence or lack of competency is established, the insurance carrier will pay the claim, there would appear to be no pressing reason why the delinquent attorney should be suspended or disbarred. Perhaps a public or private reprimand or admonition would suffice. Incidentally, in these modern days it is to be borne in mind that if the attorney represents a bank, savings institution or large public corporation, there is always the possibility of a class action which might bankrupt not only the attorney but his insurance carrier as well.

Failure to Segregate Client's Funds or Assets and Maintain Books and Records to Prove It

This offense is the first sign that a lawyer is heading for trouble —serious trouble. An attorney's first action when he starts the practice of law should be to open two separate bank accounts even if the amounts deposited are relatively small or even negligible—one is for his own personal funds and one for his client's funds. This latter one is the one in which he will hold in trust all funds belonging to a client until they are actually delivered to the client or his nominees.

It is a relatively simple rule, easy to understand, easy to abide by. Yet the public records indicate, too frequently, violations of this rule. The intermingling of personal and trust funds is the first fatal step leading to suspension or disbarment.

If your funds are low and one or more creditors are pressing you for payment, there may be an almost irrestible temptation to draw just one check on the trust account—to borrow the money for a short time—to get the creditors off your back. The best way to avoid this temptation is to have the trust account checks made up in a strikingly different color from the ones you use for your own personal funds and general expenses. Then put that particular checkbook in a different drawer or location in the office. These simple steps will alert you physically as well as mentally that you are dealing with trust funds which are sacrosanct. It is far better to put a note in the bank to tide you over when you need additional funds. Every *reputable* attorney has, or should have, an excellent credit rating at any bank in his area. There is no disgrace in being a little tight on money occasionally, or even regularly, until you strike your stride and find adequate money rolling in.

Keep Client's Escrow Funds to a Minimum

In the course of an active practice, you are bound to handle a great deal of funds which belong to clients—but my advice is to keep them to a minimum. Do not invite or encourage the holding of large sums of money in various "escrow" accounts. They not only invite temptation but inaccuracies and errors as well and add unnecessarily to your bookkeeping. With a separate deposit book and a separate checkbook for trust funds you will be safe, but it is also imperative that you maintain some form of ledgers or journals covering these funds and make a practice of having your secretary prepare a trial balance, at or near the first of every month, clearly showing a list of the various amounts and accounts which you hold in trust for an individual client, and most important of all, be sure that the bank account is in balance. More attorneys have been suspended or otherwise disciplined for failing to maintain proper books and records of their clients' funds than for any other single cause.

Don't Keep Financial Records on Scraps of Paper

Former Chief Justice Joseph Weintraub, of the New Jersey Supreme Court, in a recent address to newly admitted attorneys alerted them to the seriousness of violating these particular canons. In effect he said that if an attorney is charged with co-mingling his clients' funds with his own and dipping into them occasionally as the need arises, and all the attorney can produce and show in exoneration of these charges are a few loose sheets from a yellow pad in one or more of his files—it does not give the court very much to rely upon. In other words, the Chief Justice was saying that these factors would seem to indicate strongly that the lawyer had been guilty of a serious violation of the code.

Briefly then, it is not only the best policy to segregate clients' funds and respect their integrity—but it is the only policy if you wish to continue the practice of law.

License Is Worth from $1,000,000 To $10,000,000

When temptation arises always remember that your license to practice law is worth somewhere between $1,000,000 and $10,000,000. This fact alone should be ample incentive for respecting the sanctity of your clients' funds and obeying these canons in every respect and in every detail.

Outright Conversion, Embezzlement or Larceny

This topic certainly does not require any extended discussion. I deal with it here primarily because it follows naturally from the failure to segregate clients' funds and assets and to maintain books and records to prove it. The records seem to indicate that in many cases the violation of this canon on the segregation of funds leads logically, if not inexorably, into the offenses of conversion, embezzlement or larceny. These of course are crimes in themselves. Incidentally, they frequently involve large sums of clients' money. Not infrequently they extend over a relatively long period of time—sometimes for several years. When the facts are finally discovered and exposed, the guilty attorney either fails to answer the charge against him or frankly admits his defalcations. Such conduct in and by itself clearly indicates that the attorney is congenitally unfit to be a member of the Bar and he is summarily disbarred, but it is usually too late to protect the public and the Bar receives another black eye.

The Clients' Security Fund

This bad effect has been ameliorated somewhat by the creation of special funds by some of the courts throughout the country. Their purpose is to repay some, if not all, of the funds misappropriated by attorneys. New Jersey is fortunate in having created such a fund. It is funded by the imposition annually of a levy or tax of $25 for each practicing attorney. It is unfortunate that such a fund is necessary, but it is a well-known fact that human beings are not all perfect and that in every walk of life—in every profession—there are a few, fortunately very few, who are unable to differentiate between right and wrong. The only cure in the legal profession for this type of person is to try to weed them out in advance by screening them through the Character and Fitness Committee and then disbar those who slip through as soon as they are apprehended.

Conflicts of Interest

This subject was reserved for the last not because it is the most serious offense, but because it is the one which seems to be giving the Ethics Committees and the courts the most difficulty in establishing and enforcing a standard of conduct. Carried to the extreme, an imaginative complainant would probably establish some form of conflict of interest in practically every human transaction. Yet few if any such incidents involve any culpability or moral turpitude. Hence, the problem resolves itself into a practical decision as to precisely what relationships or transactions there are in which the client's interests are prejudiced or are likely to be prejudiced. But there must also be considered those situations in which it may appear to the public that there is an obvious and dangerous conflict of interest.

Representing a Buyer and Seller

The clearest situation involving a *potential* conflict is where the lawyer represents both the buyer and seller of a home. And yet such transactions have been consummated for many, many years with all parties being well protected and well satisfied. In many such instances the same attorney represented not only the buyer and seller, but the lending institution as well, but at the expense of the borrower. Yet because of the complexities involved in this modern age, the time is not far off, I predict, when a Disciplinary Rule will be promulgated absolutely prohibiting such dual representation. Hence, it is urgent that every attorney take extreme care to be fair and impartial to both sides in any such matter; to explain all the facts fully to both sides and put it in writing and have both sides sign and acknowledge that they have been fully appraised of all the facts and circumstances so there cannot be any charge of concealment.

Advise Clients of Their Rights in Writing

In my own State of New Jersey, the Supreme Court has made it mandatory that buyers be advised of their rights to secure Title Insurance for the full value of the property over and above the amount of the mortgage at a nominal cost. In other decisions, the Court has reprimanded an attorney for accepting and retaining a 25 percent commission from the title company on the gross costs of the title policy without fully advising the clients of that fact. RESPA has now prohibited this practice entirely.

We have attempted to meet these various criteria by sending a letter to the parties, a copy of which is set forth in this book, and to insist on it being signed and returned before we proceed with the work. A separate form of Release, Retainer and Request is also used to make a matter of record the fact that we are representing more than one of the parties, and that the borrowers are entitled to have independent counsel if they so desire. With a written record of having given all parties full notice of all the facts and with the parties' written acknowledgement of receiving same, we feel we have taken all of the precautions we can to avoid any charge of conflict of interest. However, the best protection we feel is the fact that "we lean over backwards" to be frank and fair and strictly honest and honorable in every aspect of the matter. However, if there is the slightest indication that any of the parties do not fully understand their precise rights or are unhappy or dissatisfied, we always insist that they secure the services of an attorney of their own personal selection so they are assured of independent representation.

Representing All Individual Partners or All Corporation Officials

Other illustrations of potential conflicts of interest arise where an attorney is representing all partners in a partnership or all stockholders and officers in a closed corporation. Things may start out on a basis of mutual trust and confidence only to end up with disagreements and mistrust between or among the partners. We once represented a group of professional men who had formed a syndicate to invest in a real estate venture. Matters were smooth for several years, until it became apparent that there were almost as many divergent views as there were partners. We withdrew and declined to represent any of them.

Buying an Interest in Client's Cause of Action Is Prohibited

One of the reasons that the Disciplinary Rules disapprove of any attorney purchasing a share or "buying in" on a client's project is that he thereby becomes a partner. Thus, the potential for over-reaching the layman partner becomes obvious, since the ultimate interest of the lawyer and the layman may very well conflict rather than coincide. The same difficulty may sometime arise where the attorney undertakes to represent an estate and two or more of the residuary legatees, since frequently their interests are diverse if not definitely in conflict. Many other illustrations come to mind but are too numerous to mention.

Problems Peculiar to Public Officials

In recent years, with real estate developments burgeoning across the nation, new problems involving potential conflicts of interest have arisen on all sides. This is particularly true when municipalities have been compelled by statute to create independent autonomous bodies, such as Planning Boards, Boards of Adjustment, etc., in addition to the long established Boards of Health, Boards of Education, Fair Rent Councils, Municipal Courts, etc., etc. The attorney who becomes the Municipal Attorney for the municipality is automatically prohibited from appearing before any of these agencies on behalf of a private client, and this prohibition extends to every partner and every associate connected with the Municipal Attorney's private law office. Likewise, a member of the State Legislature is automatically prohibited from appearing before any state agency. These prohibitions are not only logical but obvious as well.

Three Suggested Tests

One of the main problems, as I see it, is that the words "conflict of interest" become a catch phrase after awhile and are used to obstruct progress, confuse issues and harass honest and honorable members of the Bar in the proper practice of their profession. To meet this situation I have often recommended that the true ultimate test of what constitutes genuine conflict of interest rather than an ephemeral one is to see if the acts complained of meet these three basic tests: (1) Has the client suffered an actual or potential injury or loss by reason of the attorney's actions?; (2) Has the attorney secured an unjust profit or compensation thereby?; (3) Have items 1 and 2 been accomplished by the attorney through secret and clandestine conduct of which the client has no knowledge or at best only incomplete knowledge?

If the attorney's conduct is such that the three questions posed must be answered in the affirmative, it can be fairly assumed that the attorney's conduct constitutes a conflict of interest and was also improper and possibly illegal in the first place. But, if upon a complete review of all the facts and circumstances, it clearly appears that the client suffered no injury or loss, either actual or potential; that the lawyer made no secret, unjust profit and that the client was kept fully informed as to all facts at all times, it would appear difficult to make out any claim of conflict of interest against the attorney.

No Man Can Serve Two Masters

In the final analysis this is merely a repetition or recital or exposition of the age-old truth that "No Man Can Serve Two Masters" because he may over-reach the one or favor the other. Hence the three tests I have suggested. I know of no better way of simplifying or crystallizing the question and leading straight to the essential question—has one client been over-reached to his detriment and to the advantage of the other, thus enabling the attorney to achieve a secret and unjust profit and/or benefit? This would seem to me to be the acid test.

Offenses May Occur Outside the Practice of Law

A new and broader view of the scope of the Rules of Professional Responsibility has been developing and emerging. If you study them, you will observe that the moral sanctions imposed upon lawyers are not limited to acts arising out of and in the course of their profession. These sanctions likewise impose upon the attorney the same high ethical and moral standards which are expected of every reputable and honorable man in all walks of life. Thus, if you are a lawyer and are charged with some shady and dishonest act, such as fraud or deceit in some business matters, there is no defense for the lawyer to assert that the offense did not involve him as a lawyer or did not arise as a result of practicing law, but solely out of a personal real estate or similar deal in which he had been engaged as a private citizen or businessman. Some courts have held that irrespective of the source or origin of the offense, a lawyer is held to an even higher standard of honesty and morality than the average citizen, and may be punished accordingly. This rule is invoked by the court for the obvious purpose of establishing and protecting the Bar's reputation for honor and integrity in the marketplace as well as in the court room.

Keep Clients Advised of Progress of Case

Frankly, many attorneys are personally responsible for losing the confidence and respect of their clients by their own conduct. And this is usually the first step in the direction of having a complaint made against the attorney before an Ethics and Grievance Committee. The trouble commences when the client is not kept fully abreast of all developments in his own case. There are cases when a client does not hear from his attorney for weeks or months or sometimes for even a year or more. Court dockets may be congested; it may take a year or two for your case to be reached. You know this, but how many of your own clients understand this? Not many I am sure.

But the problem can be corrected easily. Have your secretary post the client's name in her appointment book "to bring client up to date on his case." Then make it your business to drop the client a short note periodically so he will know you are still alive. In our office we long ago made it a practice to send clients carbon copies of all correspondence which is involved in his case and which will indicate its present status. The costs are negligible, but the results are tremendous.

We also send clients copies of pleadings in many cases; copies of motions; copies of briefs and memoranda of law, etc., etc. Thus, the client is converted from a "knocker" or chronic complainer to a "booster" and warm defender not only of your obvious ability but as a staunch and active advocate of "his cause." Always remember that while you may have 50 or 100 cases pending at any given time, your client has only one—and you had better let him know you are thinking about it and working on it regularly or you will have cause to regret it. Follow the practical course always.

In conclusion I might say that the astute lawyer, whether as a neophyte or a veteran at the Bar, should so conduct his practice that he will never be confronted with the private embarrassment or public obloquy of having disciplinary proceedings filed against him. If the question of Ethics is kept foremost in the attorney's mind in all matters, he will never have this problem to contend with. But on the contrary, if some of the suggestions and recommendations I have just indicated are adopted, instead of these matters working to the disadvantage of the attorney, they may be converted into a means of improving and advancing the reputation of the individual attorney with his clients and with the public as well.

We do not include the forms in this chapter as a specific recommendation for their use, but solely as an illustration of the care and precaution which should be exercised in these areas.

FORM LETTER ADVISING ALL PARTIES
OF THEIR LEGAL RIGHTS

Re: Mortgagor:
Mortgagee: Anyville Savings and Loan Association
Premises Covered:
Amount of Mortgage:

Dear Friends:

As you know, we represent the above named lending institution in connection with the attached mortgage commitment issued to you. You will note that in the commitment the Association reserves the right to require title insurance at borrower's expense at the option of its attorney.

The laws of New Jersey require that you be advised of the following facts:

(1) That you may employ your own personal counsel, in addition to the Association's counsel, if you desire to pay this additional expense.

(2) If the Association requires a mortgagee title policy, at borrower's expense, it would only insure the Association's interest as mortgagee to the amount of their mortgage.

(3) However, should such a title policy be required, you as the owner, would also be entitled to obtain an owner's title insurance policy protecting you to the full value of your property by paying the additional cost of title premium over and above the premium charged on the mortgage title policy.

Will you therefore please advise me at the foot of this letter as to your wishes with respect to items (1) and (3) and return to me promptly?

Federal Law (Truth in Lending) also requires the attached form to be signed. Retain copy and return original with this letter.

Yours very truly,

WHITE, BLACK & BROWN, P.A.

By: JOSEPH T. WHITE

To White, Black & Brown:

We acknowledge receipt of the above notice as to our legal rights.
We do
We do not wish to employ personal counsel.
We do
We do not wish an owner's fee title insurance policy subject to above terms.

_____   _____

(Revised July 1, 197)

CONSENT, WAIVER AND RETAINER

Re: to/from

                                               to/from

                                               to/from

Gentlemen:

We, the undersigned, acknowledge receipt of notice of the various parties whom you represent in each of the above captioned matters. Your interest in each of these matters has been fully explained to us and we understand them fully.

We also acknowledge receipt of notice of the fact that we have been fully advised of our rights to retain separate, individual and independent counsel to represent each of us in each of the aforesaid matters. This would be for the purpose of eliminating any possibility of a conflict of interest.

We are satisfied to have you handle the entire transaction for each of us and expressly consent to your doing so and retain you for that purpose. We likewise waive any rights to assert any professional impropriety because of the fact that you are representing more than one interest in this transaction.

As an applicant for a mortgage loan from a financial institution which you represent, we likewise acknowledge receipt of notice that such lending institution may require a mortgage title policy, to be furnished at borrower's expense. We have likewise been advised that, should such a mortgage title policy be required, we as owners of the property would be entitled to obtain a fee title policy in our names covering the purchase price upon the payment of the additional title premium in obtaining same.

We also acknowledge that we have been given notice of the fact that you carry substantial coverage in professional liability insurance intended to protect your clients against the negligent acts of either yourself or your employees or representatives.

Yours very truly,

————————————————————————(1.S.)

————————————————————————(1.S.)

————————————————————————(1.S.)

————————————————————————(1.S.)

The complete ABA Disciplinary Rules follow for ready reference.

DISCIPLINARY RULES

of the

CODE OF PROFESSIONAL RESPONSIBILITY

of the

AMERICAN BAR ASSOCIATION*

*Copyrighted by the American Bar Association and used by special permission.

DR 1-101.   Maintaining Integrity and Competence of the Legal Profession

(A)   A lawyer is subject to discipline if he has made a materially false statement in, or if he has deliberately failed to disclose a material fact requested in connection with, his application for admission to the bar.

(B)   A lawyer shall not further the application for admission to the bar of another person known by him to be unqualified in respect to character, education, or other relevant attribute.

DR 1-102.   Misconduct

(A)   A lawyer shall not:
(1) Violate a Disciplinary Rule.
(2) Circumvent a Disciplinary Rule through actions of another.
(3) Engage in illegal conduct that adversely reflects on his fitness to practice law.
(4) Engage in conduct involving dishonesty, fraud, deceit, or misrepresentation.
(5) Engage in conduct that is prejudicial to the administration of justice.
(6) Engage in any other conduct that adversely reflects on his fitness to practice law.

DR 1-103.   Disclosure of Information to Authorities

(A)   A lawyer possessing unprivileged knowledge of a violation of DR 1-102 should report such knowledge to a tribunal or other authority empowered to investigate or act upon such violation.

DR 1-103.   Disclosure of Information to Authorities *(Continued)*

(B)   A lawyer possessing unprivileged knowledge or evidence concerning another lawyer or a judge shall reveal fully such knowledge or evidence upon proper request of a tribunal or other authority empowered to investigate or act upon the conduct of lawyers or judges.

DR 2-101.   Publicity in General

(A)   A lawyer shall not prepare, cause to be prepared, use, or participate in the use of, any form of public communication that contains professionally self-laudatory statements calculated to attract lay clients; as used herein, "Public Communication" includes, but is not limited to, communication by means of television, radio, motion picture, newspaper, magazine, or book.

(B)   A lawyer shall not publicize himself, his partner, or associate as a lawyer through newspaper or magazine advertisements, radio or television announcements, display advertisements in city or telephone directories, or other means of commercial publicity, nor shall he authorize or permit others to do so in his behalf except as permitted under DR 2-103. This does not prohibit limited and dignified identification of a lawyer as a lawyer as well as by name:

(1)   In political advertisements when his professional status is germane to the political campaign or to a political issue.

(2)   In public notices when the name and profession of a lawyer are required or authorized by law or are reasonably pertinent for a purpose other than the attraction of potential clients.

(3)   In routine reports and announcements of a bona fide business, civic, professional, or political organization in which he serves as a director or officer.

(4)   In and on legal documents prepared by him.

(5)   In and on legal textbooks, treatises, and other legal publications, and in dignified advertisements thereof.

(6)   In private communications by any of the offices or organizations enumerated in DR 2-103(D)(1) through (5), along with the biographical information permitted under DR 2-102(A)(6), in response to inquiries from a member or beneficiary of such office or organization.

(C)   A lawyer shall not compensate or give anything of value to representatives of the press, radio, television, or other communication medium in anticipation of or in return for professional publicity in a news item.

DR 2-102. Professional Notices, Letterheads, Offices, and Law Lists

(A) A lawyer or law firm shall not use professional cards, professional announcements cards, office signs, letterheads, telephone directory listings, law lists, legal directory listings, or similar professional notices or devices, except that the following may be used if they are in dignified form:

(1) A professional card of a lawyer identifying him by name and as a lawyer, and giving his address, telephone numbers, the name of his law firm, and any information permitted under DR 2-105. A professional card of a law firm may also give the names of members and associates. Such cards may be used for identification but may not be published in periodicals, magazines, newspapers, or other media.

(2) A brief professional announcement card stating new or changed associations or addresses, change of firm name, or similar matters pertaining to the professional office of a lawyer or law firm, which may be mailed to lawyers, clients, former clients, personal friends and relatives. It shall not state biographical data except to the extent reasonably necessary to identify the lawyer or to explain the change in his association, but it may state the immediate past position of the lawyer. It may give the names and dates of predecessor firms in a continuing line of succession. It shall not state the nature of the practice except as permitted under DR 2-105.

(3) A sign on or near the door or on the window of the office or on the grounds in front of the building in which the office is located and in the building directory identifying the law office. The sign shall not state the nature of the practice, except as permitted under DR 2-105.

(4) A letterhead of a lawyer identifying him by name and as a lawyer, and giving his addresses, telephone numbers, the name of his law firm and any information permitted under DR 2-105. The letterhead of a law firm may also give the names of members and associates, and names and dates relating to deceased and retired members. A lawyer may be designated "Of Counsel" on a letterhead if he has a continuing relationship with a lawyer or law firm, other than as a partner or associate. The letterhead of a law firm may give the names and dates of predecessor firms in a continuing line of succession.

(5) A listing of the office of a lawyer or law firm in the alphabetical and

DR 2-102.   Professional Notices, Letterheads, Offices, and Law Lists
     (Continued)

       classified sections of the telephone directory or directories for the geographical area or areas in which the lawyer resides or maintains offices or in which a significant part of his clientele resides, and in the city directory of the city in which his or the firm's office is located; but the listing may give only the name of the lawyer or law firm, the fact he is a lawyer, addresses, and telephone numbers. The listing shall not be in distinctive form or type. A law firm may have a listing in the firm name separate from that of its members and associates. The listing in the classified section shall not be under a heading or classification other than "Attorneys" or "Lawyers," except that additional headings or classifications descriptive of the types of practice referred to in DR 2-105 are permitted.

   (6) A listing in a reputable law list or legal directory giving brief biographical and other informative data. A law list or directory is not reputable if its management or contents are likely to be misleading or injurious to the public or to the profession. A law list is conclusively established to be reputable if it is certified by the American Bar Association as being in compliance with its rules and standards. The published data may include only the following: name, including name of law firm and names of professional associates; addresses and telephone numbers; one or more fields of law in which the lawyer or law firm concentrates; a statement that practice is limited to one or more fields of law; a statement that the lawyer or law firm specializes in a particular field of law or law practice but only if authorized under DR 2-105(A)(4); date and place of birth; date and place of admission to the bar of state and federal courts; schools attended with dates of graduation, degrees, and other scholastic distinctions; public or quasi-public offices; military service; posts of honor; legal authorships; legal teaching positions; memberships, offices, committee assignments, and section memberships in bar associations; memberships and offices in legal fraternities and legal societies; foreign language ability; names and addresses of references, and, with their consent, names of clients regularly represented.

(B) A lawyer in private practice shall not practice under a trade name, a name that is misleading as to the identity of the lawyer or lawyers practicing under such name, or a firm name containing names other than those of

DR 2-102. Professional Notices, Letterheads, Offices, and Law Lists
(Continued)

one or more of the lawyers in the firm, except that the name of a professional corporation or professional association shall comply with the laws of the State, indicating the nature of the organization, and if otherwise lawful a firm may use as, or continue to include in, its name the name or names of one or more deceased or retired members of the firm or of a predecessor firm in a continuing line of succession. A lawyer who assumes a judicial, legislative, or public executive or administrative post or office shall not permit his name to remain in the name of a law firm or to be used in professional notices of the firm during any significant period in which he is not actively and regularly practicing law as a member of the firm, and during such period other members of the firm shall not use his name in the firm name or in professional notices of the firm.

(C) A partnership shall not be formed or continued between or among lawyers licensed in different jurisdictions unless all enumerations of the members and associates of the firm on its letterhead and in other permissible listings make clear the jurisdictional limitations on those members and associates of the firm not licensed to practice in all listed jurisdictions.

(D) A lawyer who is engaged both in the practice of law and another profession or business shall not so indicate on his letterhead, office sign, or professional card, nor shall he identify himself as a lawyer in any publication in connection with his other profession or business.

(E) A lawyer who is engaged both in the practice of law and another profession or business shall not so indicate on his letterhead, office sign, or professional card, nor shall he identify himself as a lawyer in any publication in connection with his other profession or business.

(F) Nothing contained herein shall prohibit a lawyer from using or permitting the use of, in connection with his name, an earned degree or title derived therefrom indicating his training in the law.

DR 2-103. Recommendation of Professional Employment

(A) A lawyer shall not recommend employment, as a private practitioner, of himself, his partner, or associate to a non-lawyer who has not sought his advice regarding employment of a lawyer.

(B) Except as permitted under DR 2-103(C), a lawyer shall not compensate or give anything of value to a person or organization to recommend or secure his employment by a client, or as a reward for having made a recommendation resulting in his employment by a client.

(C) A lawyer shall not request a person or organization to recommend employ-

DR 2-103. **Recommendation of Professional Employment** *(Continued)*

ment, as a private practitioner, of himself, his partner, or associate, except that he may request referrals from a lawyer referral service operated, sponsored, or approved by a bar association representative of the general bar of the geographical area in which the association exists and may pay its fees incident thereto.

(D) A lawyer shall not knowingly assist a person or organization that recommends, furnishes, or pays for legal services to promote the use of his services or those of his partners or associates. However, he may cooperate in a dignified manner with the legal service activities of any of the following, provided that his independent professional judgment is exercised in behalf of his client without interference of control by any organization or other person:

(1) A legal aid office or public defender office:

    (a) Operated or sponsored by a duly accredited law school.

    (b) Operated or sponsored by a bona fide non-profit community organization.

    (c) Operated or sponsored by a governmental agency.

    (d) Operated, sponsored, or approved by a bar association representative of the general bar of the geographical area in which the association exists.

(2) A military legal assistance office.

(3) A lawyer referral service operated, sponsored, or approved by a bar association representative of the general bar of the geographical area in which the association exists.

(4) A bar association representative of the general bar of the geographical area in which the association exists.

(5) Any other non-profit organization that recommends, furnishes, or pays for legal services to its members or beneficiaries, but only in those instances and to the extent that controlling constitutional interpretation at the time of the rendition of the services requires the allowance of such legal service activities, and only if the following conditions, unless prohibited by such interpretation, are met:

    (a) The primary purposes of such organization do not include the rendition of legal services.

    (b) The recommending, furnishing, or paying for legal services to its members is incidental and reasonably related to the primary purposes of such organization.

    (c) Such organization does not derive a financial benefit from the rendition of legal services by the lawyer.

DR 2-103. **Recommendation of Professional Employment** *(Continued)*

    (d)   The member or beneficiary for whom the legal services are rendered, and not such organization, is recognized as the client of the lawyer in that matter.

    (e)   Any of the organization's members or beneficiaries is free to select counsel of his or her own choice, provided that if such independent selection is made by the client, then such organization, if it customarily provides legal services through counsel it pre-selects, shall promptly reimburse the member or beneficiary in the fair and equitable amount said services would have cost such organization if rendered by counsel selected by said organization.

    (f)   Such organization is in compliance with all applicable laws, rules of court and other legal requirements that govern its operations.

    (g)   The lawyer, or his partner, or associate, or any other lawyer affiliated with him or his firm, shall not have initiated such organization for the purpose, in whole or in part, of providing financial or other benefits to him or to them.

    (h)   The articles of organization, by-laws, agreement with counsel, and the schedule of benefits and subscription charges are filed along with any amendments or changes within sixty days of the effective date with the court or other authority having final jurisdiction for the discipline of lawyers within the state, and within sixty days of the end of each fiscal year a financial statement showing, with respect to its legal service activities, the income received and the expenses and benefits paid or incurred are filed in the form such authority may prescribe.

    (i)   Provided, however, that any non-profit organization which is organized to secure and protect Constitutionally guaranteed rights shall be exempt from the requirements of (e) and (h).

As to a qualified legal assistance organization (not described in DR 2-102(D)(1) through (4)):

    (j)   The primary purpose of such organization may be profit or non-profit and it may include the recommending, furnishing, rendering of or paying for legal services of all kinds.

    (k)   The member or beneficiary, for whom the legal services are rendered, and not such organization, is recognized as the client of the lawyer in the matter.

DR 2-103.   Recommendation of Professional Employment *(Continued)*

          (l)   Such organization is in compliance wtih all applicable laws, rules of court and other legal requirements that govern its operations.

         (m) The lawyer, or his partner, or associate, or any other lawyer affiliated with him or his firm, shall not have initiated such organization for the purpose, in whole or in part, of providing financial or other benefits to him or to them.

(E)   A lawyer shall not accept employment when he believes that the person who seeks his service does so as the result of conduct prohibited under this Disciplinary Rule.

DR 2-104.   Suggestion of Need of Legal Services

(A)   A lawyer who has given unsolicited advice to a layman that he should obtain counsel or take legal action shall not accept employment resulting from that advice, except that:

    (1) A lawyer may accept employment by a close friend, relative, former client (if the advice is germane to the former employment), or one whom the lawyer believes to be a client.

    (2) A lawyer may accept employment that results from his participation in activities designed to educate laymen to recognize legal problems, to make intelligent selection of counsel, or to utilize available legal services if such activities are conducted or sponsored by any of the offices or organizations enumerated in DR 2-103(D) (1) through (5) and to the extent and under the conditions prescribed therein.

    (3) A lawyer who is furnished or paid by any of the offices or organizations enumerated in DR 2-103(D) (1), (2), or (5) may represent a member or beneficiary thereof, to the extent and under the conditions prescribed therein.

    (4) Without affecting his right to accept employment, a lawyer may speak publicly or write for publication or legal topics so long as he does not emphasize his own professional experience or reputation and does not undertake to give individual advice.

    (5) If success in asserting rights or defenses of his client in litigation in the nature of a class action is dependent upon the joinder of others, a lawyer may accept, but shall not seek, employment from those contacted for the purpose of obtaining their joinder.

DR 2-105. Limitation of Practice

(A) A lawyer shall not hold himself out publicly as a specialist or as limiting his practice, except as permitted under DR 2-102(A) (6) or as follows:

    (1) A lawyer admitted to practice before the United States Patent Office may use the designation Patent Attorney, Patent Lawyer, Trademark Attorney, or Trademark Lawyer, or any combination of those terms on his letterhead and office sign, and a lawyer actively engaged in the admiralty practice may use the designation Admiralty or Admiralty Lawyer on his letterhead and office sign.

    (2) A lawyer may permit his name to be listed in lawyer referral system offices according to the fields of law in which he will accept referrals.

    (3) A lawyer available to act as a consultant to or as an associate of other lawyers in a particular branch of law or legal service may distribute to other lawyers and publish in legal journals a dignified announcement of such availability, but the announcement shall not contain a representation of special competence or experience. The announcement shall not be distributed to lawyers more frequently than once in a calendar year, but it may be published periodically in legal journals.

    (4) A lawyer who is certified as a specialist in a particular field of law or law practice by the authority having jurisdiction under State law over the subject of specialization by lawyers may hold himself out as such a specialist but only in accordance with the rules prescribed by that authority.

DR 2-106. Fees for Legal Services

(A) A lawyer should charge no more than a reasonable fee.

    A fee is excessive when, after a review of the facts, a lawyer of ordinary prudence would be left with a definite and firm conviction that the fee is in excess of a reasonable fee. Factors to be considered as guides in determining the reasonableness of a fee include the following:

    (1) The time and labor required, the novelty and difficulty of the questions involved, and the skill requisite to perform the legal service properly.

    (2) The likelihood, if apparent to the client, that the acceptance of the particular employment will preclude other employment by the lawyer.

DR 2-106.   Fees for Legal Services *(Continued)*

    (3) The fee customarily charged in the locality for similar legal services.

    (4) The amount involved and the results obtained.

    (5) The time limitations imposed by the client or by the circumstances.

    (6) The nature and length of the professional relationship with the client.

    (7) The experience, reputation, and ability of the lawyer or lawyers performing the services.

    (8) Whether the fee is fixed or contingent.

(B) At the request of a client, a lawyer shall submit a fee dispute to the local ethics committee for resolution.

(C) A lawyer shall not enter into an arrangement for, charge, or collect a fee for representing a defendant in a criminal case which is substantially contingent upon the result.

(D) A lawyer shall be disciplined if he shall enter into an agreement for, charge, or collect a fee so excessive as to evidence an intent to overreach his client.

DR 2-107.   Division of Fees Among Lawyers

(A) A lawyer shall not divide a fee for legal services with another lawyer who is not a partner in or associate of his law firm or law office unless:

    (1) The client consents to employment of the other lawyer after a full disclosure that a division of fees will be made.

    (2) The division is made in proportion to the services performed and responsibility assumed by each.

    (3) The total fee of the lawyers does not clearly exceed reasonable compensation for all legal services they rendered the client.

(B) This Disciplinary Rule does not prohibit payment to a former partner or associate pursuant to a separation or retirement agreement, or professional corporation stock valuation agreement.

DR 2-108.   Agreements Restricting the Practice of a Lawyer

(A) A lawyer shall not be a party to or participate in a partnership or employment agreement with another lawyer that restricts the right of a lawyer to practice law after the termination of a relationship created by the agreement, except as may be provided in a bona fide retirement plan and then only to the extent reasonably necessary to protect the plan.

(B) In connection with the settlement of a controversy or suit, a lawyer shall not enter into an agreement that restricts his right to practice law.

DR 2-109. Acceptance of Employment

(A) A lawyer shall not accept employment on behalf of a person if he knows or believes that such person wishes to:

    (1) Bring a legal action, conduct a defense, or assert a position in litigation, or otherwise have steps taken for him, merely for the purpose of harassing or maliciously injuring any person.

    (2) Present a claim or defense in litigation that is not warranted under existing law, unless it can be supported by good faith argument for an extension, modification, or reversal of existing law.

DR 2-110. Withdrawal from Employment

(A) In general

    (1) If permission for withdrawal from employment is required by the rules of a tribunal, a lawyer shall not withdraw from employment in a proceeding before that tribunal without its permission.

    (2) In any event, a lawyer shall not withdraw from employment until he has taken reasonable steps to avoid foreseeable prejudice to the rights of his client, including giving due notice to his client, allowing time for employment of other counsel, delivering to the client all papers and property to which the client is entitled, and complying with applicable laws and rules.

    (3) A lawyer who withdraws from employment shall refund promptly any part of a fee paid in advance that has not been earned.

(B) Mandatory Withdrawal

A lawyer representing a client before a tribunal, with its permission if required by its rules, shall withdraw from employment, and a lawyer representing a client in other matters shall withdraw from employment, if:

    (1) He knows or believes that his client is bringing the legal action, conducting the defense, or asserting a position in the litigation, or is otherwise having steps taken for him merely for the purpose of harassing or maliciously injuring any person.

    (2) He knows or believes that his continued employment will result in violation of a Disciplinary Rule.

    (3) His mental or physical condition renders it unreasonably difficult for him to carry out the employment effectively.

    (4) He is discharged by his client.

(C) Permissive withdrawal

If DR 2-110(B) is not applicable a lawyer may not request permission to withdraw in matters pending before a tribunal, and may not withdraw in

DR 2-110.   Withdrawal from Employment *(Continued)*

other matters, unless such request or such withdrawal is because:

(1) His client:

    (a)   Insists upon presenting a claim or defense that is not warranted under existing law and cannot be supported by good faith argument for an extension, modification, or reversal of existing law.

    (b)   Personally seeks to pursue an illegal course of conduct.

    (c)   Insists that the lawyer pursue a course of conduct that is illegal or that is prohibited under the Disciplinary Rules.

    (d)   By other conduct renders it unreasonably difficult for the lawyer to carry out his employment effectively.

    (e)   Insists, in a matter not pending before a tribunal, that the lawyer engage in conduct that is contrary to the judgment and advice of the lawyer but not prohibited under the Disciplinary Rules.

    (f)   Deliberately disregards an agreement or obligation to the lawyer as to expenses or fees.

(2) His continued employment is likely to result in a violation of a Disciplinary Rule.

(3) His inability to work with co-counsel indicates that the best interests of the client likely will be served by withdrawal.

(4) His mental or physical condition renders it difficult for him to carry out the employment effectively.

(5) His client knowingly and freely assents to termination of his employment.

(6) He believes in good faith, in a proceeding pending before a tribunal, that the tribunal will find the existence of other good cause for withdrawal.

DR 3-101.   Aiding Unauthorized Practice of Law

(A)   A lawyer shall not aid a non-lawyer in the unauthorized practice of law.

(B)   A lawyer shall not practice law in a jurisdiction where to do so would be in violation of regulations of the profession in that jurisdiction.

DR 3-102.   Dividing Legal Fees with a Non-Lawyer

(A)   A lawyer or law firm shall not share legal fees with a non-lawyer, except that:

    (1) An agreement by a lawyer with his firm, partner, or associate may provide for the payment of money, over a reasonable period of

DR 3-102.   Dividing Legal Fees with a Non-Lawyer *(Continued)*

time after his death, to his estate or to one or more specified persons.

(2) A lawyer who undertakes to complete unfinished legal business of a deceased lawyer may pay to the estate of the deceased lawyer that proportion of the total compensation that fairly represents the services rendered by the deceased lawyer.

(3) A lawyer or law firm may include non-lawyer employees in a retirement plan, even though the plan is based in whole or in part on a profit-sharing arrangement.

DR 3-103.   Forming a Partnership with a Non-Lawyer

(A)   A lawyer shall not form a partnership with a non-lawyer if any of the activities of the partnership consist of the practice of law.

DR 4-101.   Preservation of Confidences and Secrets of a Client

(A)   "Confidence" refers to information protected by the attorney-client privilege under applicable law, and "secret" refers to other information gained in the professional relationship that the client has requested be held inviolate or the disclosure of which would be embarrassing or would be likely to be detrimental to the client.

(B)   Except as permitted by DR 4-101(C), a lawyer shall not knowingly:

(1) Reveal a confidence or secret of his client.

(2) Use a confidence or secret of his client to the disadvantage of the client.

(3) Use a confidence or secret of his client for the advantage of himself or of a third person, unless the client consents after full disclosure.

(C)   A lawyer may reveal:

(1) Confidences or secrets with the consent of the client or clients affected, but only after a full disclosure to them.

(2) Confidences or secrets when permitted under Disciplinary Rules or required by law or court order.

(3) The intention of his client to commit a crime and the information necessary to prevent the crime.

(4) Confidences or secrets necessary to establish or collect his fee or to defend himself or his employees or associates against an accusation of wrongful conduct.

(D)   A lawyer shall exercise reasonable care to prevent his employees, associates, and others whose services are utilized by him from disclosing or using confidences or secrets of a client, except that a lawyer may reveal the information allowed by DR 4-101(C) through an employee.

DR 5-101.   Refusing Employment when the Interests of the Lawyer May Impair His Independent Professional Judgment

(A)   Except with the consent of his client after full disclosure, a lawyer shall not accept employment if the exercise of his professional judgment on behalf of his client will be or reasonably may be affected by his own financial, business, property, or personal interests.

(B)   A lawyer shall not accept employment in contemplated or pending litigation if he knows or believes that he or a lawyer in his firm ought to be called as a witness, except that he may undertake the employment, and he or a lawyer in his firm may testify:

(1) If the testimony will relate solely to an uncontested matter.

(2) If the testimony will relate solely to a matter of formality and there is no reason to believe that substantial evidence will be offered in opposition to the testimony.

(3) If the testimony will relate solely to the nature and value of legal services rendered in the case by the lawyer or his firm to the client.

(4) As to any matter, if refusal would work a substantial hardship on the client because of the distinctive value of the lawyer or his firm as counsel in the particular case.

DR 5-102.   Withdrawal as Counsel when the Lawyer Becomes a Witness

(A)   If, after undertaking employment in contemplated or pending litigation, a lawyer learns or believes that he or a lawyer in his firm ought to be called as a witness on behalf of his client, he shall withdraw from the conduct of the trial and his firm, if any, shall not continue representation in the trial, except that he may continue in the representation and he or a lawyer in his firm may testify in the circumstances enumerated in DR 5-101(B) (1) through (4).

(B)   If, after undertaking employment in contemplated or pending litigation, a lawyer learns or believes that he or a lawyer in his firm may be called as a witness other than on behalf of his client, he may continue the representation until it is apparent that his testimony is or may be prejudical to his client.

DR 5-103.   Avoiding Acquisition of Interest in Litigation

(A)   A lawyer shall not acquire a proprietary interest in the cause of action or subject matter of litigation he is conducting for a client, except that he may:

(1) Acquire a lien granted by law to secure his fee or expenses.

DR 5-103. Avoiding Acquisition of Interest in Litigation *(Continued)*

    (2) Contract with a client for a reasonable contingent fee in a civil case.

(B)   While representing a client in connection with contemplated or pending litigation, a lawyer shall not advance or guarantee financial assistance to his client, except that a lawyer may advance or guarantee the expenses of litigation, including court costs, expenses of investigation, expenses of medical examination, and costs of obtaining and presenting evidence.

DR 5-104. Limiting Business Relations with a Client

(A)   A lawyer shall not enter into a business transaction with a client if they have differing interests therein and if the client expects the lawyer to exercise his professional judgment therein for the protection of the client, unless the client has consented after full disclosure.

(B)   Prior to conclusion of all aspects of the matter giving rise to his employment, a lawyer shall not enter into any arrangement or understanding with a client or a prospective client by which he acquires an interest in publication rights with respect to the subject matter of his employment or proposed employment.

DR 5-105. Refusing to Accept or Continue Employment if the Interests of Another Client May Impair the Independent Professional Judgment of the Lawyer

(A)   A lawyer shall decline proffered employment if the exercise of his independent professional judgment in behalf of a client will be or is likely to be adversely affected by the acceptance of the proffered employment, except to the extent permitted under DR 5-105(C).

(B)   A lawyer shall not continue multiple employment if the exercise of his independent professional judgment in behalf of a client will be or is likely to be adversely affected by his representation of another client, except to the extent permitted under DR 5-105(C).

(C)   In situations covered by DR 5-105(A) and (B) except as prohibited by rule, opinion, directive or statute, a lawyer may represent multiple clients if he believes that he can adequately represent the interests of each and if each consents to the representation after full disclosure of the facts and of the possible effect of such representation on the exercise of his independent professional judgment on behalf of each.

(D)   If a lawyer is required to decline employment or to withdraw from employment under DR 5-105, no partner or associate of his or his firm may accept or continue such employment.

DR 5-106.   Settling Similar Claims of Clients

(A)   A lawyer who represents two or more clients shall not make or participate in the making of an aggregate settlement of the claims of or against his clients, unless each client has consented to the settlement after being advised of the existence and nature of all the claims involved in the proposed settlement, of the total amount of the settlement, and of the participation of each person in the settlement.

DR 5-107.   Avoiding Influence by Others Than the Client

(A)   Except with the consent of his client after full disclosure and provided the public interest is not adversely affected, a lawyer shall not:
    (1)   Accept compensation for his legal services from one other than his client.
    (2)   Accept from one other than his client any thing of value related to his representation of or his employment by his client.

(B)   A lawyer shall not permit a person who recommends, employs, or pays him to render legal services for another to direct or regulate his professional judgment in rendering such legal services.

DR 6-101.   Failing to Act Competently

(A)   A lawyer shall not:
    (1)   Handle a legal matter which he knows or should know that he is not competent to handle, without associating with him a lawyer who is competent to handle it.
    (2)   Handle a legal matter without preparation adequate in the circumstances.
    (3)   Neglect a legal matter entrusted to him.

DR 6-102.   Limiting Liability to Client

(A)   A lawyer shall not attempt to exonerate himself from or limit his liability to his client for his personal malpractice.

DR 7-101.   Representing a Client Zealously

(A)   A lawyer shall not knowingly:
    (1)   Fail to seek the lawful objectives of his client through reasonably available means permitted by law and the Disciplinary Rules, except as provided by DR 7-101(B). A lawyer does not violate this Disciplinary Rule, however, by acceding to reasonable requests of opposing counsel which do not prejudice the rights of his client, by

DR 7-101.   Representing a Client Zealously *(Continued)*

being punctual in fulfilling all professional commitments, by avoiding offensive tactics, or by treating with courtesy and consideration all persons involved in the legal process.

   (2) Fail to carry out a contract of employment entered into with a client for professional services, but he may withdraw as permitted under DR 2-110, DR 5-102, and DR 5-105.

   (3) Prejudice or damage his client during the course of the professional relationship, except as required under DR 7-102(B).

(B)   In his representation of a client, a lawyer may:

   (1) Where permissible, exercise his professional judgment to waive or fail to assert a right or position of his client.

   (2) Refuse to aid or participate in conduct that he believes to be unlawful, even though there is some support for an argument that the conduct is legal.

DR 7-102.   Representing a Client Within the Bounds of the Law

(A)   In his representation of a client, a lawyer shall not:

   (1) File a suit, assert a position, conduct a defense, delay a trial, or take other action on behalf of his client when he believes that such action would serve merely to harass or maliciously injure another.

   (2) Knowingly advance a claim or defense that is unwarranted under existing law, except that he may advance such claim or defense if it can be supported by good faith argument for an extension, modification, or reversal of existing law.

   (3) Conceal or knowingly fail to disclose that which he is required by law to reveal.

   (4) Knowingly use perjured testimony or false evidence.

   (5) Knowingly make a false statement of law or fact.

   (6) Participate in the creation or preservation of evidence when he believes that the evidence is false.

   (7) Counsel or assist his client in conduct that the lawyer knows to be illegal or fraudulent.

   (8) Knowingly engage in other illegal conduct or conduct contrary to a Disciplinary Rule.

(B)   A lawyer who receives information clearly establishing that:

   (1) His client has, in the course of the representation, perpetrated a fraud upon a person or tribunal shall promptly call upon his client to rectify the same, and if his client refuses or is unable to do so, he shall reveal the fraud to the affected person or tribunal.

DR 7-102. Representing a Client Within the Bounds of the Law
(Continued)

    (2) A person other than his client has perpetrated a fraud upon a tribunal shall promptly reveal the fraud to the tribunal.

DR 7-103. Performing the Duty of Public Prosecutor or Other Government Lawyer

(A) A public prosecutor or other government lawyer shall not institute or cause to be instituted criminal charges when he believes that the charges are not supported by probable cause.

(B) A public prosecutor or other government lawyer in criminal litigation shall make timely disclosure to counsel for the defendant, or to the defendant if he has no counsel, of the existence of evidence, known to the prosecutor or other government lawyer, that tends to negate the guilt to the accused, mitigate the degree of the offense, or reduce the punishment.

DR 7-104. Communicating with One of Adverse Interest

(A) During the course of his representation of a client a lawyer shall not:
    (1) Communicate or cause another to communicate on the subject of the representation with a party he knows to be represented by a lawyer in that matter unless he has the prior consent of the lawyer representing such other party or is authorized by law to do so.
    (2) Give advice to a person who is not represented by a lawyer, other than the advice to secure counsel, if the interests of such person are or have a reasonable possibility of being in conflict with the interests of his client.

DR 7-105. Threatening Criminal Prosecution

(A) A lawyer shall not present, participate in presenting, or threaten to present criminal charges to obtain an improper advantage in a civil matter.

DR 7-106. Trial Conduct

(A) A lawyer shall not disregard or advise his client to disregard a standing rule of a tribunal or a ruling of a tribunal made in the course of a proceeding, but he may take appropriate steps in good faith to test the validity of such rule or ruling.

(B) In presenting a matter to a tribunal, a lawyer shall disclose:
    (1) Legal authority in the controlling jurisdiction known to him to be

DR 7-106.   Trial Conduct *(Continued)*

directly adverse to the position of his client and which is not disclosed by opposing counsel.

(2) If relevant and unless privileged, the identities of the clients he represents and of the persons who employed him.

(C)   In appearing in his professional capacity before a tribunal, a lawyer shall not:

(1) State or allude to any matter that he has no basis to believe is relevant to the case or that will not be supported by admissible evidence.

(2) Ask any question that he has no basis to believe is relevant to the case and that is intended to degrade a witness or other person.

(3) Assert his personal knowledge of the facts in issue, except when testifying as a witness.

(4) Assert his personal opinion as to the justness of a cause, as to the credibility of a witness, as to the culpability of a civil litigant, or as to the guilt or innocence of an accused; but he may argue, on his analysis of the evidence, for any position or conclusion with respect to the matters stated herein.

(5) Fail to comply with known local customs or courtesy or practice of the bar or a particular tribunal without giving to opposing counsel timely notice of his intent not to comply.

(6) Engage in undignified or discourteous conduct which is degrading to a tribunal.

(7) Intentionally violate any established rule of procedure or of evidence.

DR 7-107.   Trial Publicity

(A)   Prior to the filing of a complaint, information or indictment, a lawyer participating in or associated with the investigation of a criminal matter shall not make or participate in making an extra-judicial statement that he expects to be disseminated by means of public communication and that does more than state without elaboration:

(1) Information contained in a public record relating to the matter.

(2) That the investigation is in progress.

(3) The general scope of the investigation including a description of the offense and, if permitted by law, the identity of the victim.

(4) A request for assistance in apprehending a suspect or assistance in other matters and the information necessary thereto.

(5) A warning to the public of any dangers.

(B)   A lawyer or law firm associated with the prosecution or defense of a crimi-

DR 7-107. Trial Publicity *(Continued)*

nal matter shall not make or participate in making an extra-judicial statement that he expects to be disseminated by means of public communication and that relates to:

(1) The character, reputation, or prior criminal record (including arrests,
indictments, or other charges of crime) of the accused.

(2) The possibility of a plea of guilty to the offense charged or to a lesser
offense.

(3) The existence or contents of any confession, admission, or statement
given by the accused or his refusal or failure to make a statement.

(4) The performance or results of any examinations or tests or the refusal
or failure of the accused to submit to examinations or tests.

(5) The identity, testimony, or credibility of a prospective witness.

(6) Any opinion as to the guilt or innocence of the accused, the evidence,
or the merits of the case.

(C)   DR 7-107(B) does not preclude a lawyer from announcing:

(1) The name, age, residence, occupation, and family status of the
accused.

(2) If the accused has not been apprehended, any information necessary
to aid in his apprehension or to warn the public of any dangers he
may present.

(3) A request for assistance in obtaining evidence.

(4) The identity of the victim of the crime.

(5) The fact, time, and place of arrest, resistance, pursuit, and use of
weapons.

(6) The identity of investigating and arresting officers or agencies and
the length of the investigation.

(7) At the time of seizure, a description of the physical evidence seized,
other than a confession, admission or statement.

(8) The nature, substance, or text of the charge.

(9) Quotations from or references to public records of the court in the
case.

(10) The scheduling or result of any step in the judicial proceedings.

(11) That the accused denies the charges made against him.

(D) During the selection of a jury or the trial of a criminal matter, a lawyer or
law firm associated with the prosecution or defense of a criminal matter
shall not make or participate in making an extra-judicial statement that he
expects to be disseminated by means of public communication and that
relates to the trial, parties, or issues in the trial or other matters that are
reasonably likely to interfere with a fair trial, except that he may quote
from or refer without comment to public records of the court in the case.

DR 7-107. **Trial Publicity** *(Continued)*

(E) After the completion of a trial or disposition without trial of a criminal matter and prior to the imposition of sentence, a lawyer or law firm associated with the prosecution or defense shall not make or participate in making an extra-judicial statement that he expects to be disseminated by public communication and that is reasonably likely to affect the imposition of sentence.

(F) The foregoing provisions of DR 7-107 also apply to professional disciplinary proceedings and juvenile delinquency proceedings when pertinent and consistent with other law applicable to such proceedings.

(G) A lawyer or law firm associated with a civil action shall not during its investigation or litigation make or participate in making an extra-judicial statement, other than a quotation from or reference to public records, that he expects to be disseminated by means of public communication and that relates to:

(1) Evidence regarding the occurrence or transaction involved.

(2) The character, credibility, or criminal record of a party, witness, or prospective witness.

(3) The performance or results of any examinations or tests or the refusal or failure of a party to submit to such.

(4) His opinion as to the merits of the claims or defenses of a party, except as required by law or administrative rule.

(5) Any other matter reasonably likely to interfere with a fair trial of the action.

(H) During the pendency of an administrative proceeding, a lawyer or law firm associated therewith shall not make or participate in making a statement, other than a quotation from or reference to public records, that he expects to be disseminated by means of public communications if it is made outside the official course of the proceeding and relates to:

(1) Evidence regarding the occurrence or transaction involved.

(2) The character, credibility, or criminal record of a party, witness, or prospective witness.

(3) Physical evidence or the performance or results of any examinations or tests or the refusal or failure of a party to submit to such.

(4) His opinion as to the merits of the claims, defenses, or positions of an interested person.

(5) Any other matter reasonably likely to interfere with a fair hearing.

(I) The foregoing provisions of DR 7-107 do not preclude a lawyer from replying to charges of misconduct publicly made against him or from participating in the proceedings of legislative, administrative, or other investigative bodies.

DR 7-107. Trial Publicity *(Continued)*

(J) A lawyer shall not permit his employees and associates to make an extra-judicial statement that he would be prohibited from making under DR 7-107.

DR 7-108. Communication with or Investigation of Jurors

(A) Before the trial of a case a lawyer connected therewith shall not communicate with or cause another to communicate with anyone he knows to be a member of the venire from which the jury will be selected for the trial of the case.

(B) During the trial of a case:
  (1) A lawyer connected therewith shall not communicate with or cause another to communicate with any member of the jury.
  (2) A lawyer who is not connected therewith shall not communicate with or cause another to communicate with a juror concerning the case.

(C) Except by leave of court no attorney shall himself or through any investigator or other person acting for him interview, examine or question any grand or petit juror with respect to any matter relating to the case.

(D) All restrictions imposed by DR 7-108 upon a lawyer shall also apply to communications with or investigations of members of a family of a venireman or a juror.

(E) A lawyer shall reveal promptly to the court improper conduct by a venireman or a juror, or by another toward a venireman or a juror or a member of his family, of which the lawyer has knowledge.

(F) All restrictions imposed by DR 7-108 upon a lawyer also apply to communications with or investigations of members of a family of a venireman or a juror.

(G) A lawyer shall reveal promptly to the court improper conduct by a venireman or a juror, or by another toward a venireman or a juror or a member of his family, of which the lawyer has knowledge.

DR 7-109. Contact with Witnesses

(A) A lawyer shall disclose any evidence that he or his client has a legal obligation to reveal or produce.

(B) A lawyer shall not advise or cause a person to secrete himself or to leave the jurisdiction of a tribunal for the purpose of making him unavailable as a witness therein.

(C) A lawyer shall not pay, offer to pay, or acquiesce in the payment of compensation to a witness contingent upon the content of his testimony.

DR 7-109. Contact with Witnesses *(Continued)*

(D) A lawyer may advance, guarantee, or acquiesce in the payment of:
    (1) Expenses reasonably incurred by a witness in attending or testifying.
    (2) Reasonable compensation to a witness for his loss of time in attending or testifying.
    (3) A reasonable fee for the professional services of an expert witness.

DR 7-110. Contact with Officials

(A) A lawyer shall not give or lend any thing of value to a judge, official, or employee of a tribunal.
(B) In an adversary proceeding, a lawyer shall not communicate, or cause another to communicate, as to the merits of the cause, with a judge or an offical before whom the proceeding is pending, except:
    (1) In the course of official proceedings in the cause.
    (2) In writing if he promptly delivers a copy of the writing to opposing counsel or to the adverse party if he is not represented by a lawyer.
    (3) Orally upon adequate notice to opposing counsel or to the adverse party if he is not represented by a lawyer.
    (4) As otherwise authorized by law.

DR 8-101. Action as a Public Official

(A) A lawyer who holds public office shall not:
    (1) Use his public position to obtain, or attempt to obtain an advantage for himself or for a client under circumstances where he believes that such action is not in the public interest.
    (2) Use his public position to influence, or attempt to influence, a tribunal to act in favor of himself or of a client.
    (3) Accept any thing of value from any person when the lawyer believes that the offer is for the purpose of influencing his action as a public official.

DR 8-102. Statements Concerning Judges and Other Adjudicatory Officers

(A) A lawyer shall not knowingly make false statements of fact concerning the qualifications of a person for appointment to a judicial office.
(B) A lawyer shall not knowingly make false accusations against a judge or other adjudicatory officer.

DR 9-101.   Avoiding Even the Appearance of Impropriety

(A) A lawyer shall not accept private employment in a matter upon the merits of which he has acted in a judicial capacity.

(B) A lawyer shall not accept private employment in a matter in which he had substantial responsibility while he was a public employee.

(C) A lawyer shall not state or imply that he is able to influence improperly or upon irrelevant grounds any tribunal, legislative body, or public official.

DR 9-102.   Preserving Identity of Funds and Property of a Client

(A) All funds of clients paid to a lawyer or law firm, other than advances for costs and expenses, and all escrow funds, shall be deposited in one or more identifiable bank accounts maintained in this State, and no funds belonging to the lawyer or law firm shall be deposited therein except as follows:

    (1) Funds reasonably sufficient to pay bank charges may be deposited therein.

    (2) Funds belonging in part to a client, a portion of which the lawyer or law firm will be entitled to receive for his own use must be deposited therein, but the portion belonging to the lawyer or law firm may be withdrawn when due unless the right of the lawyer or law firm to receive it is disputed by the client, in which event the disputed portion shall not be withdrawn until the dispute is finally resolved.

(B) A lawyer shall:

    (1) Promptly notify a client of the receipt of his funds, securities, or other properties.

    (2) Identify and label securities and properties of a client promptly upon receipt and place them in a safe deposit box or other place of safekeeping as soon as practicable.

    (3) Maintain complete records of all funds, securities, and other properties of a client coming into the possession of the lawyer and render appropriate accounts to his client regarding them.

    (4) Promptly pay or deliver to the client the funds, securities, or other properties in the possession of the lawyer which the client is entitled to receive.

Chapter 14

HOW TO USE EVIDENCE AS

A PRESTIGE BUILDER

Evidence Applies to Practically Every Field of Law . . . Where Do You Find the Laws of Evidence in Your Particular State? . . . Study the Text Covering Your Own State, if One is Available . . . Familiarity with the Law of Evidence Can Be Extremely Helpful . . . If Your Own State Adopts Its Own Code, You are Indeed Fortunate . . . Assure Leadership by Urging Adoption of a Code in Your Own State . . . Irrelevant, Immaterial and Incompetent . . . The Federal Rules of Evidence Effective July, 1975 . . . Laws of Evidence Are Basically Exclusionary Ones . . . What Is Relevant Evidence? . . . What Is Material Evidence? . . . What Is Competent Evidence? . . . Exceptions to the Hearsay Rule . . . Summary

If I were asked what in my opinion was the single most important legal subject for a lawyer to excel in, I would unhesitatingly say *"Evidence."* During my years in law school and up to the present time, the "case book" method of teaching most, if not all, subjects was used. It is still highly rated and with much justification. Probably the next most important legal subject would be "Practice and Pleading." This subject varies so widely from state to state that in my judgment, a recognized text on the subject, state by state, would be almost indispensable. But we use the case book system on the subject of evidence and at best the entire book contains probably no more than 40 or 50 cases at most. Since there are almost that many exceptions to the Hearsay Rule, such a method could hardly cover the subject adequately.

Evidence Applies to Practically Every
Field of Law

In evaluating the various legal subjects, I do not intend to belittle such basic subjects as Corporations, Taxes, Torts, Damages, Real Property, Sales, etc., but Evidence is the one subject that applies to practically all legal subjects. To get relief for any injury or any injustice in any court or other tribunal, it takes proof of facts by *evidence* to secure it. This means that a broad and thorough knowledge of the subject is imperative. Armed with specialized knowledge in this field, you will feel more at home and more prepared and hence more self-confident in any forum. Fellow practitioners and presiding judges from the lowest to the highest courts or administrative tribunals are quick to recognize and respect the practitioner who shows superior knowledge in this particular field.

Where Do You Find the Laws of Evidence in
Your Particular State?

Somehow, I must have sensed this fact early in my practice. Normally, I suppose, I would have acquired a copy of *Wigmore on Evidence* or some other similar authoritative text and used it for ready reference. But the difficulty there was that you could never be entirely sure that any given rule of evidence in *Wigmore* was the rule adopted by your own particular state. At that time in New Jersey, we had no code of evidence. Most of our law on evidence could only be found in the decisional law of the state. Occasionally the Legislature would enact some specific statute spelling out the law of evidence to apply to some particular situation. An examination of the State's Digest on this subject would be of some help, but obviously every individual rule of evidence had not been tested in the state's courts, and as to these issues, the best you could do would be to cite the prevailing rule in the other states and hope that your court would adopt it.

Study the Text Covering Your Own State,
if One Is Available

Very early in my practice I had the good fortune to acquire a textbook on the subject of ''The Law of Evidence in New Jersey.'' It was a book of about the same size and shape of the usual buckram or canvas-bound copies of the State

Reports in Law & Equity. Its author was Judge Edward McGrath who had presided over the District Court in Elizabeth, New Jersey, for many years. An examination of it indicated that it was probably a product of his own personal work, accumulated during the years he had sat as a trial judge. He probably maintained a large loose-leaf notebook and had built his own private storehouse of New Jersey citations over a long period of time. Suffice it to say that it was a veritable storehouse of extremely valuable information. I made it my Bible. I read it through not once but many times. And yet the book for some reason never gained much prestige. It is seldom cited by the upper courts. It never became a best-seller in the legal field. I don't believe that it ever went to a second edition.

Just to note the Table of Contents illustrates the wide scope of the book: Evidence in General; Judicial Notice; Presumptions; Admissions; Business Books of Original Entry; Demonstrative Evidence; Hearsay; *Res gestae*; Opinion Evidence; Evidence in Collateral Proceedings; Character and Reputation; Declarations Against Interest; Documentary Evidence; Best Evidence; Parole Evidence to Vary Writings; Sufficiency; Weight; Competence; Examination and Cross-Examination, etc.

To me it was the best single book I had ever read on a legal subject. Just to be familiar with the Table of Contents was definitely worthwhile in itself. It gave me a bird's-eye view of the whole field of the Law of Evidence, each time I consulted it or reviewed it. Each chapter had a half dozen or more sub chapters or sections and each of these was loaded with numerous citations from our own Court Reports. It was reassuring to know that there were indeed precedents in my own state on almost every facet of the Law of Evidence.

Moreover this book made it eminently clear that Demonstrative or Real Evidence was generally permitted long before Melvin Belli dramatized it so strikingly in California. *Res gestae*, Dying Declarations and Business Records were only a few of the many exceptions to the Hearsay Rule. Many of my cases were won through the years in invoking the "best evidence" rule, and the rule barring parole evidence to alter a written document and many others. Then a half century after Judge McGrath's modest work was published, New Jersey adopted its own rules of evidence. I have never ceased to marvel at the fact that the basic laws of evidence seemed virtually immutable. Most of Judge McGrath's citations are still valid today!

Familiarity with the Law of Evidence Can Be Extremely Helpful

I could cite many simple but interesting illustrations of where an intimate knowledge of evidence helped carry the day. Many times, while I was cross-examining a witness in court, my adversary would object to some question I posed on some sensitive or delicate point I wanted to bring out. Perhaps the rule he cited as the basis of his objection would, under normal circumstances, be a sound one. For a moment or two I might be stymied as the judge looked to me for a reply. I usually had a stock answer: "This question is to test the credibility of the witness." The judge would almost invariably agree that . . . "The credibility of a witness is always material; proceed with the questions."

If Your Own State Adopts Its Own Code, You Are Indeed Fortunate

Today in my state there is no longer any need for the trial lawyer to carry a textbook on evidence to the Court House or other hearing place. All he need have with him is a copy of the New Jersey Rules of Evidence. It was the product of the joint efforts of the Supreme Court and the Legislature over a long period of time. It first went into effect in its complete form in September, 1967, by order of Chief Justice Joseph Weintraub. Now when a question of the admissibility of evidence comes up, the lawyer does not need to cite textbooks or decisional law but merely cite the rule of evidence by number covering the point at issue, and the Court will make an immediate ruling, at least most of the time.

Assure Leadership by Urging Adoption of a Code in Your Own State

If your own state has adopted a similar Code of Evidence you are indeed fortunate. By all means read it and study it regularly so you know it almost by heart. If your own state has not as yet adopted such a Code, this is a wonderful opportunity for any ambitious lawyer who would like to become a recognized leader at the Bar or at least in the field of evidence. I would respectfully suggest that you publicly urge your own state to adopt such a Code promptly. Your letters might very well be adressed not only to the Chief Justice of your own highest court but to the President of the State Senate, the Speaker of the House and the Governor as well. I guarantee that this will get the ball rolling. If you know how to follow through properly, you may wind up as a member of the Committee or Commission appointed to study the matter and make recommendations—and not only receive favorable and *proper* recognition in the press and other news media—but you will meet some of the other leading members of the Legislature and the Bench and Bar of your state. What do you have to lose?

Irrelevant, Immaterial and Incompetent

We have all heard the stereotyped objection of the lawyer to some offered evidence: "Objection! This is irrelevant, immaterial and incompetent." Unfortunately, many practicing attorneys go through life without ever becoming sufficiently familiar with the laws of evidence to successfully answer such a challenge. Some of them do not know the basic distinctions between the three. Some lawyers use the three categories interchangeably which is a flagrant admission that their knowledge of the subject leaves much to be desired. And yet it is surprising how few lawyers take time out to learn and *recognize* the distinctions between the three. Even the courts on some occasions fall into the same error and treat the terms almost as if they were interchangeable. The astute lawyer will learn the difference and thus fortify himself in every forum.

The Federal Rules of Evidence—
Effective July, 1975

Today the average lawyer has a very simple way of learning more about the laws of evidence in one day than the older lawyer could learn in a year. For the *first time*, uniform rules of evidence have been adopted by the Congress of the United States for use by the Federal Courts in all 50 states. They are applicable in both Civil and Criminal cases. They took effect on July 1, 1975.

Once again a cursory review of the Table of Contents indicates that the entire field of evidence is covered: General Provisions; Judicial Notice, Relevancy; Privilege; Witnesses; Opinion and Expert Testimony; Hearing Authorities and Identification; Best Evidence; Contents of Writings, Recordings and Photos, etc., etc., etc. Up to that time the Federal Courts usually made a practice of following the substantive laws and the laws of evidence of the specific states embraced in their particular district. However, they followed their own uniform rules of Practice and Procedure which they had adopted long ago. I believe that the first step for a wide-awake ambitious lawyer is to make a detailed study of these new Federal Rules of Evidence and compare them with those in effect in his own state. The chances are that in most instances they coincide with the prevailing rule in most states. If there are some differences, make note of them by all means. Here is a simple yet effective way for becoming an authority on evidence with a minimum amount of study and effort.

Laws of Evidence Are Basically Exclusionary Ones

To begin with basics, the laws of evidence consist largely of a set of primary rules *excluding* testimony which on its face might seem to be relevant and material but which must be excluded for practical reasons, plus another set of exceptions to these exclusionary rules to prevent a miscarriage of justice and to help the court and jury in its search for the truth. Hence it is these exclusionary functions which form the basic Law of Evidence.

What Is Relevant Evidence?

What is "Relevant Evidence" is always determined by what facts are actually in issue. Hence, testimony which has a logical tendency to prove or disprove the fact actually at issue should be admitted. Thus, when the issue as framed by the pleadings requires the establishment of a certain fact, then any other fact is relevant to it—if taken by itself or in connection with other facts—is so related that in the common course of events, it proves or renders probable the basic fact in issue. Stated differently, testimony which can have no effect on the issues as framed by the pleadings is obviously irrelevant and should be excluded. For instance, the new Federal Rules of Evidence define what is relevant evidence as follows: "Relevant Evidence means evidence having any tendency to make the existence of any fact that is of consequence to the determination of the action more probable or less probable than it would be without the evidence."

For example, a little girl is struck and fatally injured by a large truck. Suit is instituted by the parents for damages. As the trial is about to commence, the defendants admit liability. The plaintiffs try to prove that the truck was traveling 50 miles an hour in a 15-miles-an-hour school zone and that the child was struck on a crosswalk. The defendants object to this testimony on the ground that it is irrelevant. The Court sustains the objection since "negligence" has been admitted and hence is no longer an issue in the case. Only damages are now in issue.

What Is Material Evidence?

What is material testimony is also circumscribed by what facts are in issue. Even evidence which appears on its face to be material may be too remote to be considered and hence might only serve to confuse the jury. Under such circumstances, the trial court has wide discretion in determining what is material and what is not. A good, old-fashioned test may be that the defendant or the Court is led to automatically say—"Assuming the facts offered are true—so what?", or they may say—"What difference does it make?" If the facts do not have some reasonable relationship to the issue or are not necessary to prove the point at issue, they are subject to rejection by the Court as immaterial, and the Appellate Court will usually sustain the trial court on such rulings unless there has been an obvious abuse of discretion.

What Is Competent Evidence?

What is competent evidence is clearly dependent upon specific rules of evidence. Suppose a woman steps into a break or crack in a public sidewalk, fractures her ankle and sues the property owner for damages. At the trial she offers in evidence a photograph of the property owner with a trowel and batch of cement repairing the break in the sidewalk on the morning following the accident. This would certainly seem relevant and material also, but it is nevertheless incompetent because the laws of evidence make such testimony inadmissible on grounds of public policy. Were it not for such a rule, any dangerous condition might remain in disrepair until the Statute of Limitations ran out for fear that the very act of repairing it constituted an admission that it was a dangerous condition. However, even this testimony could be admitted for a very limited purpose. Thus, if a property owner denied that he had possession, custody or control over the property, his acts in repairing it might be evidential for the very limited purpose of establishing that he *was* in control of same.

Exceptions to the Hearsay Rule

Without doubt the exclusionary rule of evidence against the admission of Hearsay testimony is subject to the most exceptions to any basic rule of evidence. I could list many of them. Here are some of the typical exceptions to the Hearsay Rule: previous statements; spontaneous and contemporary utterances (*Res gestae*); dying declarations; admissions; vicarious admissions; declarations against interest; routine business entries; filed official records; certificates of marriage; judgments of record; former history; reputation as to character; commercial publications; statutes of foreign states; declarations unavailable because of death; etc., etc. Knowledge of these specific exceptions to the basic rule of excluding Hearsay evidence comes in very handy in getting into evidence or keeping out of evidence some important testimony which may mean victory or defeat.

Summary

To recapitulate, I can only say that I know of no other area of the law where mastery can be achieved more quickly and with less effort than in the field of evidence. The ambitious lawyer, whether neophyte or veteran, will find that the study and comprehension of this branch of the law will not only bring quick and favorable recognition by the Court and your fellow practitioners, but will add to his skill, his prestige and his income as well.

Here are the Federal Rules of Evidence for review and ready reference:

FEDERAL RULES OF EVIDENCE

Effective Date: July 1, 1975

To establish rules of evidence for certain courts and proceedings.

Be it enacted by the Senate and House of Representatives of the United States of America in Congress assembled, That the following rules shall take effect on the one hundred and eightieth day beginning after the date of the enactment of this Act. These rules apply to actions, cases, and proceedings brought after the rules take effect. These rules also apply to further procedure in actions, cases, and proceedings then pending, except to the extent that application of the rules would not be feasible, or would work injustice, in which event former evidentiary principles apply.

TABLE OF CONTENTS

Article XI. Miscellaneous Rules

(Continued)

Rule 1102. Amendements.

Rule 1103. Title.

RULES OF EVIDENCE FOR UNITED STATES COURTS AND MAGISTRATES

ARTICLE I. GENERAL PROVISIONS

Rule 101. Scope

These rules govern proceedings in the courts of the United States and before United States magistrates, to the extent and with the exceptions stated in rule 1101.

Rule 102. Purpose and Construction

These rules shall be construed to secure fairness in administration, elimination of unjustifiable expense and delay, and promotion of growth and development of the law of evidence to the end that the truth may be ascertained and proceedings justly determined.

Rule 103. Rulings on Evidence

(a) Effect of erroneous ruling.—Error may not be predicated upon a ruling which admits or excludes evidence unless a substantial right of the party is affected, and

(1) Objection.—In case the ruling is one admitting evidence, a timely objection or motion to strike appears of record, stating the specific ground of objection, if the specific ground was not apparent from the context; or

(2) Offer of proof.—In case the ruling is one excluding evidence, the substance of the evidence was made known to the court by offer or was apparent from the context within which questions were asked.

(b) Record of offer and ruling.—The court may add any other or further statement which shows the character of the evidence, the form in which it was offered, the objection made, and the ruling thereon. It may direct the making of an offer in question and answer form.

(c) Hearing of jury.—In jury cases, proceedings shall be conducted, to the extent practicable, so as to prevent inadmissible evidence from being suggested to the jury by any means, such as making statements or offers of proof or asking questions in the hearing of the jury.

(d) Plain error.—Nothing in this rule precludes taking notice of plain errors affecting substantial rights although they were not brought to the attention of the court.

Rule 104. Preliminary Questions

(a) Questions of admissibility generally.—Preliminary questions concerning the qualification of a person to be a witness, the existence of a privilege, or the admissibility of evidence shall be determined by the court, subject to the provisions of subdivision (b). In making its determination it is not bound by the rules of evidence except those with respect to privileges.

(b) Relevancy conditioned on fact.—When the relevancy of evidence depends upon the fulfillment of a condition of fact, the court shall admit it upon, or subject to, the introduction of evidence sufficient to support a finding of the fulfillment of the condition.

(c) Hearing of jury.—Hearings on the admissibility of confessions shall in all cases be conducted out of the hearing of the jury. Hearings on other preliminary

Rule 104. Preliminary Questions
(Continued)

matters shall be so conducted when the interests of justice require or, when an accused is a witness, if he so requests.

(d) Testimony by accused.—The accused does not, by testifying upon a preliminary matter, subject himself to cross-examination as to other issues in the case.

(e) Weight and credibility.—This rule does not limit the right of a party to introduce before the jury evidence relevant to weight or credibility.

Rule 105. Limited Admissibility

When evidence which is admissible as to one party or for one purpose but not admissible as to another party or for another purpose is admitted, the court, upon request, shall restrict the evidence to its proper scope and instruct the jury accordingly.

Rule 106. Remainder of or Related Writings or Recorded Statements

When a writing or recorded statement or part thereof is introduced by a party, an adverse party may require him at that time to introduce any other part or any other writing or recorded statement which ought in fairness to be considered contemporaneously with it.

ARTICLE II. JUDICIAL NOTICE

Rule 201. Judicial Notice of Adjudicative Facts

(a) Scope of rule.—This rule governs only judicial notice of adjudicative facts.

(b) Kinds of facts.—A judicially noticed fact must be one not subject to reasonable dispute in that it is either (1) generally known within the territorial jurisdiction of the trial court or (2) capable of accurate and ready determination by resort to sources whose accuracy cannot reasonably be questioned.

(c) When discretionary.—A court may take judicial notice, whether requested or not.

(d) When mandatory.—A court shall take judicial notice if requested by a party and supplied with the necessary information.

(e) Opportunity to be heard.—A party is entitled upon timely request to an opportunity to be heard as to the propriety of taking judicial notice and the tenor of the matter noticed. In the absence of prior notification, the request may be made after judicial notice has been taken.

(f) Time of taking notice.—Judicial notice may be taken at any stage of the proceeding.

(g) Instructing jury.—In a civil action or proceeding, the court shall instruct the jury to accept as conclusive any fact judicially noticed. In a criminal case, the court shall instruct the jury that it may, but is not required to, accept as conclusive any fact judicially noticed.

ARTICLE III. PRESUMPTIONS IN CIVIL ACTIONS AND PROCEEDINGS

Rule 301. Presumptions in General in Civil Actions and Proceedings

In all civil actions and proceedings not otherwise provided for by Act of Congress or by these rules, a presumption imposes on the party against whom it is directed the burden of going forward with evidence to rebut or meet the presumption, but does not shift to such party the burden of proof in the sense of the risk of nonpersuasion, which remains throughout the trial upon the party on whom it originally cast.

Rule 302. Applicability of State Law in Civil Actions and Proceedings

In civil actions and proceedings, the effect of a presumption respecting a fact which is an element of a claim or defense as to which State law supplies the rule of decision is determined in accordance with State law.

ARTICLE IV. RELEVANCY AND ITS LIMITS

Rule 401. Definition of "Relevant Evidence"

"Relevant evidence" means evidence having any tendency to make the existence of any fact that is of consequence to the determination of the action more probable or less probable than it would be without the evidence.

Rule 402. Relevant Evidence Generally Admissible; Irrelevant Evidence Inadmissible

All relevant evidence is admissible, except as otherwise provided by the Constitution of the United States, by Act of Congress, by these rules, or by other rules prescribed by the Supreme Court pursuant to statutory authority. Evidence which is not relevant is not admissible.

Rule 403. Exclusion of Relevant Evidence on Grounds of Prejudice, Confusion, or Waste of Time

Although relevant, evidence may be excluded if its probative value is substantially outweighed by the danger of unfair prejudice, confusion of the issues, or misleading the jury, or by considerations of undue delay, waste of time, or needless presentation of cumulative evidence.

Rule 404. Character Evidence Not Admissible To Prove Conduct; Exceptions; Other Crimes

(a) Character evidence generally. —Evidence of a person's character or a trait of his character is not admissible for the purpose of proving that he acted in conformity therewith on a particular occasion, except:

(1) Character of accused.—Evidence of a pertinent trait of his character offered by an accused, or by the prosecution to rebut the same;

(2) Character of victim.—Evidence of a pertinent trait of character of the victim of the crime offered by an accused, or by the prosecution to rebut the same, or evidence of a character trait of peacefulness of the victim offered by the prosecution in a homicide case to rebut evidence that the victim was the first aggressor;

(3) Character of witness.—Evidence of the character of a witness, as provided in rules 607, 608, 609.

(b) Other crimes, wrongs, or acts. —Evidence of other crimes, wrongs, or acts is not admissible to prove the character of a person in order to show that he acted in conformity therewith. It may, however, be admissible for other purposes, such as proof of motive, opportunity, intent, preparation, plan, knowledge, identity, or absence of mistake or accident.

Rule 405. Methods of Proving Character

(a) Reputation or opinion.—In all cases in which evidence of character or a trait of character of a person is admissible, proof may be made by testimony as to reputation or by testimony in the form

Rule 405. Methods of Proving Character *(Continued)*

of an opinion. On cross-examination, inquiry is allowable into relevant specific instances of conduct.

(b) Specific instances of conduct.—In cases in which character or a trait of character of a person is an essential element of a charge, claim, or defense, proof may also be made of specific instances of his conduct.

Rule 406. Habit; Routine Practice

Evidence of the habit of a person or of the routine practice of an organization, whether corroborated or not and regardless of the presence of eyewitnesses, is relevant to prove that the conduct of the person or organization on a particular occasion was in conformity with the habit or routine practice.

Rule 407. Subsequent Remedial Measures

When, after an event, measures are taken which, if taken previously, would have made the event less likely to occur, evidence of the subsequent measures is not admissible to prove negligence or culpable conduct in connection with the event. This rule does not require the exclusion of evidence of subsequent measures when offered for another purpose, such as proving ownership, control, or feasibility of precautionary measures, if controverted, or impeachment.

Rule 408. Compromise and Offers to Compromise

Evidence of (1) furnishing or offering or promising to furnish, or (2) accepting or offering or promising to accept, a valuable consideration in compromising or attempting to compromise a claim which was disputed as to either validity or amount, is not admissible to prove liability for or invalidity of the claim or its amount. Evidence of conduct or statements made in compromise negotiations is likewise not admissible. This rule does not require the exclusion of any evidence otherwise discoverable merely because it is presented in the course of compromise negotiations. This rule also does not require exclusion when the evidence is offered for another purpose, such as proving bias or prejudice of a witness, negativing a contention of undue delay, or proving an effort to obstruct a criminal investigation or prosecution.

Rule 409. Payment of Medical and Similar Expenses

Evidence of furnishing or offering or promising to pay medical, hospital, or similar expenses occasioned by an injury is not admissible to prove liability for the injury.

Rule 410. Offer To Plead Guilty; Nolo Contendere; Withdrawn Plea of Guilty

Except as otherwise provided by Act of Congress, evidence of a plea of guilty, later withdrawn, or a plea of nolo contendere, or of an offer to plead guilty or nolo contendere to the crime charged or any other crime, or of statements made in connection with any of the foregoing pleas or offers, is not admissible in any civil or criminal action, case, or proceeding against the person who made the plea or offer. This rule shall not apply to the introduction of voluntary and reliable statements made in court on the record in connection with any of the foregoing pleas or offers where offered for impeachment purposes or in a subsequent

Rule 410. Offer To Plead Guilty; Nolo Contendere; Withdrawn Plea of Guilty
(Continued)

prosecution of the declarant for perjury or false statement.

This rule shall not take effect until August 1, 1975, and shall be superseded by any amendment to the Federal Rules of Criminal Procedure which is inconsistent with this rule, and which takes effect after the date of the enactment of the Act establishing these Federal Rules of Evidence.

Rule 411. Liability Insurance

Evidence that a person was or was not insured against liability is not admissible upon the issue whether he acted negligently or otherwise wrongfully. This rule does not require the exclusion of evidence of insurance against liability when offered for another purpose, such as proof of agency, ownership, or control, or bias or prejudice of a witness.

ARTICLE V. PRIVILEGES

Rule 501. General Rule

Except as otherwise required by the Constitution of the United States or provided by Act of Congress or in rules prescribed by the Supreme Court pursuant to statutory authority, the privilege of a witness, person, government, State, or political subdivision thereof shall be governed by the principles of the common law as they may be interpreted by the courts of the United States in the light of reason and experience. However, in civil actions and proceedings, with respect to an element of a claim or defense as to which State law supplies the rule of decision, the privilege of a witness, person, government, State, or political subdivision thereof shall be determined in accordance with State law.

ARTICLE VI. WITNESSES

Rule 601. General Rule of Competency

Every person is competent to be a witness except as otherwise provided in these rules. However, in civil actions and proceedings, with respect to an element of a claim or defense as to which State law supplies the rule of decision, the competency of a witness shall be determined in accordance with State law.

Rule 602. Lack of Personal Knowledge

A witness may not testify to a matter unless evidence is introduced sufficient to support a finding that he has personal knowledge of the matter. Evidence to prove personal knowledge may, but need not, consist of the testimony of the witness himself. This rule is subject to the provisions of rule 703, relating to opinion testimony by expert witnesses.

Rule 603. Oath or Affirmation

Before testifying, every witness shall be required to declare that he will testify truthfully, by oath or affirmation administered in a form calculated to awaken his conscience and impress his mind with his duty to do so.

Rule 604. Interpreters

An interpreter is subject to the provisions of these rules relating to qualification as an expert and the administration of an oath or affirmation that he will make a true translation.

Rule 605. Competency of Judge as Witness

The judge presiding at the trial may not testify in that trial as a witness. No objection need be made in order to preserve the point.

Rule 606. Competency of Juror as Witness

(a) At the trial.—A member of the jury may not testify as a witness before that jury in the trial of the case in which he is sitting as a juror. If he is called so to testify, the opposing party shall be afforded an opportunity to object out of the presence of the jury.

(b) Inquiry into validity of verdict or indictment.—Upon an inquiry into the validity of a verdict or indictment, a juror may not testify as to any matter or statement occurring during the course of the jury's deliberations or to the effect of anything upon his or any other juror's mind or emotions as influencing him to assent or to dissent from the verdict or indictment or concerning his mental processes in connection therewith, except that a juror may testify on the question whether extraneous prejudicial information was improperly brought to the jury's attention or whether any outside influence was improperly brought to bear upon any juror. Nor may his affidavit or evidence of any statement by him concerning a matter about what he would be precluded from testifying be received for these purposes.

Rule 607. Who May Impeach

The credibility of a witness may be attacked by any party, including the party calling them.

Rule 608. Evidence of Character and Conduct of Witness

(a) Opinion and reputation evidence of character.—The credibility of a witness may be attacked or supported by evidence in the form of opinion or reputation, but subject to these limitations: (1) the evidence may refer only to character for truthfulness or untruthfulness, and (2) evidence of truthful character is admissible only after the character of the witness for truthfulness has been attacked by opinion or reputation evidence or otherwise.

(b) Specific instances of conduct. —Specific instances of the conduct of a witness, for the purpose of attacking or supporting his credibility, other than conviction of crime as provided in rule 609, may not be proved by extrinsic evidence. They may, however, in the discretion of the court, if probative of truthfulness or untruthfulness, be inquired into a cross-examination of the witness (1) concerning his character for truthfulness or untruthfulness, or (2) concerning the character for truthfulness or untruthfulness of another witness as to which character the witness being cross-examined has testified.

The giving of testimony, whether by an accused or by any other witness, does not operate as a waiver of his privilege against self-incrimination when examined with respect to matters which relate only to credibility.

Rule 609. Impeachment by Evidence of Conviction of Crime

(a) General rule.—For the purpose of attacking the credibility of a witness, evidence that he has been convicted of a crime shall be admitted if elicited from him or established by public record during cross-examination but only if the crime (1) was punishable by death or imprisonment in excess of one year under the law under which he was convicted, and the court determines that the probative value of admitting this evidence outweighs its prejudicial effect to the defendant, or (2) involved dishonesty or false statement, regardless of the punishment.

(b) Time limit.—Evidence of a convic-

Rule 609. Impeachment by Evidence of Conviction of Crime
(Continued)

tion under this rule is not admissible if a period of more than ten years has elapsed since the date of the conviction or of the release of the witness from the confinement imposed for that conviction, whichever is the later date, unless the court determines, in the interests of justice, that the probative value of the conviction supported by specific facts and circumstances substantially outweighs its prejudicial effect. However, evidence of a conviction more than 10 years old as calculated herein, is not admissible unless the proponent gives to the adverse party sufficient advance written notice of intent to use such evidence to provide the adverse party with a fair opportunity to contest the use of such evidence.

(c) Effect of pardon, annulment, or certificate of rehabilitation.—Evidence of a conviction is not admissible under this rule if (1) the conviction has been the subject of a pardon, annulment, certificate of rehabilitation, or other equivalent procedure based on a finding of the rehabilitation of the person convicted, and that person has not been convicted of a subsequent crime which was punishable by death or imprisonment in excess of one year, or (2) the conviction has been the subject of a pardon, annulment, or other equivalent procedure based on a finding of innocence.

(d) Juvenile adjudications.—Evidence of juvenile adjudications is generally not admissible under this rule. The court may, however, in a criminal case allow evidence of a juvenile adjudication of a witness other than the accused if conviction of the offense would be admissible to attack the credibility of an adult and the court is satisfied that admission in evidence is necessary for a fair determination of the issue of guilt or innocence.

(e) Pendency of appeal.—The pendency of an appeal therefrom does not render evidence of a conviction inadmissible. Evidence of the pendency of an appeal is admissible.

Rule 610. Religious Beliefs or Opinions

Evidence of the beliefs or opinions of a witness on matters of religion is not admissible for the purpose of showing that by reason of their nature his credibility is impaired or enhanced.

Rule 611. Mode and Order of Interrogation and Presentation

(a) Control by court.—The court shall exercise reasonable control over the mode and order of interrogating witnesses and presenting evidence so as to (1) make the interrogation and presentation effective for the ascertainment of the truth, (2) avoid needless consumption of time, and (3) protect witnesses from harrassment or undue embarrassment.

(b) Scope of cross-examination. —Cross-examination should be limited to the subject matter of the direct examination and matters affecting the credibility of the witness. The court may, in the exercise of discretion, permit inquiry into additional matters as if on direct examination.

(c) Leading questions.—Leading questions should not be used on the direct examination of a witness except as may be necessary to develop his testimony. Ordinarily leading questions should be permitted on cross-examination. When a party calls a hostile witness, an adverse party,

Rule 611. Mode and Order of Interrogation and Presentation
(Continued)

or a witness identified with an adverse party, interrogation may be by leading questions.

Rule 612. Writing Used To Refresh Memory

Except as otherwise provided in criminal proceedings by section 3500 of title 18, United States Code, if a witness uses a writing to refresh his memory for the purpose of testifying, either—

(1) while testifying, or

(2) before testifying, if the court in its discretion determines it is necessary in the interests of justice,

an adverse party is entitled to have the writing produced at the hearing, to inspect it, to cross-examine the witness thereon, and to introduce in evidence those portions which relate to the testimony of the witness. If it is claimed that the writing contains matters not related to the subject matter of the testimony the court shall examine the writing in camera, excise any portions not so related, and order delivery of the remainder to the party entitled thereto. Any portion withheld over objections shall be preserved and made available to the appellate court in the event of an appeal. If a writing is not produced or delivered pursuant to order under this rule, the court shall make any order justice requires, except that in criminal cases when the prosecution elects not to comply, the order shall be one striking the testimony or, if the court in its discretion determines that the interests of justice so require, declaring a mistrial.

Rule 613. Prior Statements of Witnesses

(a) Examining witness concerning prior statement.—In examining a witness concerning a prior statement made by him, whether written or not, the statement need not be shown nor its contents disclosed to him at that time, but on request the same shall be shown or disclosed to opposing counsel.

(b) Extrinsic evidence of prior inconsistent statement of witness.—Extrinsic evidence of a prior inconsistent statement by a witness is not admissible unless the witness is afforded an opportunity to explain or deny the same and the opposite party is afforded an opportunity to interrogate him thereon, or the interests of justice otherwise require. This provision does not apply to admissions of a party-opponent as defined in rule 801(d)(2).

Rule 614. Calling and Interrogation of Witnesses by Court

(a) Calling by court.—The court may, on its own motion or at the suggestion of a party, call witnesses, and all parties are entitled to cross-examine witnesses thus called.

(b) Interrogation by court.—The court may interrogate witnesses, whether called by itself or by a party.

(c) Objections.—Objections to the calling of witnesses by the court or to interrogation by it may be made at the time or at the next available opportunity when the jury is not present.

Rule 615. Exclusion of Witnesses

At the request of a party the court shall order witnesses excluded so that they cannot hear the testimony of other witnes-

Rule 615. Exclusion of Witnesses
(Continued)

ses, and it may make the order of its own motion. This rule does not authorize exclusion of (1) a party who is a natural person, or (2) an officer or employee of a party which is not a natural person designated as its representative by its attorney, or (3) a person whose presence is shown by a party to be essential to the presentation of his cause.

ARTICLE VII. OPINIONS AND EXPERT TESTIMONY

Rule 701. Opinion Testimony by Lay Witnesses

If the witness is not testifying as an expert, his testimony in the form of opinions or inferences is limited to those opinions or inferences which are (a) rationally based on the perception of the witness and (b) helpful to a clear understanding of his testimony or the determination of a fact in issue.

Rule 702. Testimony by Experts

If scientific, technical, or other specialized knowledge will assist the trier of fact to understand the evidence or to determine a fact in issue, a witness qualified as an expert by knowledge, skill, experience, training, or education, may testify thereto in the form of an opinion or otherwise.

Rule 703. Bases of Opinion Testimony by Experts

The facts or data in the particular case upon which an expert bases an opinion or inference may be those perceived by or made known to him at or before the hearing. If of a type reasonably relied upon by experts in the particular field in forming opinions for inferences upon the subject, the facts or data need not be admissible in evidence.

Rule 704. Opinion on Ultimate Issue

Testimony in the form of an opinion or inference otherwise admissible is not objectionable because it embraces an ultimate issue to be decided by the trier of fact.

Rule 705. Disclosure of Facts or Data Underlying Expert Opinion

The expert may testify in terms of opinion or inference and give his reasons therefor without prior disclosure of the underlying facts or data, unless the court requires otherwise. The expert may in any event be required to disclose the underlying facts or data on cross-examination.

Rule 706. Court-Appointed Experts

(a) Appointment.—The court may on its own motion or on the motion of any party enter an order to show cause why expert witnesses should not be appointed, and may request the parties to submit nominations. The court may appoint any expert witnesses agreed upon by the parties, and may appoint expert witnesses of its own selection. An expert witness shall not be appointed by the court unless he consents to act. A witness so appointed shall be informed of his duties by the court in writing, a copy of which shall be filed with the clerk, or at a conference in which the parties shall have opportunity to participate. A witness so appointed shall advise the parties of his findings, if any; his deposition may be taken by any party; and he may be called to testify by the court or any party. He shall be subject to cross-examination by each party, including a party calling him as a witness.

Rule 706. Court-Appointed Experts
(Continued)

(b) Compensation.—Expert witnesses so appointed are entitled to reasonable compensation in whatever sum the court may allow. The compensation thus fixed is payable from funds which may be provided by law in criminal cases and civil actions and proceedings involving just compensation under the fifth amendment. In other civil actions and proceedings the compensation shall be paid by the parties in such proportion and at such time as the court directs, and thereafter charged in like manner as other costs.

(c) Disclosure of appointment.—In the exercise of its discretion, the court may authorize disclosure to the jury of the fact that the court appointed the expert witness.

(d) Parties' experts of own selection.—Nothing in this rule limits the parties in calling expert witnesses of their own selection.

ARTICLE VIII. HEARSAY

Rule 801. Definitions

The following definitions apply under this article:

(a) Statement.—A "statement" is (1) an oral or written assertion or (2) nonverbal conduct of a person, if it is intended by him as an assertion.

(b) Declarant.—A "declarant" is a person who makes a statement.

(c) Hearsay.—"Hearsay" is a statement, other than one made by the declarant while testifying at the trial or hearing, offered in evidence to prove the truth of the matter asserted.

(d) Statements which are not hearsay.—A statement is not hearsay if—

(1) Prior statement by witness. —The declarant testifies at the trial or hearing and is subject to cross-examination concerning the statement, and the statement is (A) inconsistent with his testimony, and was given under oath subject to the penalty of perjury at a trial, hearing, or other proceeding, or in a deposition, or (B) consistent with his testimony and is offered to rebut an express or implied charge against him of recent fabrication or improper influence or motive, or

(2) Admission by party-opponent. —The statement is offered against a pary and is (A) his own statement, in either his individual or a representative capacity or (B) a statement of which he has manifested his adoption or belief in its truth, or (C) a statement by a person authorized by him to make a statement concerning the subject, or (D) a statement by his agent or servant concerning a matter within the scope of his agency or employment, made during the existence of the relationship, or (E) a statement by a co-conspirator of a party during the course and in furtherance of the conspiracy.

Rule 802. Hearsay Rule

Hearsay is not admissible except as provided by these rules or by other rules prescribed by the Supreme Court pursuant to statutory authority or by Act of Congress.

Rule 803. Hearsay Exceptions; Availability of Declarant Immaterial

The following are not excluded by the hearsay rule, even though the declarant is available as a witness:

(1) Present sense impression.—A statement describing or explaining an

Rule 803. Hearsay Exceptions; Availability of Declarant Immaterial
(Continued)

event or condition made while the declarant was perceiving the event or condition, or immediately thereafter.

(2) Excited utterance.—A statement relating to a startling event or condition made while the declarant was under the stress of excitement caused by the event or condition.

(3) Then existing mental, emotional, or physical condition.—A statement of the declarant's then existing state of mind, emotion, sensation, or physical condition (such as intent, plan, motive, design, mental feeling, pain, and bodily health), but not including a statement of memory or belief to prove the fact remembered or believed unless it relates to the execution, revocation, identification, or terms of declarant's will.

(4) Statements for purposes of medical diagnosis or treatment.—Statements made for purposes of medical diagnosis or treatment and describing medical history, or past or present symptoms, pain, or sensations, or the inception or general character of the cause or external source thereof insofar as reasonably pertinent to diagnosis or treatment.

(5) Recorded recollection.—A memorandum or record concerning a matter about which a witness once had knowledge but now has insufficient recollection to enable him to testify fully and accurately, shown to have been made or adopted by the witness when the matter was fresh in his memory and to reflect that knowledge correctly. If admitted, the memorandum or record may be read into evidence but may not itself be received as an exhibit unless offered by an adverse party.

(6) Records of regularly conducted activity.—A memorandum, report, record, or data compilation, in any form, of acts, events, conditions, opinions, or diagnoses, made at or near the time by, or from information transmitted by, a person with knowledge, if kept in the course of a regularly conducted business activity, and if it was the regular practice of that business activity to make the memorandum, report, record, or data compilation, all as shown by the testimony of the custodian or other qualified witness, unless the source of information or the method or circumstances of preparation indicate lack of trustworthiness. The term "business" as used in this paragraph includes business, institution, association, profession, occupation, and calling of every kind, whether or not conducted for profit.

(7) Absence of entry in records kept in accordance with the provisions of paragraph (6).—Evidence that a matter is not included in the memoranda reports, records, or data compilations, in any form, kept in accordance with the provisions of paragraph (6), to prove the nonoccurrence or nonexistence of the matter, if the matter was of a kind of which a memorandum, report, record or data compilation was regularly made and preserved, unless the sources of information or other circumstances indicate lack of trustworthiness.

(8) Public records and reports. —Records, reports, statements, or data compilations, in any form, of public offices or agencies, setting forth (A) the activities of the office or agency, or (B) matters observed pur-

Rule 803. Hearsay Exceptions; Availability of Declarant Immaterial
(Continued)

suant to duty imposed by law as to which matters there was a duty to report, excluding, however, in criminal cases matters observed by police officers and other law enforcement personnel, or (C) in civil actions and proceedings and against the Government in criminal cases, factual findings resulting from an investigation made pursuant to authority granted by law, unless the sources of information or other circumstances indicate lack of trustworthiness.

(9) Records of vital statistics.—Records or data compilations, in any form, of births, fetal deaths, deaths, or marriages, if the report thereof was made to a public office pursuant to requirements of law.

(10) Absence of public record or entry.—To prove the absence of a record, report, statement, or data compilation, in any form, or the nonoccurrence or nonexistence of a matter of which a record, report, statement, or data compilation, in any form, was regularly made and preserved by a public office or agency, evidence in the form of a certification in accordance with rule 902, or testimony, that diligent search failed to disclose the record, report, statement, or data compilation, or entry.

(11) Records of religious organizations.—Statements of births, marriages, divorces, deaths, legitimacy, ancestry, relationship by blood or marriage, or other similar facts of personal or family history, contained in a regularly kept record of a religious organization.

(12) Marriage, baptismal, and similar certificates.—Statements of fact contained in a certificate that the maker performed a marriage or other ceremony or administered a sacrament, made by a clergyman, public official, or other person authorized by the rules or practices of a religious organization or by law to perform the act certified, and purporting to have been issued at the time of the act or within a reasonable time thereafter.

(13) Family records.—Statements of fact concerning personal or family history contained in family Bibles, genealogies, charts, engravings on rings, inscriptions on family portraits, engravings on urns, crypts, or tombstones, or the like.

(14) Records of documents affecting an interest in property.—The record of a document purporting to establish or affect an interest in property, as proof of the content of the original recorded document and its execution and delivery by each person by whom it purports to have been executed, if the record is a record of a public office and an applicable statute authorizes the recording of documents of that kind in that office.

(15) Statements in documents affecting an interest in property.—A statement contained in a document purporting to establish or affect an interest in property if the matter stated was relevant to the purpose of the document, unless dealings with the property since the document was made have been inconsistent with the truth of the statement or the purport of the document.

(16) Statements in ancient documents.—Statements in a document in existence twenty years or more the authenticity of which is established.

Rule 803. Hearsay Exceptions; Availability of Declarant Immaterial
(Continued)

(17) Market reports, commercial publications.—Market quotations, tabulations, lists, directories, or other published compilations, generally used and relied upon by the public or by persons in particular occupations.

(18) Learned treatises.—To the extent called to the attention of an expert witness upon cross-examination or relied upon by him in direct examination, statements contained in published treatises, periodicals, or pamphlets on a subject of history, medicine, or other science or art, established as a reliable authority by the testimony or admission of the witness or by other expert testimony or by judicial notice. If admitted, the statements may be read into evidence but may not be received as exhibits.

(19) Reputation concerning personal or family history.—Reputation among members of his family by blood, adoption, or marriage, or among his associates, or in the community, concerning a person's birth, adoption, marriage, divorce, death, legitimacy, relationship by blood, adoption, or marriage, ancestry, or other similar fact of his personal or family history.

(20) Reputation concerning boundaries or general history.—Reputation in a community, arising before the controversy, as to boundaries of or customs affecting lands in the community, and reputation as to events of general history important to the community or State or nation in which located.

(21) Reputation as to character.—Reputation of a person's character among his associates or in the community.

(22) Judgment of previous conviction.—Evidence of a final judgment, entered after a trial or upon a plea of guilty (but not upon a plea of nolo contendere), adjudging a person guilty of a crime punishable by death or imprisonment in excess of one year, to prove any fact essential to sustain the judgment, but not including, when offered by the Government in a criminal prosecution for purposes other than impeachment, judgments against persons other than the accused. The pendency of an appeal may be shown but does not affect admissibility.

(23) Judgment as to personal, family or general history, or boundaries.—Judgments as proof of matters of personal, family or general history, or boundaries, essential to the judgment, if the same would be provable by evidence of reputation.

(24) Other exceptions.—A statement not specifically covered by any of the foregoing exceptions but having equivalent circumstantial guarantees of trustworthiness, if the court determines that (A) the statement is offered as evidence of a material fact; (B) the statement is more probative on the point for which it is offered than any other evidence which the proponent can procure through reasonable efforts; and (C) the general purposes of these rules and the interests of justice will best be served by admission of the statement into evidence. However, a statement may not be admitted under this exception unless the proponent of it makes known to the adverse party sufficiently in advance of the trial or hearing to provide the adverse party with a fair opportunity to prepare to meet it, his intention

**Rule 803. Hearsay Exceptions;
Availability of Declarant Immaterial**
(Continued)

to offer the statement and the particulars of it, including the name and address of the declarant.

**Rule 804. Hearsay Exceptions:
Declarant Unavailable**

(a) Definition of unavailability.
—"Unavailability as a witness" includes situations in which the declarant—

(1) is exempted by ruling of the court on the ground of privilege from testifying concerning the subject matter of his statement; or

(2) persists in refusing to testify concerning the subject matter of his statement despite an order of the court to do so; or

(3) testifies to a lack of memory of the subject matter of his statement; or

(4) is unable to be present or to testify at the hearing because of death or then existing physical or mental illness or infirmity; or

(5) is absent from the hearing and the proponent of his statement has been unable to procure his attendance (or in the case of a hearsay exception under subdivision (b) (2), (3), or (4), his attendance or testimony) by process or other reasonable means.

A declarant is not unavailable as a witness if his exemption, refusal, claim of lack of memory, inability, or absence is due to the procurement or wrongdoing of the proponent of his statement for the purpose of preventing the witness from attending or testifying.

(b) Hearsay exceptions.—The following are not excluded by the hearsay rule if the declarant is unavailable as a witness:

(1) Former testimony.—Testimony given as a witness at another hearing of the same or a different proceeding, or in a deposition taken in compliance with law in the course of the same or another proceeding, if the party against whom the testimony is now offered, or, in a civil action or proceeding, a predecessor in interest, had an opportunity and similar motive to develop the testimony by direct, cross, or redirect examination.

(2) Statement under belief of impending death.—In a prosecution for homicide or in a civil action or proceeding, a statement made by a declarant while believing that his death was imminent, concerning the cause or circumstances of what he believed to be his impending death.

(3) Statement against interest.—A statement which was at the time of its making so far contrary to the declarant's pecuniary or proprietary interest, or so far tended to subject him to civil or criminal liability, or to render invalid a claim by him against another, that a reasonable man in his position would not have made the statement unless he believed it to be true. A statement tending to expose the declarant to criminal liability and offered to exculpate the accused is not admissible unless corroborating circumstances clearly indicate the trustworthiness of the statement.

(4) Statement of personal or family history.—(A) A statement concerning the declarant's own birth, adoption, marriage, divorce, legitimacy, relationship by blood, adoption, or marriage, ancestry, or other similar fact of personal or family history, even though declarant had no means of acquiring personal knowledge of the matter stated; or (B) a statement concern-

Rule 804. Hearsay Exceptions; Declarant Unavailable
(Continued)

ing the foregoing matters, and death also, of another person, if the declarant was related to the other by blood, adoption, or marriage or was so intimately associated with the other's family as to be likely to have accurate information concerning the matter declared.

(5) Other exceptions.—A statement not specifically covered by any of the foregoing exceptions but having equivalent circumstantial guarantees of trustworthiness, if the court determines that (A) the statement is offered as evidence of a material fact; (B) the statement is more probative on the point for which it is offered than any other evidence which the proponent can procure through reasonable efforts; and (C) the general purposes of these rules and the interests of justice will best be served by admission of the statement into evidence. However, a statement may not be admitted under this exception unless the proponent of it makes known to the adverse party sufficiently in advance of the trial or hearing to provide the adverse party with a fair opportunity to prepare to meet it, his intention to offer the statement and the particulars of it, including the name and address of the declarant.

Rule 805. Hearsay Within Hearsay

Hearsay included within hearsay is not excluded under the hearsay rule if each part of the combined statements conforms with an exception to the hearsay rule provided in these rules.

Rule 806. Attacking and Supporting Credibility of Declarant

When a hearsay statement, or a statement defined in Rule 801(d)(2), (C), (D), or (E), has been admitted in evidence, the credibility of the declarant may be attacked, and if attacked may be supported, by any evidence which would be admissible for those purposes if declarant had testified as a witness. Evidence of a statement or conduct by the declarant at any time, inconsistent with his hearsay statement, is not subject to any requirement that he may have been afforded an opportunity to deny or explain. If the party against whom a hearsay statement has been admitted calls the declarant as a witness, the party is entitled to examine him on the statement as if under cross-examination.

ARTICLE IX. AUTHENTICATION AND IDENTIFICATION

Rule 901. Requirement of Authentication or Identification

(a) General provision.—The requirement of authentication or identification as a condition precedent to admissibility is satisfied by evidence sufficient to support a finding that the matter in question is what its proponent claims.

(b) Illustrations.—By way of illustration only, and not by way of limitation, the following are examples of authentication or identification conforming with the requirements of this rule:

(1) Testimony of witness with knowledge.—Testimony that a matter is what it is claimed to be.

(2) Nonexpert opinion on hand-

Rule 901. Requirement of Authentication or Identification
(Continued)

writing.—Nonexpert opinion as to the genuineness of handwriting, based upon familiarity not acquired for purposes of the litigation.

(3) Comparison by trier or expert witness.—Comparison by the trier of fact or by expert witnesses with specimens which have been authenticated.

(4) Distinctive characteristics and the like.—Appearance, contents, substance, internal patterns, or other distinctive characteristics, taken in conjunction with circumstances.

(5) Voice identification.—Identification of a voice, whether heard firsthand or through mechanical or electronic transmission or recording, by opinion based upon hearing the voice at any time under circumstances connecting it with the alleged speaker.

(6) Telephone conversations. —Telephone conversations, by evidence that a call was made to the number assigned at the time by the telephone company to a particular person or business, if (A) in the case of a person, circumstances, including self-identification, show the person answering to be the one called, or (B) in the case of a business, the call was made to a place of business and the conversation related to business reasonably transacted over the telephone.

(7) Public records or reports. —Evidence that a writing authorized by law to be recorded or filed and in fact recorded or filed in a public office, or a purported public record, report, statement, or data compilation, in any form, is from the public office where items of this nature are kept.

(8) Ancient documents or data compilation.—Evidence that a document or data compilation, in any form, (A) is in such condition as to create no suspicion concerning its authenticity, (B) was in a place where it, if authentic, would likely be, and (C) has been in existence 20 years or more at the time it is offered.

(9) Process or system.—Evidence describing a process or system used to produce a result and showing that the process or system produces an accurate result.

(10) Methods provided by statute or rule.—Any method of authentication or identification provided by Act of Congress or by other rules prescribed by the Supreme Court pursuant to statutory authority.

Rule 902. Self-authentication

Extrinsic evidence of authenticity as a condition precedent to admissibility is not required with respect to the following:

(1) Domestic public documents under seal.—A document bearing a seal purporting to be that of the United States, or of any State, district, Commonwealth, territory, or insular possession thereof, or the Panama Canal Zone, or the Trust Territory of the Pacific Islands, or of a political subdivision, department, officer, or agency thereof, and a signature purporting to be an attestation or execution.

(2) Domestic public documents not under seal.—A document purporting

Rule 902. Self-Authentication
(Continued)

to bear the signature in his official capacity of an officer or employee of any entity included in paragraph (1) hereof, having no seal, if a public officer having a seal and having official duties in the district or political subdivision of the officer or employee certifies under seal that the signer has the official capacity and that the signature is genuine.

(3) Foreign public documents.—A document purporting to be executed or attested in his official capacity by a person authorized by the laws of a foreign country to make the execution or attestation, and accompanied by a final certification as to the genuineness of the signature and official position (A) of the executing or attesting person, or (B) of any foreign official whose certificate of genuineness of signature and official position relates to the execution or attestation or is in a chain of certificates of genuineness of signature and official position relating to the execution or attestation. A final certification may be made by a secretary of embassy or legation, consul general, consul, vice consul, or consular agent of the United States, or a diplomatic or consular official of the foreign country assigned or accredited to the United States. If reasonable opportunity has been given to all parties to investigate the authenticity and accuracy of official documents, the court may, for good cause shown, order that they be treated as presumptively authentic without final certification or permit them to be evidenced by an attested summary with or without final certification.

(4) Certified copies of public records.—A copy of an official record or report or entry therein, or of a document authorized by law to be recorded or filed and actually recorded or filed in a public office, including data compilations in any form, certified as correct by the custodian or other person authorized to make the certification, by certificate complying with paragraph (1), (2), or (3) of this rule or complying with any Act of Congress or rule prescribed by the Supreme Court pursuant to statutory authority.

(5) Official publications.—Books, pamphlets, or other publications purporting to be issued by public authority.

(6) Newspapers and periodicals. —Printed materials purporting to be newspapers or periodicals.

(7) Trade inscriptions and the like.—Inscriptions, signs, tags, or labels purporting to have been affixed in the course of business and indicating ownership, control, or origin.

(8) Acknowledged documents. —Documents accompanied by a certificate of acknowledgment executed in the manner provided by law by a notary public or other officer authorized by law to take acknowledgments.

(9) Commercial paper and related documents.—Commercial paper, signatures thereon, and documents relating thereto to the extent provided by general commercial law.

(10) Presumptions under Acts of Congress.—Any signature, document, or other matter declared by Act of Congress to be presumptively or prima facie genuine or authentic.

Rule 903. Subscribing Witness' Testimony Unnecessary

The testimony of a subscribing witness is not necessary to authenticate a writing unless required by the laws of the jurisdiction whose laws govern the validity of the writing.

ARTICLE X. CONTENTS OF WRITINGS, RECORDINGS, AND PHOTOGRAPHS

Rule 1001. Definitions

For purposes of this article the following definitions are applicable:

(1) Writings and recordings. —"Writings" and "recordings" consist of letters, words, or numbers, or their equivalent, set down by handwriting, typewriting, printing, photostating, photographing, magnetic impulse, mechanical or electronic recording, or other form of data compilation.

(2) Photographs.—"Photographs" include still photographs, X-ray films, video tapes, and motion pictures.

(3) Original.—An "original" of a writing or recording is the writing or recording itself or any counterpart intended to have the same effect by a person executing or issuing it. An "original" of a photograph includes the negative or any print therefrom. If data are stored in a computer or similar device, any printout or other output readable by sight, shown to reflect the data accurately, is an "original."

(4) Duplicate.—A "duplicate" is a counterpart produced by the same impression as the original, or from the same matrix, or by means of photography, including enlargements and miniatures, or by mechanical or electronic re-recording, or by chemical reproduction, or by other equivalent techniques which accurately reproduces the original.

Rule 1002. Requirement of Original

To prove the content of a writing, recording, or photograph, the original writing, recording, or photograph is required, except as otherwise provided in these rules or by Act of Congress.

Rule 1003. Admissibility of Duplicates

A duplicate is admissible to the same extent as an original unless (1) a genuine question is raised as to the authenticity of the original or (2) in the circumstances it would be unfair to admit the duplicate in lieu of the original.

Rule 1004. Admissibility of Other Evidence of Contents

The original is not required, and other evidence of the contents of a writing, recording, or photograph is admissible if—

(1) Originals lost or destroyed. —All originals are lost or have been destroyed, unless the proponent lost or destroyed them in bad faith; or

(2) Original not obtainable.—No original can be obtained by any available judicial process or procedure; or

(3) Original in possession of opponent.—At a time when an original was under the control of the party against whom offered, he was put on notice, by the pleadings or otherwise, that the contents would be a subject of proof at the hearing, and he does not produce the original at the hearing; or

(4) Collateral matters.—The writing, recording, or photograph is not closely related to a controlling issue.

Rule 1005. Public Records

The contents of an official record, or of a document authorized to be recorded or filed and actually recorded or filed, including data compilations in any form, if otherwise admissible, may be proved by copy, certified as correct in accordance with rule 902 or testified to be correct by a witness who has compared it with the original. If a copy which complies with the foregoing cannot be obtained by the exercise of reasonable diligence, then other evidence of the contents may be given.

Rule 1006. Summaries

The contents of voluminous writings, recordings, or photographs which cannot conveniently be examined in court may be presented in the form of a chart, summary, or calculation. The originals, or duplicates, shall be made available for examination or copying, or both, by other parties at reasonable time and place. The court may order that they be produced in court.

Rule 1007. Testimony or Written Admission of Party

Contents of writings, recordings, or photographs may be proved by the testimony or deposition of the party against whom offered or by his written admission, without accounting for the nonproduction of the original.

Rule 1008. Functions of Court and Jury

When the admissibility of other evidence of contents of writings, recording, or photographs under these rules depends upon the fulfillment of a condition of fact, the question whether the condition has been fulfilled is ordinarily for the court to determine in accordance with the provisions of rule 104. However, when an issue is raised (a) whether the asserted writing ever existed, or (b) whether another writing, recording, or photograph produced at the trial is the original, or (c) whether other evidence of contents correctly reflects the contents, the issue is for the trier of fact to determine as in the case of other issues of fact.

ARTICLE XI.
MISCELLANEOUS RULES

Rule 1101. Applicability of Rules

(a) Courts and magistrates.—These rules apply to the United States district courts, the District Court of Guam, the District Court of the Virgin Islands, the District Court for the District of the Canal Zone, the United States courts of appeals, the Court of Claims, and to United States magistrates, in the actions, cases, and proceedings and to the extent hereinafter set forth. The terms ''judge'' and ''court'' in these rules include United States magistrates, referees in bankruptcy, and commissioners of the Court of Claims.

(b) Proceedings generally.—These rules apply generally to civil actions and proceedings, including admiralty and maritime cases, to criminal cases and proceedings, to contempt proceedings except those in which the court may act summarily, and to proceedings and cases under the Bankruptcy Act.

(c) Rule of privilege.—The rule with respect to privileges applies at all stages of all actions, cases, and proceedings.

(d) Rules inapplicable.—The rules (other than with respect to privileges) do not apply in the following situations:

Rule 1101. Applicability of Rules
(Continued)

(1) Preliminary questions of fact.—The determination of questions of fact preliminary to admissibility of evidence when the issue is to be determined by the court under rule 104.

(2) Grand jury.—Proceedings before grand juries.

(3) Miscellaneous proceedings. —Proceedings for extradition or rendition; preliminary examinations in criminal cases; sentencing, or granting or revoking probation, issuance of warrants for arrest, criminal summonses, and search warrants; and proceedings with respect to release on bail or otherwise.

(e) Rules applicable in part.—In the following proceedings these rules apply to the extent that matters of evidence are not provided for in the statutes which govern procedure therein or in other rules prescribed by the Supreme Court pursuant to statutory authority: the trial of minor and petty offenses by United States magistrates; review of agency actions when the facts are subject to trial de novo under section 706(2)(F) of title 5, United States Code; review of orders of the Secretary of Agriculture under section 2 of the Act entitled "An Act to authorize association of producers of agricultural products" approved February 18, 1922 (7 U.S.C. 292), and under sections 6 and 7(c) of the Perishable Agricultural Commodities Act 1930 (7 U.S.C. 499f, 499g(c)); naturalization and revocation of naturalization under sections 310-318 of the Immigration and Nationality Act (8 U.S.C. 1421-1429); prize proceedings in admiralty under sections 7651-7681 of title 10, United States Code; review of orders of the Secretary of the Interior under section 2 of the Act entitled "An Act authorizing associations of producers of aquatic products" approved June 25, 1934 (15 U.S.C. 522); review of orders of petroleum control boards under section 5 of the Act entitled "An Act to regulate inter-state and foreign commerce in petroleum and its products by prohibiting the shipment in such commerce of petroleum and its products produced in violation of State law, and for other purposes," approved February 22, 1935 (15 U.S.C. 715d); actions for fines, penalties, or forfeitures under part V of title IV of the Tariff Act of 1930 (19 U.S.C. 1581-1624), or under the Anti-Smuggling Act (19 U.S.C. 1701-1711); criminal libel for condemnation, exclusion of imports, or other proceedings under the Federal Food, Drug, and Cosmetic Act (21 U.S.C. 301-392); disputes between seamen under sections 4079, 4080 and 4081 of the Revised Statutes (22 U.S.C. 256-258; habeas corpus under sections 2241-2254 of title 28, United States Code; motions to vacate, set aside or correct sentence under section 2255 of title 28, United States Code; actions for penalties for refusal to transport destitute seamen under section 4578 of the Revised Statutes (46 U.S.C. 679); actions against the United States under the Act entitled "An Act authorizing suits against the United States in admirality for damage caused by and salvage service rendered to public vessels belonging to the United States, and for other purposes," approved March 3, 1925 (46 U.S.C. 781-790), as implemented by section 7730 of title 10, United States Code.

Rule 1102. Amendments

Amendments to the Federal Rules of Evidence may be made as provided in sec-

Rule 1102. Amendments
(Continued)

tion 2076 of title 28 of the United States Code.

Rule 1103. Title

These rules may be known and cited as the Federal Rules of Evidence.

Sec. 2 (a) Title 28 of the United States Code is amended—

(1) by inserting immediately after section 2075 the following new section:

"§2076. Rules of Evidence."

"The Supreme Court of the United States shall have the power to prescribe amendments to the Federal Rules of Evidence. Such amendments shall not take effect until they have been reported to Congress by the Chief Justice at or after the beginning of a regular session of Congress but not later than the first day of May, and until the expiration of one hundred and eighty days after they have been so reported; but if either House of Congress within that time shall by resolution disapprove any amendment so reported it shall not take effect. The effective date of any amendment so reported may be deferred by either House of Congress to a later date or until approved by Act of Congress. Any rule whether proposed or in force may be amended by Act of Congress. Any provision of law in force at the expiration of such time and in conflict with any such amendment not disapproved shall be of no further force or effect after such amendment has taken effect. Any such amendment creating, abolishing, or modifying a privilege shall have no force or effect unless it shall be approved by Act of Congress"; and

(2) by adding at the end of the table of sections of chapter 131 the following new item:

"2076. Rules of Evidence."

(b) Section 1732 of title 28 of the United States Code is amended by striking out subsection (a), and by striking out "(b)".

(c) Section 1733 of title 28 of the United States Code is amended by adding at the end thereof the following new subsection:

"(c) This section does not apply to cases, actions, and proceedings to which the Federal Rules of Evidence apply."

Sec. 3. The Congress expressly approves the amendments to the Federal Rules of Civil Procedure, and the amendments to the Federal Rules of Criminal Procedure, which are embraced by the orders entered by the Supreme Court of the United States on November 20, 1972, and December 18, 1972, and such amendments shall take effect on the one hundred and eightieth day beginning after the date of the enactment of this Act.

Chapter 15

HOW TO MAKE PROFICIENCY
IN PUBLIC SPEAKING
PRODUCE PROFITS

A Key to Increased Income . . . Why Some Lawyers Outdistance Others . . . A Law Degree Does Not Automatically Make You a Speaker . . . You Can Achieve Proficiency in a Wide Variety of Ways . . . Entering Public Life One of Surest Methods . . . The Four Most Common Handicaps . . . Shun the Polysyllabic Vocabulary . . . Seek Clarity and Brevity and a Common-Sense Approach . . . How to Prepare for Your Talk . . . How to Acquire Enthusiasm . . . How to Overcome Lack of Self-Confidence . . . The Four Modes of Delivery . . . Selecting Your Own Type of Speaking . . . The Extemporaneous Talk Gives Flexibility . . . How to Use the Outline Effectively . . . Woodrow Wilson's Rule . . . Pointers on Effective Delivery . . . Use the "Tricks of the Trade" . . . Ten Recommended Rules for Sharpening Your Speaking Skills . . . Words Can Be Equally Effective in Promoting Profits . . . The Profit Potential of the Spoken Word

A Key to Increased Income

A lawyer may be a genius in his field, but if he cannot express himself simply, clearly, cogently, logically, and coherently in public, the chances are 10

295

to 1 that he will never hit the magic goal of $100,000 per annum. He will almost certainly be relegated to a position of mediocrity in his profession. But if he has learned the art of public speaking, he has taken an important step in increasing his income as an attorney. Ignore this talent or belittle it, or fail to develop it, and this handicap will dog your footsteps throughout your career.

Why Some Lawyers Outdistance Others

While a few lawyers make the grade without this talent, we have all observed lawyers who seem to have forged ahead more rapidly than others and to have won success in their practice and preferment in public life and even in the judiciary. Many of them did not possess the endowments or the mental acuity of their contemporaries whom they had surpassed. Just investigate a little and you will be surprised to learn that early in their careers, these fortunate few had cultivated the art of public speaking. While this may not be a guarantee to pre-eminence at the bar or to build up a profitable practice, many times it is a deciding factor—all other things being equal. An attorney is not called a "mouthpiece" in the vernacular without good reason.

A Law Degree Does Not Automatically
Make You a Speaker

A law degree does not automatically make you a speaker. The mistake many attorneys make is to ignore this, either because they lack this talent, or don't know how to develop it, or because they have the idea that they are accomplished speakers. Some even have the mistaken notion that a degree from a law school carries with it *automatically* a certification of proficiency in public speaking. If you are in this category, the sooner you check up on yourself and take a proficiency test by some qualified person—or better still, ask some disinterested, but candid observer, to give you an informal rating—the better it will be for for you. I would suggest that perhaps the best investment you can make at this point would be to buy a tape recorder and a few cassettes, transcribe one of your public utterances, and then play it back for your own study and analysis.

There is an analogy here between the old adage relating to the importance between tact and talent. Tact carries the day every time. In many instances, talk carries the day over talent in the field of law and this fact is necessarily reflected in the income an attorney is able to produce. In many instances, it is related directly, if not geometrically to this capacity to speak in public.

You Can Achieve Proficiency in a Wide
Variety of Ways

When I graduated from law school, I had little or no training in public speaking. I had treated it lightly in high school and in college. The law school had provided only a club where embryo speakers used the "hit or miss" or "trial and error" method by practicing on each other without either teacher or text. It was of little value and, when I was eventually projected into the practice of law, the realization of my total lack of training struck me. I began a rigorous study of every book on the subject available. I visited the libraries of all nearby cities. I read every volume available on the subject. Next I signed up at a local extension course at Rutgers University for a 16-week course, one night a week.

Gradually, it dawned on me that only practice and more practice would give me the proficiency and fluency I needed. My law practice at that time was too meager to afford me much range in the field of public speaking. I began accepting speaking engagements whenever and wherever they were tendered. I was agreeably surprised to learn that many of these were productive from a professional standpoint. There was scarcely a speaking engagement I accepted where I was not accosted by one of the audience who had a legal problem on his mind that he wanted to discuss informally. In many instances, these people later became clients, and profitable ones too.

However, in order to extend my field of operation, I ran for the Legislature. This was, in fact, adopting the old "sink or swim" theory. Catapulted into an extremely hard-fought campaign, I was out on the trail every night, speaking in 25 different communities. After a grueling four-months' campaign, which involved 6 to 12 speaking engagements a day, I began to learn the fine points of the art—in fact, I began to like it—and I won the election to boot.

Entering Public Life One of Surest Methods

Now I had a ready-made forum to display my newly developed talents. There were 60 members in the lower House—15 in the minority and 45 in the majority. As a minority member, I considered this to mean that I could speak three times as often as a majority member—and I usually did! In the third year, one address I made was believed to be of sufficient value to have it printed in lots of 10,000 and circulated throughout the state to assist in the gubernatorial campaign of that year.

Meanwhile, I found that as I spoke to clients in the office I instinctively organized my facts, dressed up my presentation so that it was clear, cogent and chronological—and greatly improved my powers of persuasion. There were all kinds of special knacks and techniques that I had acquired on the political platform and in the halls of the Legislature which were helpful in my professional life. Before a jury, the use of these same newly-acquired talents and techniques was even more apparent to me.

I doubt that this change was obvious to my listeners, since they had never heard me before, but I was immediately conscious of a new power of presenting facts with more clarity and with a greater power of persuasion. Favorable verdicts began to come in regularly in substantial amounts. In one instance in an uncontested case, my arguments were apparently so persuasive that the jury stayed out for more than four hours on the sole question of how large a verdict to bring in. And in another case, where the client I was defending in an automobile negligence case lost courage and failed to appear in court to testify in his own behalf, I was still able to persuade the jury to bring in a verdict favorable to him *in absentia.*

The Four Most Common Handicaps

Public speakers are not born—but they certainly can be developed. Bear always in mind that as a lawyer your income depends in large measure upon your speaking talents. Usually, inability to speak effectively in public is due to four simple handicaps vis: (1) lack of confidence, (2) lack of vocabulary, (3) lack of preparation and (4) lack of enthusiasm. With these four handicaps properly overcome, the task should be relatively simple.

Shun the Polysyllabic Vocabulary

To skip to the second handicap—I made the mistake early in my career in believing that I had to use polysyllabic words to make my talk impressive. I actually cultivated the habit of never using a simple word when a larger one could be introduced. I believe I acquired this unhappy trait from one of the old-time law professors who had served as a U.S. District Court Judge for years. He not only employed this technique himself, but he was the most stentorian, rhetorical, redundant and repetitious speaker I ever knew.

He had apparently developed this particular habit over the years through his numerous charges to the juries. In his dedication to this task, "he told them what he was going to tell them—then he told them—and then he told them what he had told them." Moreover, he displayed an unusual proficiency for using synonyms and invariably, he gave three or four variations of the same word with slightly different shades of meaning and delicate nuances whenever he could. But his talks always sounded so impressive—so magnificent—like the voice coming from Mt. Sinai—and I made the mistake of emulating him.

Seek Clarity and Brevity and a Common Sense Approach

I soon learned that this is not the way to talk in public. What a listener wants is clarity and brevity. Keep the words short and simple. Keep the sentences and the paragraphs equally simple. For example, consider President Lincoln's Gettysburg Address which has become a classic through the years. It contains only 270 words. 70 percent of these are of one syllable. Only 15 percent are of two syllables, leaving only 15 percent of more than two syllables. Hence, my admonition is to reverse the process of developing a vocabulary of long words. Cultivate short, concise, pungent, strong words. It is difficult to beat the good old-fashioned Anglo-Saxon words in this respect. Make a game of studying words and utilizing them. The *Readers Digest* publishes a list of 20 words each month. It gives you four choices as to the meaning of each word. Utilizing this list alone as a basis for enlarging your vocabulary is an excellent practice. Over a period of a few years, you may acquire hundreds of new words which you might otherwise not have occasion to adopt.

How to Prepare for Your Talk

As to preparation, nothing will make you more restless and uneasy than a lack of preparation. No one can speak about anything without thought and preparation. If gifted men, like Winston Churchill, prepare their talks, why should an ordinary individual depend upon sudden inspiration which seldom, if ever, comes? As a professional, the lawyer is recognized as being skilled and qualified in the field of research. Law is not the only subject which requires, or deserves, research. Every subject upon which you attempt to speak in public should also be thoroughly researched.

But, there is no necessity for making a federal project out of it. If you keep abreast of current events, subscribe to and read a few leading newspapers or magazines, your mind should be full of ideas demanding public discussion. Perhaps many of these may have a legal sidelight or highlight. It is important just to make certain that your audience is always aware of the fact that you are a lawyer. Always remember this simple advice—a good speech is 90 percent preparation and 10 percent inspiration.

I have found it advisable to maintain files, or even scrapbooks, on subjects which appeal to my interests. It takes but a moment to mark an item in a newspaper or magazine to be clipped out and filed by a secretary. After a short time, you will have acquired a wealth of data on as wide a variety of subjects as you are interested in. Hopefully all, or most of these will have a legal angle. A cardinal rule is not to speak on any subject in which you are not actually interested. If you attempt to do so, you are doomed to defeat before you start. Your talk will lack enthusiasm, as well as sincerity. No one enjoys listening to a speaker who does not radiate enthusiasm for his subject. And how do you acquire enthusiasm? Let's examine this subject.

How to Acquire Enthusiasm

When I first attended public speaking courses at Rutgers University, that was one of the first questions I asked the professor. The course was conducted by Richard J. Reager, author of one of the best books on the subject, "You Can Talk Well." His answer was simple and concise. "Never," he admonished, "attempt to talk on any subject in which you are not vitally interested."

The answer for lawyers would seem to be simple and obvious. Always select a subject that does have legal overtones—and prospects of doing you and your practice some good eventually. Why do you suppose attorneys accept invitations to address the Parlin Women's Club on "Wills—And Who Should Draw Them"? Or why do they accept invitations to address the Men's Executive Club on "Estate Planning to Save Taxes"? These subjects will not only give you enthusiasm, but are bound to inspire your audience with admiration for your erudition. While I had trouble building up enthusiasm, I am now frank to admit that I can now become enthusiastic about such mundane subjects as the weather with little or no difficulty.

How to Overcome Lack of Self-Confidence

To return to handicap #1, i.e., lack of self-confidence, this is invariably rooted in handicaps #2, #3 and #4. You will find that as soon as you have developed an adequate vocabulary; prepared your material properly and thoroughly; have built up enthusiasm to expound or explain the matter to your audience—you will possess ample self-confidence to deliver a speech without difficulty. Speeches usually fall into five categories viz: (a) to inform, (b) to explain, (c) to inspire, (d) to persuade and (e) to entertain. A good speech may, and frequently does, embody some of the characteristics of all five.

The Four Modes of Delivery

Delivery is probably the most important single element to develop. Countless volumes have been written on this subject. If you are aware of the potential handicaps previously discussed and have eliminated them at least to a substantial extent, you are now ready for action. Your first decision is to elect which method of delivery you intend to pursue. There are only four methods, namely: (a) impromptu, (b) extemporaneous, (c) written and memorized and (d) written and read.

The impromptu, as the name suggests, implies that you are suddenly called upon without any advance warning to stand up and speak. It is the most difficult and can be the most disastrous type. Only the most voluble can usually achieve it. Frost once said: "Half the world is composed of people who have something to say and cannot say it. The other half are people who have nothing to say—and keep on saying it." Impromptu speakers usually fall into the latter category.

I once made the mistake of inviting a distinguished jurist to address a group. He insisted that he would speak impromptu and could not give me a text or even the title of his talk. It certainly was impromptu. It had no beginning and no end and contributed little except boredom to the program.

Selecting Your Own Type of Speaking

The second type of talk, while called extemporaneous, is actually a well-thought-out, coherent, comprehensive, dissertation on a given subject. It may have been carefully written out, or at least outlined before hand. However, it is definitely not memorized and the speaker does extemporize in the framing of his sentences and paragraph structure. He is usually guided only by his outlines.

The third method is the speech that is written and memorized. This is difficult since it requires an excellent memory and, if you lose your place or forget your line, you can also lose your audience. It is like an actor following a script, but it is usually stilted, artificial and ineffective. This type of talk lacks the warmth and sincerity and spontaneity required to have a good effect upon an audience.

The speech that is written and read has all the drawbacks of the previous one. The only exception is that the speaker frankly admits that it is a prepared speech and prepares to read it. While this method is widely followed, particularly by many political candidates and public officials, it is nowhere nearly as effective as a speech should be. While reading the manuscript the speaker necessarily has his eyes cast down. He has lost an important contact with his audience. Sometimes he even forgets to look up as he comes to the end of a sentence or makes a particularly strong point.

The Extemporaneous Talk Gives Flexibility

The best and most effective form is unquestionably the extemporaneous talk. It is the type which the lawyer has, or must train himself, to use in both the trial and appellate courts. Can you visualize a lawyer standing up before a judge or jury and speaking impromptu? It would be either futile or suicidal. Or, can you imagine a lawyer writing out a legal memorandum, or argument, in support of, or in opposition to a motion before a single judge—or in support of, or in opposition to an appeal before an appellate tribunal of 3 or 7 or 9 justices, and then memorizing it for delivery? Impossible! The judges may pose questions not covered in your memorized talk. As for preparing and reading your message, this method does not play any valued role in the lawyer's world today. That is precisely what Briefs are for. This written form of communication is excellent. But, it is the effective oral argument that usually "carries the day."

How to Use the Outline Effectively

So it is wise for the lawyer to use the extemporaneous method both in the courtroom and on the public platform. It is unimportant in which forum you develop this skill, but you should develop it by all means and use it exclusively —for both results and *profit*. The outline may be as simple or complex as you wish it to be. Some veteran speakers stand up with an outline consisting of only three major points. Others will require 12 major points. Still others require a half dozen sub-heads under each of the major points to make certain that they cover the ground. Whatever you find that you personally need in the way of an outline —prepare it.

It is not always easy to prepare an outline. I write the speech out first and the outline second. I then discard or file the written speech—and retain only the outline. I have it available before me when I stand up. If I need to refer to it, I have it. But I seldom need to refer to it. Item by item, point by point, sub-point by sub-point, the speech is delivered extemporaneously. This method lends to the speaker a freedom of development and a freedom of expression, without losing the thread or the theme of the talk, which cannot be otherwise achieved. This is precisely what a lawyer must do in court, whether he is arguing a motion, making an opening or closing statement to the jury, or arguing an appeal.

Woodrow Wilson's Rule

The importance of preparation is probably best illustrated by a story about Woodrow Wilson. He was once invited to make an address. He inquired how soon the talk was scheduled and how long—or how short—it was to be. His visitor inquired if these elements were important. Wilson replied: "If I have to talk ten minutes, I will need two weeks to prepare it. If I have to talk 20 minutes, I will need one week. But if you want me to talk two hours—I am ready now."

Pointers on Effective Delivery

The mode or manner of delivery is also important if you are to gain confidence and enthusiasm. As a precaution, it is recommended that you conserve your strength and stamina. If you are the featured speaker at the end of a parade, do not march! Either ride, or arrange your schedule so as to arrive when the speaking program starts. Do not exhaust your energy in advance. Listen to the other speakers. Observe the reaction of the audience. Note the subject matter that appeals to them. When you stand up, be sure that you speak clearly and distinctly so that *everyone* in the audience can hear you. Use the microphone by all means, that is what it is there for.

Bear always in mind that audiences are there to listen—but you must make them want to listen. Your message has a purpose. Follow the old rule of the news reporter. Tell them who, what, when, where, why—and even how. You must emanate sincerity, cordiality and enthusiasm. This is not always an easy task. As you approach the podium, tell yourself that you like the audience and they like you. You will find that this attitude is infectious. They will respond. I have seen speakers appearing before hostile audiences apply this method effectively. If you employ this technique, you, too, can convey to any audience a spirit of warmth and friendliness.

Use the "Tricks of the Trade"

As you speak, do not remain fixed and rigid in one spot. If the audience is small and a microphone is not required, move about occasionally, but do it gracefully and naturally. Use gestures if they come *naturally*; otherwise eliminate them entirely. Change the pitch and tempo and the tone of voice as the text or subject matter suggests. "There is as much eloquence in the tone of your voice —in the eye—in the air of the speaker, as in his words," says Rochefoucauld.

Avoid the monotone at all costs. A whisper well placed commands more attention than a bellow or a shout. Embellish your talks generously with anecdotes, illustrations and short stories provided they are apt and are not "immaterial, irrelevate or incompetent." Avoid the off-color story, the one with an ethnic or religious overtone. Try to be felicitous at all times. Avoid the acute angle. Say something gracious not only about your friends, but even about your adversaries occasionally. It will surprise them, it may shock them, and hopefully it may disarm them.

When making a point, do not be indirect about it. Make it! When Sir Winston Churchill was instructing the Prince of Wales in public speaking, he is reported to have told him: "If you have an important point to make, don't try to be subtle or clever—use a pile driver. Hit the point once. Then come back and hit it again. Then hit it a third time—a tremendous whack."

Ten Recommended Rules for Sharpening Your Speaking Skills

Through years of trial and error, I have developed a few rules of my own which I call "Karcher's 10 Rules for Sharpening your Public Speaking Skills," viz:

(1) Know your subject.
(2) Study your audience.
(3) Speak clearly and audibly.
(4) Be logical, coherent and chronological.
(5) Use timbre, tone and volume to suit the subject matter.
(6) Move about gracefully and naturally.
(7) Use natural gestures—or none at all.
(8) Avoid monotony by an occasional pause, whisper and similar techniques.
(9) Illustrate your talks with appropriate anecdotes and aphorisms.
(10) Know when to stop, and do it.

"The power of words is immense," says DeGirardin. "A few well chosen words have often sufficed to stop a fleeing army; to change defeat into victory—and save an empire." History is rich with illustrations of the truth of this declaration. Witness, for instance, such immortal quotes as "Give me liberty or give me death," "We have nothing to fear but fear itself," "I have nothing to offer you but blood, sweat and tears," etc.

Words Can Be Equally Effective in Promoting Profits

Words can be equally effective in the everyday affairs of the lawyer's life and practice—even if less dramatic. You do not want to stop an army; save an empire; give resolution to a revolution, give hope to a faltering nation in the slough of economic despond; or to inspire courage when a nation has its back to the wall. Your objectives are much simpler and also much more easy to realize. All you want is to have thinking members of your audience say: ''That lawyer makes sense. If and when I need one, he's my man!'' Or, to have a juror say as soon as he has heard your exposition of the case: ''I *knew* he was right. I didn't have to hear the other side. The way he put it—justice was clearly on his side.'' These are the rewards that come to the lawyer who has sharpened his speaking skills and uses them constantly. The reflection in his income is bound to be automatic and gratifying.

The Profit Potential of the Spoken Word

A realization of the important part public speaking can play in increasing a lawyer's practice and income came early in my career. I was attending an open political rally in New Brunswick. It was a relatively small audience—not more than 100 at most. I had just completed an old-fashioned slashing attack upon the opposition party. Being in the minority party at the time, and out of office I felt that I had to carry the fight to the ''enemy.'' After cataloging a long list of what I claimed were highly questionable acts by men in high office I concluded my address with the typical plea ''Send me to Trenton as your representative before they steal the gold dome off the State Capitol!''

Shortly afterward as the meeting broke up I was approached by a member of the audience. He identified himself as the secretary of a civic group which needed the services of an attorney. I listened intently. As the story unfolded, I realized that the case had great potential. I asked him why he sought me out. His answer was simple. ''I liked your talk! You're a fighter.'' That was enough. I accepted the case. The legal fee eventually earned ran into five figures! But this was only one isolated case. Similar situations have occurred regularly throughout my career.

I have even had people look me up and retain me solely because of reading an account of one of my addresses in the press. Some others have come to me through the recommendations of friends who heard one of my talks. Appearance on TV and radio have had even more dramatic results. Thus, the effects of an attorney's facility in public speaking can be far reaching indeed. It is not limited to the immediate audience by any means. Today with radio and TV carrying your message to unseen millions, the power of the spoken word is greater than ever before. Hence, my advice to all lawyers, young and old, is—*"Use it* for prestige—power—and *profit!"*

Chapter 16

HOW TO TURN PARLIAMENTARY LAW
INTO A PROFESSIONAL ASSET

*Can Be Made to Pay Substantial Dividends in New Clients and
Larger Fees . . . Powerless at Public Meetings Without It . . .
Essential to Corporate Clients . . . Don't Miss Greater Oppor-
tunity for Bigger and Better Fees . . . How Clients Use Par-
liamentary Procedure to Comply with the Law . . . A Well-
Organized Corporation Can Grow into a Prosperous Client . . .
Labor Union Clients Need Parlimentary Skills . . . Compensation
Cases Can Lead to Profitable Third-Party Suits . . . Less than a
Dozen Motions in Frequent Use . . . The 12 Subsidiary
Motions . . . The 8 Incidental Motions . . . The 5 Privileged
Motions . . . The 9 Motions Most Frequently Made . . . Always
Arm Yourself with a Chart . . . A Powerful Weapon in Building a
Practice and Increasing Fees*

Can Be Made to Pay Substantial Dividends
in New Clients and Larger Fees

Nobody every studied parliamentary law without a good reason. I can
give you one of the best reasons in the world, i.e., it will help you build up your
law practice *and your income*. The difficulty is that many lawyers view the
subject as inane, uninteresting and of little practical or professional value. Nothing could be further from the facts. It is a fairly simple subject, which if used
properly can be made to pay substantial dividends in attracting new clients and
increased fees.

Some other attorneys labor under the mistaken assumption that they know all that is to be known about the subject—or at least all they need to know to get by.

Many of them would be surprised as to how little they really do know about it—and how much at a loss they would be—how absolutely out-classed they would be, if they were to meet up with an adversary who had any degree of skill in this particular area.

Powerless at Public Meetings Without It

If you want to check up on your knowledge in this field, just attend any session of a deliberative body from the local Township Committee to the U.S. Congress—and watch what happens. On the local level, every step in the proceedings is covered by parliamentary procedure from the simple receipt and disposition of a letter to the enactment of a million-dollar bond issue. At the highest level, every intricate move the bill, or law, takes from its conception in the mind of the author to its signing or veto by the President must follow a maze of parliamentary procedure. In some instances, these regulations are governed by the Rules of Order of the body itself. In the absence of such special regulations, basic Parliamentary Procedure prevails, and nothing is accomplished unless these rules are followed. To follow them, you must first know and master them. Since lawyers usually occupy a majority of the positions in most deliberative bodies above the county level, it follows that lawyers above all others, should study and master these rules if they expect to take their rightful part in these proceedings.

Essential to Corporate Clients

But it is not only public bodies where these standard rules of parliamentary procedure prevail. They are an integral part of practically every assemblage, from the initial meeting of the incorporators of a family corporation to an annual stockholders meeting of such corporate giants as General Motors or American T. & T. Co. These rules are essential tools in carrying out these legal functions so that they will stand up in court.

When a lawyer organizes a corporation, whether large or small, he must immediately begin to use at least the elementary rules. A temporary chairman, or secretary, must be selected. A motion must be made to elect directors; to appoint tellers; and a judge of the election. Appropriate action must be taken to announce the results of the election and the induction of the directors into office; the consideration of routine stockholder business—and finally, adjournment. If a lawyer sloughs off all these routine procedures as useless red tape, he is doing a disservice to the law, to his clients and to himself. He does not *earn* a decent fee for the incorporation. He does not *deserve* a decent fee. Usually he does not *receive* a decent fee.

Don't Miss Greater Opportunity for Bigger and Better Fees

To carry the illustration further—the same is true when the directors have been elected by the shareholders and want to begin to function. An "organization meeting" must be held. The directors must elect an entire slate of officers; adopt bylaws; adopt the corporate seal; adopt resolutions covering bank depositories and signatures on checks; determine management policies for the operation of the business; approve the form of and adopt a close corporation stockholders' purchase agreement to protect each other; etc. To assure their legality, all of these procedures should follow parliamentary procedure. Regretfully in most corporate organizations, most of these extremely important matters are adopted in a purely, simple *pro forma* manner supervised by an over-busy attorney who ignores these formalities and strives primarily to get the proper forms and papers signed "to make it all legal."

I have had dealings with many corporate officials who confide to me that they never had a regular and formal directors meeting in their entire business careers, never properly made or entertained a motion—and are totally unaware of the proper parliamentary procedure for conducting a corporate meeting or properly adopting a corporate resolution. I do not know what fees the attorneys representing these corporate executives charge for their services—but I do know that such attorneys are wasting golden opportunities for charging bigger and better fees for doing the job properly.

How Clients Use Parliamentary Procedure to Comply with the Law

An astute lawyer, in the first place, wants to protect his client by making certain that the client complies with the law. In the second place, he should take his incorporating clients through the proper ritual at least once. He should show them how to meet; how to make motions and second them; how to permit debate or discussion; how to record the vote; how to keep the minutes; etc. The attorney should then go over the bylaws with his incorporating clients item by item. Finally, he should make certain that the board, or perhaps each director, has at least one copy of a simple handbook on parliamentary law for guidance—and that they *refer to it occasionally.*

I have had many attorney friends who make a practice of giving each board of directors a copy of some recognized handbook on Parliamentary Law. This thoughtfulness on the part of the counsel cannot help but favorably impress the clients with the thoroughness and competence of their attorney. The clients are more ready and willing to accept and pay a far more substantial fee for the corporate organization, than if this important work is cranked out like a grist mill, or the assembly line in an automobile factory. I urge every attorney to try my recommended method at least once. I feel that he will never go back to the mail-order method of incorporation.

In my judgment, the low minimum fee frequently fixed by local bar associations for "incorporating a domestic corporation" is the fault of the lawyers themselves. They have failed to fulfill their full duties as officers of the court to instruct their clients in the art of conducting a simple, ordinary, corporate business meeting in accordance with standard parliamentary procedure.

A Well-Organized Corporation Can Grow into a Prosperous Client

I have frequently found that corporations which are started out correctly, i.e., with a proper introduction in parliamentary law, seem to progress better. The officers and directors have a better and more enlightened comprehension of their obligation to the stockholders. The stockholders are happier because they sense this fact and thus have greater confidence that the business of the corporation is being conducted in an orderly and legal manner—and *it usually is.*

Given a conscientious set of officers and directors and a group of happy stockholders, a sound corporation can grow into a substantial and profitable enterprise. And who are these corporate executives going to use as their counsel (hopefully on an annual retainer), or as special counsel as the need arises? It will be the lawyer who has made them feel that they were an important cog in the corporate structure of their company. If you don't believe that parliamentary law *can be* a professional asset and add substantially to your professional income, *just try it!*

Labor Union Clients Need Parliamentary Skills

In recent years, labor unions have grown to great proportions. Their memberships are usually large and their meetings well attended. The average working man knows about as much—if not more—about parliamentary procedure than the average stockholder. He is vitally interested in the election of officers and delegates; election of stewards; selection of the wage negotiations committees; consideration and approval of wage and benefit contracts, etc. All of these items, and more, make up the daily life of the average union worker.

These items are his bread and butter in the real sense. Hence, there is a thirst for knowledge in this field by most members of the unions. The union officers, and particularly the young, ambitious members who hope to become officers, find this subject fascinating. The business of representing unions can be a veritable gold mine. Extended maneuvering for increased wages and benefits; the long-drawn-out negotiations; the long-drawn-out bargaining sessions; the hearings on grievances and disputed elections; all lend themselves to extensive and profitable legal work.

Workmen's compensation cases flow from union contacts by the hundreds; perhaps thousands. Third party suits where, in addition to collecting on his compensation claim, the injured workman can also sue one or more third parties have proven to be the most lucrative of all.

Many labor lawyers also make a practice of giving the newly-elected officers of a union a complimentary copy of some recognized handbook on parliamentary law. I have had the honor of having my own "Handbook on Parliamentary Law" used in this manner on many occasions. I find that it recommends itself by its sheer simplicity. It was actually designed to take most of the red tape and hocus-pocus out of the subject. Apparently the union leaders found it helpful. They were grateful to their counsel for his thoughtfulness. Incidentally, the use of a handbook also assisted the attorney in guiding the officers and members in the proper conduct of their union meetings.

Compensation Cases Can Lead to
Profitable Third-Party Suits

This is by way of illustrating the point that workmen's compensation cases can lead to attractive third-party suits. A compensation case came into our office involving the death of a man with a wife and three children, one of whom was an infant. The death occurred only a few days before Christmas. It was caused when a back hoe got out of control coming down a steep hill made slippery by snow and ice and crashed into a pit where the men were working, killing two of them. The workmen's compensation claim at that time was only worth approximately $40,000—but a third-party claim proved to be worth more than four times that amount, or $160,000.

Investigation showed that there were four other defendants who could have been at least partly responsible and all of them were "blue chip" defendants. We thereupon sued the owner of the plant property; the owner and operator of the back hoe; the company who had allowed a heavy pipe on the boom of the back hoe; the company who had built the steep access road, etc. They all contributed to the final settlement. This was a unique case in that the depositions were so extensive and intensive that they were conducted in the library of the courthouse and took 20 full days to complete. The costs of the depositions ran to several thousands of dollars for each participant. The case was so thoroughly tried by means of these depositions that the Court-recommended negotiated settlement, just before trial, was practically inevitable.

Less than a Dozen Motions in Frequent Use

In my years of study of parliamentary law, I have found that there are less than a dozen motions in general use which cover practically every situation which might arise at a meeting. But you have to know these motions and know how to use them. To begin with, there are only four categories of motions viz: 12 Subsidary Motions, 8 Incidental Motions, 5 Privileged Motions and approximately 4 Unclassified. Each of these is important when the issue involves that particular motion; its application and its precedence or priority. But the odds are a thousand to one that more than one of these involved questions will ever arise in the ordinary meeting.

The 12 Subsidiary Motions

To begin with, the Main Motion is the important one since it sets the stage for action and sets the other motions into operation. All other motions heretofore referred to are addressed to the Main Motion. Fortunately, there can only be *one Main Motion* pending at a time. In practically all cases, it has to be seconded. Then it is considered to be "before the meeting" and "open to discussion or debate."

This is where the fun begins. The main motion may be subject to a series of subsidiary motions and as the name implies they are subordinate and must be disposed of before the main motion can be voted upon. The subsidiary motions in the inverse order of their propriety are: (1) to postpone indefinitely; (2) to amend; (3) to amend the amendment; (4) to substitute for the whole; (5) to refer to committee; (6) to postpone to a certain time; (7) to limit or extend debate; (8) the previous question and (9) to lay on the table.

The first few of these are the regular, routine, ordinary motions in constant use. As their priority increases, they become less routine, more complicated and difficult to enforce. But it is extremely unusual to have more than one or two subsidiary motions addressed to the main motion pending at any one time.

The Incidental Motions

The incidental motions are much less difficult or complex. Their main purpose is to clarify, simplify and expedite the procedure with a minimum of inconvenience to the body. As the name implies, they are actually "incidental" to the debate on the main motion before its passage or defeat. In the inverse order of their precedence, these motions are: (1) withdrawal of motion; (2) preliminary inquiry; (3) division of the question; (4) division of the vote; (5) objection to consideration of the question; (6) suspension of the rules; (7) point of order; (8) appeal from the decision of chair. Reviewing these items, you will recognize a number which are designed primarily to be helpful rather than contentious. This is true at least until you get up to the "point of order" and "appeal from the chair." Sometimes these motions can be more lively and interesting than the routine ones.

The Five Privileged Motions

The privileged motions, as their name implies, take priority or precedence over all the incidental and subsidiary motions. Fortunately they are relatively few. Their application is fairly clear and simple. Listed in the inverse order of their priority they are: (1) orders of the day; (2) question of privilege; (3) recess; (4) adjournment; and (5) fixing time to which to adjourn. Most of these are also familiar to the average lawyer and to the average person. However, their application, their priority or precedence, can be rather tricky and must be studied if they are to be mastered.

As to the unclassified motions, these usually include: (1) to take from the table; (2) to ratify; (3) to rescind; (4) to reconsider, etc.

Reviewing all of the foregoing motions, it might be feared that the subject is so complex and difficult that it should be shied away from. This would be a grievous mistake. The lawyer who knows his parliamentary law can usually achieve his will, or his way, in any gathering anywhere in the country. Parliamentary procedure is more or less uniform in its adoption throughout the 50 states.

The Nine Motions Most Frequently Made

More important still, there are relatively few motions ever brought into play. Thus, of the subsidiary motions, the "motion to amend" and "to refer to committee" are the most commonly used of all and are of low priority. "The previous question" and "to lay on the table" are the most common in use of the higher proceedings. Thus, we have only four out of 12 which are in frequent use.

As to the incidental motions, the most commonly used are the "parliamentary inquiry" and "call for the division of the question." These motions are granted automatically in most cases. "Point of order" and "appeal from the decision of the chair" are the next most commonly used and are somewhat more contentious. So, once again, we have only two motions, which might offer a little difficulty in their application, out of a total of nine.

As to the privileged motions, "the point of privilege," "recess" and "adjournment" are the most commonly used. "Privilege" and "recess" are almost universally granted and "adjournment" is usually unanimous unless the motion is made for the purpose of killing a pending motion. Thus, we have three out of five in common use.

As to the unclassified motions, they are usually treated the same as main motions and do not require extended discussion. Thus, we have a total of only nine motions which are habitually used and with which the lawyer should certainly familiarize himself. I am certain that there is more power in knowing how to use these nine motions properly and effectively than anyone could ever dream of. I have seen important legislation blocked; elections controlled; and entire programs thwarted. On the other hand, I have seen entire programs ratified and approved, sending their sponsors on to greater achievements, all through the astute, skillful use of these few rules of parliamentary procedure.

Always Arm Yourself with a Chart

I believe that the task of mastering parliamentary law can be reduced to a very simple formula for all practical purposes. The basic structures of the rules can be set forth in a single chart. Most authors include such a chart somewhere in their textbooks on the subject. I have done likewise in *Karcher's Handbook on Parliamentary Law*.

What I do is to have this chart reproduced, folded up to fit in my wallet and carry it with me at all times. It is the manner in which you utilize this chart that will make the difference between success and failure in utilizing your skills in this field. Thus, I am armed to meet any conceivable situation which might arise.

This is true whether I attend a meeting as corporate counsel of a municipality, director or counsel of a domestic corporation, a Bar Association meeting, a hostile public body whose acts I am challenging, or even a political convention. I am able to stand up with confidence and self-assurance and participate actively in any parliamentary maneuvers which may be in progress. A full text is not always required. It can be sought as an authority and referred to later. The important point is to know the proper form of the motions, their order of precedence and how to utilize them effectively. Armed with such a chart, you immediately are head and shoulders over all your contemporaries.

**A Powerful Weapon in Building a
Practice and Increasing Fees**

Don't sell Parliamentary Law short. It is a powerful weapon in the hands of an enemy. It can be of great help in the hands of a friend. It follows that any procedure carrying with it this tremendous power, carries with it corresponding responsibility. The lawyer owes it to his clients and to himself to become at least something of an expert in this field. Only in this manner can he achieve real leadership, leadership that will be recognized and rewarded. Parliamentary Law is indeed a valuable professional asset. Its proper use will build up your practice and your professional income. *This I guarantee you.*

CHART SHOWING SYNOPSIS OF RULES AND ORDER OF PRECEDENCE*

	Must be sec-onded	Can be de-bated	Can be amend-ed	Motions to which it can be applied	Motions which can be applied to it	Can be made when another has floor	Vote re-quired to carry	Can be recon-sidered
PRIVILEGED MOTIONS								
To fix time to adjourn to	Yes	No[1]	Yes	None	To Amend	No	Majority	Yes
To adjourn	Yes	No	No	None	None	No	Majority	No
To recess	Yes	No[1]	Yes	None	None[2]	No	Majority	No
Raising question of privilege[25]	No	No[3]	No	None	No Limit[28]	Yes	Majority	No
Call for orders of the day[6,26]	No	No	No	None	Usually None[5]	Yes	None[4]	No
INCIDENTAL MOTIONS								
Appeal from decision of Chair	Yes	Yes	No	No Limit[28]	To Table[7] To Reconsider	Yes	Majority	Yes
Point of order	No	No	No	No Limit[28]	None[9]	Yes	None	No
Suspension of rules	Yes	No	No	No Limit[10,28]	None	None	2/3	No
Objection to consideration of question	No	No	No	All Main[12]	To Reconsider[11]	Yes	2/3	Yes[11]
Division of vote or assembly	No	No	No	No Limit[13,28]	None	Yes	None[14]	No
Division of question	Yes[15]	No	Yes	All Main & Amendments	Amend	No[15]	None[14]	No
Parliamentary and other inquiries	No	No	No	No Limit[28]	None	Yes	None[14]	No
Leave to withdraw motion	No	No	No	No Limit[28]	To Reconsider	No	Majority	Yes[16]
SUBSIDIARY MOTIONS								
To lay on the table	Yes	No	No	All Main[17]	None	No	Majority	No
The previous question	Yes	No	No	No Limit[19,23]	To Reconsider	No	2/3	Yes[18]
To limit (or extend) debate	Yes	No	Yes	No Limit[20,28]	To Amend To Reconsider	No	2/3	Yes

Motion				Applicable to	Limit of Debate		Vote	
To postpone to certain time	Yes	Yes	Yes	All Main & Subord. Appeals	(See [24])	No	Majority	Yes
To refer to committee	Yes	Yes	Yes	All Main	(See[24])	No	Majority	Yes[21]
Amendment to amendment	Yes	Yes[22]	No	To Amendment of 1st degree	(See[27])	No	Majority	Yes
To amend	Yes	Yes[22]	Yes	All Main	(See[24])	No	Majority	Yes
To postpone indefinitely	Yes	Yes	No	All Main — Question of Privilege and Orders of Day	(See[27])	No	Majority	See[28]
ALL MAIN MOTIONS	Yes	Yes	Yes	None	No Limit	No	Majority	Yes

1. Debatable if no other motion is pending.
2. Except as to period of time.
3. When motion re Privilege is made and stated, it is to be treated as a Main motion.
4. 2/3 vote to postpone special order.
5. Except to suspend, change or postpone orders.
6. When motion is to fix orders of the day, it is to be treated as Main motion.
7. Yields to points of orders and privileged motions.
8. When Chair is in doubt and majority vote required.
9. Yields to Privileged motions and to Table.
10. If no motion pending or is relevant to pending motion.
11. Negative vote only can be reconsidered.
12. Provided made before debate is started.
13. Provided vote is by Viva Voce or show of hands.
14. Formal vote usually not required.
15. Many groups provide for division of complicated questions on demand of any member.
16. Affirmative vote cannot be reconsidered.
17. Also to questions of privilege, appeal and reconsider in certain cases.
18. Unless a vote has been taken under it.
19. Provided question is amendable or debatable.
20. Provided question is debatable.
21. Unless committee has begun to act on matter.
22. Unless motion to which it is applied is undebatable.
23. A negative vote cannot be reconsidered.
24. To amend, to reconsider, previous question, limit or extend debate.
25. Question of Privilege (when made and stated) is treated as Main and not Privileged Motion.
26. Fixing or Approving Orders of the Day treated as a Main and not Privileged Motion.
27. To reconsider, previous question, limit or extend debate.
28. For all Practical Purposes.

*Copyrighted and used by permission of the Michie Co., Charlottesville, Virginia.

Chapter 17

A SPECIAL WORD TO

THE YOUNGER LAWYER*

Young Lawyer Needs This Book–Only More So . . . Profit by the Mistakes of Others . . . Associate–Partner or Sole Practitioner? . . . Some Advantages of Delaying Solo Practice . . . Will You Win a Partnership? . . . Let a Sole Practitioner Find His "Acres of Diamonds" . . . Should Young Lawyers Join Forces as Partners? . . . Some Suggestions on Solo Practice . . . Avoid Establishing Office in Home . . . Main Theme–the Proper Desk-Side Manner . . . Avoid Excessive Hirsute Adornments . . . Show Empathy with and Sympathy for the Client . . . Don't Play Hard to Get via Phone . . . Does Single Scrawled Hieroglyphic Suffice as a Signature? . . . Secretary's Signature and Rubber Stamps . . . Love Work–Work Hard . . . Continued Legal Education Mandatory . . . A Lawyer's Letter to His Lawyer Son and Daughter . . . Rule I–Be Healthy . . . Rule II–Be Studious . . . Rule III–Be Hard-Working . . . Rule IV–Be Friendly . . . Rule V–Be Dedicated . . . Rule VI–Be Public-Spirited . . . Rule VII–Be Reasonable . . . Rule VIII–Be Generous . . . Rule IX–Be Honest . . . Rule X–Be Happy

Young Lawyer Needs This Book—Only More So

This book has been written for the benefit of the average lawyer, irrespective of age, education, location, experience or other circumstances. If this

---

*Portions of this chapter were previously published in the *New Jersey State Bar Journal* and are used here with the permission of the copyright owner.

is true, you may wonder why there is any need for this special chapter. The answer is that the young lawyer needs all of the guidance, advice and assistance that the average practicing lawyer does—*only more so*. Throughout my life I have felt a special interest in, and concern and sympathy for, the neophyte lawyer. This may be as a result of the keen recollection I have of the obstacles and problems I had to contend with and overcome myself. Or perhaps it may be due to the fact that I have a son and daughter of my own who are now practicing attorneys. In any event, I have spoken to many young lawyers and have written a number of articles on the subject. These include such articles as "A Lawyer's Advice to His Children" in the *New Jersey State Bar Journal*; "Ten Rules for the Young Lawyer in Developing a Successful Practice" in the *Practical Lawyer*; "Advice to Young Lawyers in Becoming a Trial Lawyer" in the *American Bar Association Journal*, and many others. Hence, this chapter may very well be a composite or synthesis of all of these various other articles.

Profit by the Mistakes of Others

Some wit has said that a foolish man profits by his own mistakes, but a wise man profits by the mistakes of others. The principal thrust of this book has been to help all lawyers by charting a course which will help them avoid the shoals and rocks upon which the professional careers of some of their predecessors may have foundered. Many times I have looked back on my own career in shock and amazement at how ill-prepared or unprepared I was for meeting and solving many of my own personal problems, much less the problems of the clients who placed the solution of their larger and manifold problems in my lap. Apparently they did so with absolute trust and confidence in me and in my capability to solve them with ease and dispatch.

Associate—Partner or Sole Practitioner?

The lawyer just admitted to practice has many decisions to make which may advance or retard his ultimate success. These include the decision on whether he is to seek employment or association with some lawyer or law firm; or strike out for himself and try solo practicing—or seeking a partnership with some other practicing attorney. There are some good and bad features in all of these which require careful study and evaluation. The easiest way of launching your career is to spend a year or two as an associate or employee with some well-established law firm with a general and well-diversified practice. If you decide to follow this course, I would suggest that you try to avoid being tied down to one field. Be quick to volunteer to aid in the handling of any and every matter that comes into the office. Knowledge that there are other experienced lawyers in the office who will guide you and review your final work product, should and will give you a degree of confidence you would otherwise lack if you were practicing alone.

Some Advantages of Delaying Solo Practice

If you are reasonably diligent and reasonably observant, in the course of a year or two you should have learned the basic rules for conducting a law office on a business-like basis, and how to handle various types of legal matters in such a manner as to produce a reasonable profit for the office, without the necessity of charging exorbitant fees. In previous chapters, the methods of determining what is a reasonable fee in specific cases has been fully developed. Always bear in mind that you must produce and complete, or at least complete through your own efforts and ability, legal work assigned to you which will produce fees for the firm amounting to approximately twice the compensation you are paid. This is so because it has been definitely established that a new lawyer in an office generates approximately as much overhead expense as his own salary and sometimes more.

Will You Win a Partnership?

How effective you are in meeting this test will go a long way toward satisfying the attorney you are working for, and thus lead to early recognition, periodic increases in salary or indications that you may eventually be considered for a partnership. I urge all newly admitted attorneys to read and study Elbert Hubbard's classic "A Message to Garcia" and emulate the example set by the indomitable messenger in every task assigned to you. If you do so, it will guarantee you not only recognition and advancement, but increased financial rewards as well. Eventually you will realize that the real rewards which the law offers can only be achieved as a partner or a sole practitioner, regardless of the size of the salary or other fringe benefits employment may offer.

Let a Sole Practitioner Find His "Acres of Diamonds"

When I first commenced the practice of law, I was actually frightened at the prospects of starting out as a solo practitioner. But I was left no other choice. The great Depression was at our doorstep. No openings were available in any of the law offices at any salary. My mentor or preceptor, in whose office I had served a rather negative and uninspiring clerkship, advised me, "You will soon find out if you are going to be a success or a failure." To change the metaphor somewhat, this was a plain case of being thrown overboard and left to either sink or swim. Fortunately, I made it but it wasn't exactly easy. To bolster my own courage when my spirits were low, I read and reread Russell Conwell's "Acres of Diamonds" until I could recite it almost by heart.

The particular quote in this famous lecture, which I returned to again and again, is:

> "If you wish to be great, you must begin *where* you are and with *what* you are *now*! He who can give to his city any blessing, he who can be a good citizen while he lives there . . . whatever be his life, he who would be great anywhere, must *first* be great in his home community. *Right here. Right now.*"

Try this on yourself sometime and see how it can help work miracles.

Should Young Lawyers Join Forces as Partners?

Lately there seems to be an inclination on the part of some new practitioners to join one or more other young attorneys in starting a partnership of their own, and striking out together to find fame and fortune in the field of law. This procedure has a number of things to commend it to you for consideration: (a) it divides the cost of rent, secretarial help, library, etc.; (b) if one, or more, of the parties has had some specialized training in one field of law, he will bring this added knowledge and acumen into the firm and thus share it with the other partners. It seems to add something to the prestige of the attorney to be listed wtih a firm—no matter how small it may be or how lacking in experience and reputation it may be.

Some Suggestions on Solo Practice

If you decide to try practicing alone, as most attorneys apparently eventually do, in my judgment, your own town or city is the best locale in which to start. Your roots are there. Your family and friends are there. You may count on their loyalty and support at least until you have become eminent and successful. By that time they will probably be helping out some other struggling attorney and you may very well be able to and willing to do likewise. The ancient adage that "All the world loves a lover" sometimes can be rephrased to read "Everyone loves a *young* lawyer."

I have seen this sentiment put into action countless times. Even the veteran lawyer in court will hesitate to try to over-reach his young opponent. If any attempts are made to do so, the judge first, and then the jury finally will demonstrate sympathy for the young lawyer and a desire to give him a helping hand, as he climbs the ladder to scale the heights to professional proficiency and financial success.

Avoid Establishing Office in Home

Here are a few more preliminary admonitions to the young lawyer. Do not open your office in your home, unless it happens to be located in, or immediately adjacent to, the local business district. The public will sense that you do not have much confidence in yourself—so rent an office of your own separate from your residence. Try to get the right kind of secretary, who not only respects you, but is somehow able to pass on and inspire that same respect in your clients, as she ushers them into your private office. The more respect a client has for you, the more willing he is to pay you an adequate fee.

Main Theme—The Proper Desk-Side Manner

Also be careful that your office help as well as you yourself maintain and exhibit the proper "desk-side manner." When a person comes to a lawyer's office, he is usually in trouble—sometimes in plenty of trouble. Nothing is more disconcerting and disheartening to a prospective client than to have the girl in the reception room ignore his entrance entirely or to get interested in a file or telephone call or actually turn her back on the client to perform some type of errand. She may think that this is impressing the client with how busy the office is. Believe me when I tell you—he won't be. Therefore, greet the client with a friendly and reassuring smile. Inquire solicitously as to the purpose of his visit. Make him comfortable while he waits for a few minutes or so.

When he is ushered into the attorney's office, it is then the attorney's task to demonstrate his best desk-side manner. Hopefully, the attorney will be neatly dressed in a conventional business suit, so that the client does not feel that he may lose the attorney's interest to some delayed golf game or tennis match.

Avoid Excessive Hirsute Adornments

In these days of hirsute facial adornments, it is also to be hoped that if the attorney is not clean-shaven, that at least a major portion of his face is visible, and he does not look as if his beard, mustache and sideburns were made up for him as a contestant in a "Gay Nineties Production" or for a part in a "Barber Shop Quartet Contest." His hair may, of course, be reasonably long to conform to present customs, provided it is well-combed and well-groomed, so that it has the appearance of being "molded or sculped," rather than indicating that the individual is somewhat eccentric.

Show Empathy with and Sympathy for the Client

Listen to the client's story attentively. Do not consult files or read correspondence or permit extended interruptions of any kind. Let the client know that he not only has your undivided attention but your empathy and sympathy as well. However, it is not right or wise to have your secretary block all incoming phone calls (assuming that there are some), by saying "Sorry, he is in conference." Even older and successful attorneys do not use this blunt technique. If the attorney is actually tied up at a title closing or in taking a deposition, that is a legitimate excuse in itself. Or perhaps the attorney is on a long-distance phone call—this of course is a legitimate excuse for not accepting the incoming call immediately. In any event, it is better if the secretary not only expresses her regret, but assures the person calling that she will have the attorney call him back just as soon as he is free.

Don't Play Hard to Get via Phone

Incidentally, some of the most prominent and successful attorneys are much easier to reach than some newly-admitted attorneys are who hope to give the impression that they are much busier than they really are. You can usually get through to former Senator John E. Toolan much more quickly than you can get through to Joe Doakes, Esq. I sometimes put my own phone calls through when all the girls are tied up and behind in their work. Occasionally, I would phone a prominent and extremely successful defense lawyer in an adjoining city. Sometimes he would answer the phone directly. It was such a pleasure that my respect for that man went up immediately. I said, "George, how come you are so democratic as to be answering your own phone? Don't tell me you have fallen upon hard times?" He laughed and said, No, Joe, I do this often. It helps hold down my ego. I hear the phone ring, and I know the chances are 10 to 1 that it is some poor fellow who wants to talk to me. Why should I make it harder for him?"

Does Single Scrawled Hieroglyphic Suffice as a Signature?

While I am on the subject of law office etiquette or practice, let me say a word or two on signatures to letters sent out by lawyers. They seem to be fairly legible when the young lawyer first starts out to practice. He seems happy and pleased to be able to project his own name in ink. However, within a few months it sometimes becomes an illegible scrawl, but at least the separation of the first name and the last name by some initial is still discernible. But it seems that after he has practiced a year or so the alleged signature in many cases becomes a mere scrawl which looks somewhat like a Chinese or Egyptian hieroglyphic. I have noticed some recently where barely the first initial of the first name is indicated. Even that tapers off into a faint line that looks as if it were intended to illustrate and perhaps emphasize that the attorney signing same was just taking off by jet plane to keep a professional appointment which was far more important than reading, much less signing, the letter addressed to me.

Believe me when I tell you that this type of signature is utterly worthless if it is intended to impress laymen or other lawyers with the importance of the signer. It has the opposite effect on all persons with normal reactions. It is perfectly legitimate to have a distinctive signature which would be hard to forge. John Hancock had such a signature when he appended it to the Declaration of Independence, but it was still very legible. Come to think of it—every signature on that immortal document was written in a legible handwriting. I have what I think is a very distinctive signature, but I am proud of it. Hence, it is always legible and I have signed as many as 500 letters at one sitting in emergencies. I have always felt that a dignified, distinct and *legible* signature always adds to the style of a professional letter.

Secretary's Signature and Rubber Stamps

It seems to me that it is much better to let a secretary sign your name in ink after you have checked the letter and added a simple check mark or some other symbol to indicate that you have checked and approved it and authorized your signature to be annexed to it. If worst comes to worst, let your secretary use a rubber stamp facsimile of your signature. But she will use insufficient ink on it and stamp it angularly and thus add confirmation to the fact that it is only a "rubber stamp signature."

Love Work—Work Hard

While you may feel that many of these admonitions cover trifles only, I can only politely disagree with you. As I have said before in this volume, recalling the ancient aphorism, "Trifles make perfection—but perfection is no trifle." In law there are no such things as trifles or "small" things *per se*. But of course these small things should not distract you from the main thrust of this book which is to emphasize that if you wish for success, financial as well as professional, it will depend in large measure on learning to love work and work hard —and welcome it, and to continue your legal education in every avenue available—every day of your life.

Continued Legal Education Mandatory

Incidentally, the courts and the bar associations across the nation are now giving serious consideration to making continued legal education mandatory under the threat of having all attorneys take new Bar Examinations periodically, if they wish to retain the right to practice law. So you may very well get used to the idea and learn to enjoy it before it becomes mandatory.

A Lawyer's Letter to His Lawyer Son and Daughter

I once wrote a message to my son and daughter as they were starting out in the practice of law. It was published in the New Jersey State Bar Journal and reprinted widely in other Bar Journals throughout the nation. I have reviewed it and attempted to improve upon it by means of either deletions or additions or substitutions. I could not do it. I found that I could not improve upon it. I can not state or restate the ten points more succinctly, more clearly or more sincerely. Here they are for your personal help and guidance.

RULE I—BE HEALTHY

Health is important in any field of human endeavor. Law is no exception. You may have heard of the handicapped lawyer who nevertheless was a success. This is the exception, not the rule. The practice of law can be grueling. It takes reasonably good health to keep up the pace. You cannot do your best if you are ill. Therefore, treasure your health. Take stock of your strengths and weaknesses. Buttress yourself against these weaknesses by moderation in everything—particularly tobacco and alcohol. Don't worry about a "nervous breakdown" from overwork. There is no such malady if the work is done right and under the proper rules.

RULE II—BE STUDIOUS

When you receive your license to practice law—please don't think that your legal education is complete. It is only beginning. Law is a very broad subject. No lawyer, no matter how studious he may be, can hope to master all that is to be known in even one branch of the law. Even the specialist whose practice is limited to one field must keep abreast of the statutes and current decisions which are constantly being enacted or decided. Hence your success will depend in large measure on keeping abreast of the law. To do so you must be studious.

RULE III—BE HARD-WORKING

The practice of law is not a profession which may be pursued in a desultory fashion. Since you are in effect your own boss, it requires rigorous self-discipline. You cannot go to the office when you choose—see only the clients you want to see—handle only the cases that suit your taste—and still be a genuine success. The client who comes in with a good case is usually one whom you have served—and served satisfactorily—in a minor case. Unless you are willing to dedicate yourself to hard work, law is not the profession for you. Take up something else.

RULE IV—BE FRIENDLY

By that I mean be democratic. Remember Kipling's trenchant line: ". . . if you can walk with kings—nor lose the common touch." Develop the faculty of being able to deal with people in every walk of life—from prince to pauper—from aristocrat to peasant. They are all equal under the law—and they are all potential clients. While I always was glad to welcome a substantial estate to the office or a large corporate matter, the bread and butter business usually comes from the rank and file clients. Besides, not infrequently, these same "poor" clients may bring in some exceptionally worthwhile negligence claim. This has been my experience many times over. And don't look down on negligence cases. It is my view that more leaders of the Bar should take a greater interest in this field of the law.

RULE V—BE DEDICATED

Law is a profession in which you cannot be passive. The adversary system inspires dedication to the cause you espouse. But first it would be wise to make sure that the cause is a just one. Dedication to an unjust cause—or to one which does not promote public welfare, or is against public policy generally—is misplaced dedication. First be sure you are right—or rather that your cause is right—and then give that cause all of the dedication and devotion of which you are capable. If you have no faith in the claim, disclose this fact to your client at once and do not accept the case. There are too many worthy causes crying for an able advocate for you to waste your time on an unworthy cause.

RULE VI—BE PUBLIC-SPIRITED

Every member of the Bar becomes an Officer of the Court the day he is sworn in. As such he is an essential cog in the administration of justice. While this branch of government is important, so are the others. The lawyer by virtue of his education, training and prestige owes a duty of leadership in his community. Hence he should be public-spirited—willing to contribute his time and talent and energies on public matters which will promote the public good.

This can be done in many ways: running for election to office itself; serving as Counsel to elected Boards, Bodies or Officers; or as Counsel to reform elements when conditions require it. He should gladly contribute these services without thought of profit. Of course he cannot set himself up as a charitable institution and sacrifice a large proportion of his time *gratis*. But he can and should contribute a fair portion of his time, effort and energy to such worthy causes *gratis*—and as much more as the gravity of the situation requires—at cost or at "break-even" fees. I have found that you get back what you give out—and usually in the same proportion.

In my own case, instead of moving to a larger city to improve my fortune through larger fees, I stayed in my own small hometown, and built up around me. It is one of the most genuine gratifications that the practice of law lends itself to this type of endeavor.

RULE VII—BE REASONABLE

Never over-reach yourself in seeking a fee. It may be a key to failure rather than to success. Never speculate on "how much the traffic will bear"—and charge accordingly. If you do so, you are inviting trouble. You cannot generate respect for yourself or the profession in this manner. If a negligence case is handled by you on a contingency basis and the fee you charge is out of proportion to what the claimant receives, you are courting trouble. If a client wonders whose accident it was—yours or his—you have definitely violated this rule.

Be reasonable in all your charges. Do not over-estimate them. By the same token do not under-estimate them. The size of the fee must bear some logical and clearly discernible relationship not only to the time and effort expended, the novelty of the points of law involved and the size of the subject matter—*but to the results you have obtained for your client*. The sharp issue always must be—how much good have you really done for your client—and what is it reasonably worth? If you can answer these questions fairly and frankly, you will have few arguments with clients about fees. You will have been reasonable.

RULE VIII—BE GENEROUS

There are times when your fee may have to be substantially less than the value of the work involved. There may be some cases where no fee at all should be charged. In such cases do the work as devotedly and assiduously and as graciously and good-naturedly as if you were being well-paid for it. This applies not only to cases where you are assigned to defend some indigent person accused of crime, but to many other situations as well. For instance, if a widow with a large family and a small estate comes in and asks you to help her, do it!—even if you can charge her only half the normal fee. If the janitress in your office building asks you to prepare her will to dispose of all her worldly possessions, don't charge her a week's salary for the instrument—even if the minimum Bar Association rates indicate such a fee as being fair and reasonable. Pat her on the back and say: "I don't need this fee. There is no charge." You'll get more self-satisfaction out of this than from any fee you could collect.

Generosity is a cardinal virtue. In law it pays large dividends in the knowledge that you've done someone a good turn, in self-satisfaction and sometimes in much more practical ways. Always be generous in your private life and in the profession of law—even with your adversary. Life is too short to be small or mean in any matter.

RULE IX—BE HONEST

While I have listed this rule near the end—it is probably the one basic and most important rule of all. Don't deviate from it—or you will regret it all your life. There is no profession where the opportunity and temptation for dishonesty are greater. I have always taken a keen personal pride in the strength of character it takes to ignore these opportunities and resist these temptations. It is generally recognized that these opportunities and temptations increase in direct proportion to your activities in public office—whether the same be appointive or elective.

All such overtures are to be strongly resisted. Permit yourself to succumb once to these temptations and you are forever afterwards at the mercy of your clients. Moreover, you will probably lose such dangerous clients anyway. They will know that you cannot be trusted.

Sooner or later the truth always comes out. If you have been absolutely honest and frank and aboveboard in all your professional dealings, you will fear no man, you will maintain your own self-respect, and you will be able to sleep soundly at night. Surely these are rewards worth seeking. Hence, absolute honesty is the only policy for a lawyer to pursue in seeking real and genuine success.

RULE X—BE HAPPY

I saved this one for the last because I liked it the best. Of what possible value are all other attributes, if you are not happy? Life is a constant search for happiness. It is what we all seek. Success in your chosen profession will be very helpful in achieving happiness. From a strictly material standpoint, success will also bring you the pecuniary rewards which you justly deserve from your observance of these rules. Once you obtain all of the money you need to satisfy your own needs and those of your family, money will mean—or should mean—less and less to you. Hence you will have more time to devote to your home and family and friends; to literature and the arts and public affairs; and to all those pursuits which are or should be the natural inclinations of the cultured man and woman. You will be able to achieve happiness not only in your work but in your leisure as well. I say in your work because work is never burdensome—unless you would rather be doing something else. Sir Winston Churchill speaks of "Fortune's favored people." For them, says he, "the working hours are never long enough. Each day is a holiday—and ordinary holidays, when they come, are grudged as enforced interruptions in an absorbing vocation." I can truthfully say that this has been my experience in life. I have enjoyed the hours, the days and the years I have spent in the practice of law. I have been happy. And you will be too—if you follow these ten simple rules.

Chapter 18

HOW TO SET THE GOAL—
AND ACHIEVE IT!

You Are Greater than You Think . . . "We Grow Great by Dreams"—PLUS! . . . Your Legal Training Is Worth Millions . . . The Brain—Inexhaustible Font of Treasure . . . Do You Come Anywhere Near Exhausting Your Resources? . . . "Who Is the Wise Man?" Asks the Talmud . . . Learn to Like Reading—and to Love Study . . . Recognize Opportunity When It Comes . . . Every Lawyer Must Also Be a Salesman . . . Work —the Magic Ingredient of Success . . . Work Can Really Be Play—or Even a Religion . . . Your Work Can Constitute a Rewarding Challenge . . . Find the Need—and Fill It . . . Be Frugal with Your Time . . . Perseverance as an Asset . . . Don't Coast When You Reach the Goal . . . The Futility of Money Alone . . . Find Out How to Serve—for a Fee . . . Service and Achievement Bring Rich Rewards Automatically

You Are Greater than You Think

It is well to follow the admonition of the famous evangelist, Norman Vincent Peale. His constant admonition is to "Never forget this basic fact about yourself—you are greater and finer than you think!" He is, of course, addressing himself to the spiritual side of man. But this fact is equally true and useful in the social, political and economic fields as well. I do not mean to suggest that the attorney should merely throw out his chest and proclaim his superiority without any basis to support it. This would only prove futile and fatal in his efforts to achieve the $100,000 per annum mark. He must work to make himself worthy of public confidence and approbation by developing the latent powers within him and putting them to practical, constructive, worthwhile use.

"We Grow Great by Dreams"—PLUS!

"We grow great by dreams—all great men are dreamers—they see things in the soft haze of a Spring day or in the red fire of a long Winter evening."—says Woodrow Wilson. This is fine. There is never any objection to seeing the pot of gold at the rainbow's end. The point to bear in mind is that you do not realize these dreams or reach this pot of gold except through hard work. Few men in public life worked harder than Wilson. He had dreams indeed but he backed them up with the fruits of a fine, highly trained and organized mind plus plenty of hard work.

And don't be concerned about the possibility of failure in your endeavors. Some failures are bound to beset you. They are a normal incident of life. No one is a failure unless and until he gives up hope and gives up trying. Just remember that as Martin Vantree has so well said, "It is better to aim high and *miss* than to aim low and *hit*."

Your Legal Training Is Worth Millions

Some years ago we used to be reminded of the fact that our entire body was made up of a few chemicals having a market value of less than $1.00. Today it might be $2.00 or even $3.00 but the point of the message is still appropriate. Yet properly used that body can produce $100,000 per annum for you—and without too much difficulty. You have the essential educational background—the only test is how you put it to use—or if you ever really do put it to use.

We all know from our own knowledge, the economic value of an education. Throughout life a high school education should have a minimum economic value, over those who do not possess it of $200,000 to $500,000. A college education should have an economic value of $1,000,000 and up. A post-graduate education should have a minimum value of several million dollars if properly used. In fact, the sky is the limit in today's market place. As a matter of fact even this limitation should not be placed upon it today. The astronauts have demolished this old saw by their exploits.

The Brain—Inexhaustible Font of Treasure

But as Professor William James of Harvard said "Compared with what we ought to be, we are only half awake—we are making use of only a small part of our physical and mental resources." And this is particularly true of our mental resources. At least you have heard it said many times, and medical records prove it, that any part of the body which is not used regularly as nature intended, tends to atrophy.

If this is true of the body and its members, it is probably equally true of the brain. It may seem strange, but it is nevertheless true, that the brain is an inexhaustible source of strength, power, ideas, production. The more gold you mine from it, the more there remains. Up to very near the end of life when degeneration of the blood vessels sets in and senility approaches, the human brain remains practically an inexhaustible source of precious, priceless thoughts and ideas. These faculties seem to actually multiply with use. So the lesson is obvious—use them.

Do You Come Anywhere Near Exhausting
Your Resources?

It was Admiral Richard E. Byrd who observed that "Few men during their lifetime come anywhere near exhausting the resources dwelling within them. There are deep wells of strength in all of us that we never use!" He was undoubtedly thinking of physical and perhaps spiritual resources as he reviewed the vast, silent, awesome expanses of the frozen Arctic regions he had explored. But in like manner these same mental resources lie more or less dormant in the average lawyer as he sits behind his desk asking himself the question "Can I increase my income to $100,000 per annum?" The answer is a definite, positive, reassuring *yes*.

"Who Is the Wise Man?" Asks the Talmud

Nothing worthwhile is ever achieved without adequate preparation. This does not apply merely to an isolated case pending in the office. It applies to every worthwhile endeavor in life. The Talmud poses the question "Who is the wise man?" It proceeds to answer the question "He who learns from all men." You don't learn much by accident or by osmosis. The learning process must be deliberate, planned, continuous. It will not come to you automatically or by inspiration. Lloyd George clinched the point when he said "The shortest road to inspiration—is preparation." In other words inspiration flows from preparation. It is not a substitute for it.

Learn to Like Reading—and to Love Study

Hence, one of the first rules of preparation is to cultivate a liking for reading and a veritable love for study. Become an omnivorous reader. Don't limit your study to law. Study everything from nature in your backyard to the human drives motivating your children or the individual man you meet on the street.

Endowed with this appreciation of reading and love of learning I can guarantee you several important things, viz: You will never be lonesome; never be bored; never be out-classed by your contemporaries—and you will never want for a substantial income. But I can only give you this assurance if you have applied what you have read and what you have learned to the solution of the problems that have crossed your desk as a practicing lawyer.

Recognize Opportunity When It Comes

Never count on sheer luck. Luck is a vague, ephemeral, illusory thing. It is what you may derisively attribute as the basic cause of the success of some of your competitors. Actually as E. G. Leterman puts it "Luck is what happens when preparation meets opportunity." So first you must have the preparation to be ready for the opportunity. And one of the magic things about preparation is that it enables you to recognize opportunity when it presents itself. Without this foundation and background of preparation, the average man frequently does not recognize a golden opportunity when it is actually knocking on his door. He views it only as another unwelcome and unnecessary salesman intruding upon his somnambulant lethargy.

Every Lawyer Must Also Be a Salesman

And speaking of a salesman, a lawyer should always bear in mind that he too is a salesman of sorts. Hence his reading and studying should also embrace such subjects as salesmanship; advertising; layout; art; publishing; the media generally and all such related fields.

All of this basic material can be effectively used or adapted in the practice of law. This would not, of course, be directly in the field of advertising or publication itself, but the principles of capturing the imagination of the public; of winning their confidence; of satisfying their wants; earning their approbation (and their compensation)—are all extremely helpful.

Charles Schwab once observed "We are all salesmen everyday of our lives. We are selling our ideas, our plans, our energies, our enthusiasms to those we come in contact with." How true this is so far as the lawyer is concerned! He is selling himself to the public first; next to his client; next to the judge and perhaps finally to the jury. If he is not selling himself finally to the 12 stalwarts sitting in the jury box, then at least figuratively he is selling himself to the jury of public opinion. The average lawyer's income will keep pace and grow in direct proportion to his capacity for salesmanship in the areas indicated.

Work—the Magic Ingredient of Success

Next to preparation for the day when the opportunity arrives, and the perception to recognize the opportunity when it does present itself, there is a further essential ingredient to success, i.e., *work*. The sweet victory of success is already half won when you have acquired not only the *habit* of work, but *love* for the work you are doing. If a lawyer loves his work (aside from any question of success or compensation), the gods have blessed him indeed.

There has been a growing tendency in recent years to denigrate work as though it were something to be sneered at or downgraded or avoided. But this merely shows a false sense of values. It was Joseph Conrad who observed that "Man is a worker. If he is not that—he is nothing." And Vauvenargues expressed the same thought when he said "The fruit derived from labor is the sweetest of all pleasure."

I can see a five-day week at least for the office staff and perhaps eventually a four-day week. But I cannot see closing a professional office on Wednesday as well or having it run by the staff while the boss plays golf. I once had a client who retired at age 40. He insisted on boasting of the fact that he did not work—at anything. It is difficult to envision a more futile, empty or frustrating way of life unless you are unfortunate enough to be born just plain lazy. It was Nicolas Murray Butler who said "I am more interested in the 40-hour day than the 40-hour week."

Work Can Really Be Play—or Even a Religion

A lawyer who loves his work does not consider his effort as work. J. H. Patterson put it this way "It is only those who do not *know how to work* that do not love it. To those who do it is better than play—it is religion." This is the attitude I long ago developed toward my own work. I can enjoy a holiday, a long weekend or an occasional vacation. but when these are over, I return to the busy humming office without regrets. In fact I look forward to each Monday morning as a new and thrilling experience. Every letter that comes in may bring with it a check covering a substantial verdict or settlement. Each phone call has great possibilities. One of them may be the forerunner of a new, important, challenging and profitable matter.

Your Work Can Constitute a Rewarding Challenge

In fact every matter that crosses my desk brings with it a certain degree of satisfaction. Each of these matters constitutes a problem—or challenge. The ability to meet that challenge—to solve that problem—makes life worth living. And this is true, irrespective of the monetary rewards which may flow from this effort. My office has prospered on "tough" cases. We love them.

Try to adopt this attitude toward your work. If you do, then the distant clatter of the battery of electric typewriters will sound like music to your ears. And when 5:00 p.m. comes and the office staff departs, you will be able to lean back in your chair and review the day's happenings in retrospect with pride and satisfaction, in the fact that you are playing a live and vital and telling part in the happenings about you, which we usually refer to euphoniously as "the passing scene."

It was the much-quoted Charles A. Schwab again who said "The man who does not work for the love of work—but only for money—is not likely to make money nor to find much fun in life either." To this I say—Amen!

Find the Need—and Fill It

A lawyer has really reached success when he has recognized the crying need for his services—and has proceeded to fill that need to the best of his skill and competence. The fact that he is well paid for it should be purely secondary. In other words, progress and success depend upon growth—growth and service to your community, to society and to your fellow man. Not just some service or any service—but essential, worthwhile, outstanding service rendered by you to the best of your ability and capacity. All of this can be accomplished only by work. So work must be recognized as a blessing rather than a curse. Adopt this attitude and you are well on your way to success.

Be Frugal with Your Time

And the amount of work you can produce depends in the first instance on the element of time. Lord Chesterfield put it well when he said "Know the true value of time. Snatch, seize, use, enjoy every moment of it. No idleness, no laziness, no procrastination. Never put off until tomorrow what you can do today." Now this may sound like heresy coming from one lawyer to another but it is an admonition which is long overdue. Failure to observe this very advice is one of the underlying reasons for many lawyers not reaching the goal of $100,000 per annum. Always bear in mind this simple fact that irrespective of how rich or poor you may be, we are all allotted only an equal amount of time. There is just so much of it—and no more. Hence, the wise man will respect it, conserve it and use it sparingly.

Perseverance as an Asset

And while I am on the subject, let me put in a word for perseverance. You may be surprised to know that a poet, of all persons, with the background of Longfellow should have made this observation on the subject: "Perseverance is the greatest element of success. If you only knock long enough and loud enough at the gate, you are sure to wake up somebody." This is good sound logic coming from an eminent source. He is not advising that you sit inside and wait for opportunity to come knocking on your door. His advice is to go out and hammer at the other fellow's gate—long and loud—until you have awakened someone.

Don't Coast When You Reach the Goal

The final admonition—when you have eventually reached the much sought for goal of $100,000—don't rest on your laurels. The moment you begin to relax, you will begin to decline. If you entertain the idea that having reached the goal you have reached perfection, you are wrong. Perfection is unattainable. We may strive for it mightily, but we can never achieve it. Hence, when your income reaches the bench mark set, you must continue with the same effort, energy and enterprise as you did before reaching the goal. If you fail to do this, you will automatically find yourself slipping below it. Goals are not self-sustaining or self-perpetuating. Keep up the tempo of your race. The rewards are sweet and so is the race.

The Futility of Money Alone

Some people make the mistake of thinking they have made a success of life when all they have really done is just made a lot of money. There is a great deal of difference indeed. As evidence of the ultimate futility of garnering money alone, we have only to remember the inevitable approach of the income tax collector and the undertaker. You not only cannot take it with you, you cannot hold on to it here, very long, either.

Find Out How to Serve—for a Fee

Dr. Albert Schweitzer summed it up neatly when he said "The one thing I know—'The only ones among you who will really be happy are those who will have sought—and *have found how to serve*''.'' And we don't all have to be Albert Schweitzers, or go to Africa, or live like hermits in order to serve the poor and the less fortunate than ourselves. There are almost as many opportunities for service to our fellow man, *right on Main Street*. And these people do not want you to serve for nothing. Most of them are ready, *willing and able to pay you handsomely*. In fact, you can fix your own price and your own terms. All they want of you is your dedication, your devotion to their cause—and the expenditure of at least some of your time and energy in solving their problems, and in protecting their rights. And, incidentally, this is some of the time which you might otherwise waste or fritter away on some less worthy cause.

Service and Achievement Bring Rich Rewards Automatically

So in conclusion I would like to say that if you want success, if you want a happy well-balanced life—as well as the $100,000 per annum income —money should not be the only objective sought. Money should be the by-product of a more worthy and worthwhile objective.

And money, like happiness, is frequently achieved in much the same manner. Seek ways and means of rendering service to those who need it. Not just ordinary routine service such as can be obtained anywhere. Make it distinguished, outstanding service—pressed down and running over—over and above the call of duty. Seek ways and means, through your work as a lawyer, of accomplishing something worthy, constructive and worthwhile for your community, your state, your nation, for society itself—and you will have found the key to both happiness and material reward as well.

Render these services—achieve these accomplishments—and monetary rewards will *inevitably* follow. This rule is almost as inexorable as death itself. Thus, you will have a double-edged satisfaction and a double-edged reward—achievement plus the $100,000 per annum you have sought.

Epilogue

HOW TO DEVELOP A

PHILOSOPHY FOR LIVING*

My Message Is Not Crass Materialism . . . Only the "Love" of Money Is Evil . . . Law Is Not Only a "Learned," but a "Great Profession" . . . The Work of Justice . . . How to Achieve True Greatness . . . Service to Fellow Man Can Be Source of Personal Happiness . . . The Lawyer Has the Opportunity of Acting as the Good Samaritan Many Times in His Lifetime . . . Show Me a "Regular Loser" and I'll Show You a Failure . . . Lawyers Can Aspire to Greatness at Every Level of Endeavor . . . Serve Thy Fellow Man Through Law! . . . "The Victory of Justice over Force" . . . "A Cause Greater than Yourself" . . . Opportunities for Service at County and Municipal Levels . . . Bring Honor to the Marketplace . . . The Duty of Leadership . . . The Five Functions of the Real Lawyer . . . What Good May I Do in It? . . . New Vistas–New Horizons–for the Lawyer! . . . Fighting for Ideals Can Also Bring Rich Rewards

My Message Is Not Crass Materialism

Perhaps you may believe that the primary thrust of my message has been materialistic. While there have been occasional references to the high ideals of service, which should motivate the true lawyer, they may have been more or

---

*A portion of this chapter was first published by the *New Jersey State Bar Journal* and is used by special permission of the copyright owners.

338

less oblique or collateral. However, if you feel that the single point made in this volume is to get that $100,000 cash per annum irrespective of consequence, that is not my intention.

Only the "Love" of Money Is Evil

Money or wealth, in and of itself, is not the root of all evil. Wealth is a blessing devoutly to be wished. It is only the obsessive *love* of money that is destructive. You can seek and achieve adequate and perhaps generous income to which you are entitled, without compromising your character, integrity and honor—or the ideals of the lawyer.

Law Is Not Only a "Learned," but a "Great Profession"

Law has always been recognized as a learned profession. But it is also a path to greatness for those with the vision to see its potentialities for service. People usually come to a lawyer when they are in trouble. Hence, the great calling is to extend help to those in trouble. Nor does it merely mean the individual in trouble. A corporation, an institution, or a division of government may find itself in trouble. These entities merely represent aggregates of individual persons. Thus, both the opportunity and the responsibility for service are multiplied and magnified. When it happens to be a state or nation or society itself which finds itself in trouble, a real challenge to service and to greatness presents itself. We are living in such a period today.

The Work of Justice

Unlike the physician's training, this aspect of the lawyer's lifework (i.e., service to society itself through "The work of justice") is not sufficiently stressed either in his academic training or in his clerkship or apprenticeship to older practitioners. Perhaps it is taken for granted and considered unnecessary. Implicit in the aspirations to join the learned professions of the clergy, medicine, law, science or teaching should be the desire to serve your fellow man. But we must all bear in mind George Eliot's admonition:

"Who shall put his finger on the work of Justice and say, 'It is there?' Justice is like the kingdom of God: it is not without us as a fact; it is within us as a great yearning."

How to Achieve True Greatness

Too often we strive for the accumulation of wealth long after we have reached our original goal of $100,000 per annum and the need for such accumulation is apparent to no one except ourselves. It somehow seems that we seek to convince ourselves and our associates of our professional success by the mere yardstick of our income. Or perhaps some of us confuse the search for ever-increasing income with the search for happiness—or the search for money with the search for achievement. This chapter is intended as a challenge to those who may have fallen into these errors, to improve their ways while there is still time to serve their fellow man—and in so doing to achieve true greatness, not only for themselves but for their profession as well.

Service to Fellow Man Can Be Source of Personal Happiness

Many great writers have described the futility of deliberately searching for happiness. They have pointed out that only when you lose yourself in the service of others, you may suddenly find that happiness has found you. There is a strong analogy in the practice of law. Strain for success, for the sole pleasure and profit you may obtain from it, and you will probably never attain either, no matter how numerous or great your clients or your retainers may be. But lose yourself in a worthy cause, and quite probably you will find not only pleasure and profit but lasting satisfaction as well, and the consolation of knowing that you have been true to the highest ideals of your profession. These are the sentiments which motivate many lawyers who give up lucrative practices to serve on the bench or in some public office. But there is no valid reason why the application of these ideals should be limited to the judiciary or to public office. Every lawyer is in a unique position to serve his fellow man in this regular everyday practice. It was Abraham Lincoln who advised:

> "Discourage litigation. Persuade your neighbor to compromise wherever you can. As a peacemaker the lawyer has a superior opportunity of being a great man. There will still be business enough."

The Lawyer Has the Opportunity of Acting as the Good Samaritan Many Times in His Lifetime

Every man who comes to a lawyer's office when he is in trouble needs understanding, compassion and help. He is our neighbor. The lawyer has the opportunity of playing the part of the Good Samaritan on countless occasions in the course of his lifetime. The question is how often do we rise to the occasion?

I am too practical and hard-bitten to ask the members of the legal profession to take all of the admonitions of the "Great Teacher" literally. For instance, when He says in His Sermon on the Mount, "Blessed are the poor in spirit," He was not so impractical as to recommend poverty as a virtue *per se*. There is nothing either virtuous or beneficial or uplifting or inspirational in poverty in and by itself.

What He was saying was "You can still be happy if you are *poor in spirit*." You may own and drive a Cadillac and own a country home and yet not be so puffed up, egotistical, selfish or self-centered that you lose sight of the fact that the things of the spirit are always more important, and more enduring and more satisfying in the long run, than pure material things such as money—believe it or not! What we lawyers must never lose is *the common touch*. We must recognize not only the dignity of man as a laudable theory, but the dignity of each and every man as an essential fact of life.

Show Me a "Regular Loser" and I'll Show You a Failure

I have a dear friend who practices law. Often he has said to me, "You should not become emotionally involved in your client's problems. Always keep your professional distance." To me this seems like apostasy or heresy. I am sure that he was not suggesting that I should be impersonal as to whether my client won or lost. I certainly had to believe in his case to take it in the first place—and if it is lost, then obviously there has been a miscarriage of justice, in my judgment at least. I hope he was not trying to tell me to be a "good loser," because I have always held that if you show me a good loser, I will show you a regular loser——and a regular loser is obviously a failure.

I do not admire "poor losers" nor lawyers who can only see one side of the case, nor those who make a career of every case they handle. However, I want to see a lawyer who realizes that once he has undertaken the prosecution or defense of a case, he has a solemn duty to perform, a solemn obligation to discharge, and that he must give to that case every ounce of effort, energy, enterprise, dedication and devotion of which he is capable.

Lawyers Can Aspire to Greatness at Every Level of Endeavor

I realize that every member of the legal profession cannot be a leader or hope to achieve enduring fame. A Lincoln arises only once in a nation's history. But we can all aspire to greatness in the everyday work we are doing in our profession, regardless of what social or economic or professional level we may find ourselves in. The point to remember, it seems to me, should always be to weigh the importance of what we are doing against its value not only to the individual or corporation or public entity we represent, but to society as a whole and act accordingly.

Serve Thy Fellow Man Through Law!

Historically no profession ever offered so many opportunities to "serve thy fellow man." The last Suez or Panama Canal has not been built nor has the last greatest railroad or steamship or airline or the last flight ship to the moon or Mars been conceived and built. While these and similar projects are basically engineering achievements, legal minds played a large role in their conception, financing and execution.

Think of the great services rendered by lawyers through the intervention of governmental agencies. Those with lesser vision may feel that at its best these activities represent governmental intervention, and that at its worse—rank socialism. But the dedicated lawyer working on the solution of such massive problems as the rehabilitation of slums; the providing of decent homes for those in the middle and lower economic brackets; care for the aged, the poor, the sick and the dying; providing educational advantages for those who need it and deserve it and yet cannot afford it; securing the enjoyment of civil rights for all, regardless of race, creed or color; establishment of ethical principles and practices in government; or perhaps the securing of peace—must derive enormous satisfaction from his application of legal talents to achieve these worthy objectives.

"The Victory of Justice over Force"

The human race has reached some degree of unity and accord on such mundane subjects as the law of the sea; air flights; postal regulations; diplomatic immunity and the like. Is it too much to hope that some day disputes between nations can be settled by appeals to law and reason—without the resultant carnage and destruction which always follow when mankind resorts to war to settle their differences by force and violence?

"A Cause Greater than Yourself"

Opportunities for service present themselves on every level of government, state, county, municipal and even down to the very voting district in which the lawyer lives and practices. Offer your aid and support to the Legal Aid

Society; accept assignemtns to defend indigent defendants; volunteer your services in promoting and defending civil rights, etc., etc. But it must be deeper and broader and stronger and on a much more universal scale. The real lawyer must bring this spirit of service into every aspect of his life—personal as well as professional. It is up to every individual lawyer to see the opportunity; seize it as an outlet for his services; to pour into it his strength and vigor. This is what is meant by losing yourself in a "cause greater than yourself."

Untold opportunities for service lie in state government. Most governors and legislatures are lawyers. Our court systems are crying for improvement. Our juries can be made more effective in achieving real justice. Our rules of evidence can be modernized and simplified to make trials a genuine search for the truth. Our probate laws can be made less archaic to secure efficiency, speed and economy in the administration of estates and distribution of the assets to the beneficiaries with a minimum of delay and expense.

Opportunities for Services at County and Municipal Levels

On the county and municipal levels, new and improved concepts of ethics for public officials can be promulgated and enforced. In many areas there is a crying need for a revision of voting laws and procedures to insure honest elections and the widest participation in government by our citizens. Why haven't these objectives been realized? If the lawyers actually dominate the legislative bodies, they should and must assume full responsibility for achieving these reforms promptly. While these basic reforms remain unrealized, we find many new current problems arising constantly and demanding solution, such as: elimination of air and water pollution; protection against massive electrical power failures which can paralyze the activities of millions; adequate protection for the public against the inherent danger arising from careless or inadequate auto design; adequate protection of the public against the health hazards involved in excessive smoking, drinking, use of hallucinatory and other forms of drugs. The list is legion. While some of these problems may seem to fall into categories other than the law, enabling or regulatory laws are usually the first step toward their solution. Moreover, dedicated lawyers can also lead in the field of implementation, administration, execution and enforcement of such laws.

Bring Honor to the Marketplace

But in the last analysis, if the lawyer wants to improve society and thus serve his fellow man, he should begin with himself, in his own office, in his own practice, with his own clients. Historically the lawyer's task has been to bring honor to the marketplace. Let the client know that the lawyer is dedicated to this objective in fact as well as in theory. Let the lawyer instill in every client's mind the fact that unless the client's cause is a just one, he should not and cannot hope to win—that the ultimate objective of every litigation is to see that justice prevails! I realize that this procedure may very well lose a lawyer some of his clients, but in the long run, he will be better off without such clients. A rigid observance of these principles by the bar as a whole would have a stimulating, refreshing and perhaps a somewhat purifying effect upon society as a whole.

The Duty of Leadership

The message I am trying to develop is a simple, old-fashioned one—the lawyer will be judged in the last analysis not by what he proposes or professes or preaches, but by how he personally measures up to the responsibilities of the profession.

Hence, it is not enough for the lawyer merely to observe the usual or routine requirements of the responsible, reputable and reliable citizen. As a leader in the community, he owes the duty of acting as a leader, of setting a good example for those about him—and the best place to begin is with his individual clients. But in addition to dedication to the high principles of his profession in the course of his routine practice, he owes a further duty as Woodrow Wilson put it:

"To advance society by at least the full measure of a generation's progress."

The Five Functions of the Real Lawyer

The lawyer can do this by following the admonitions of the late Chief Justice Arthur T. Vanderbilt as to the five functions of the real lawyer: (1) to be a wise counselor; (2) to be a skilled advocate; (3) to improve their profession; (4) to lead public opinion; (5) to answer the call to public duty. It is in these latter two, leading public opinion and in answering the call to public duty, that the lawyer can best hope to serve his fellow man.

What Good May I Do in It?

Benjamin Franklin really summed it all up in a single sentence when he said: "He who shall introduce into public affairs the principles of even *primitive* Christianity will revolutionize the world." He tried to refine it still further when he said: "The noblest question in all the world is '*What good may I do in it?*'"—and he proved his dedication to these principles by a lifetime dedicated to serving his fellow man in a wide diversity of fields.

New Vistas—New Horizons—for the Lawyer!

This documentation of just a few of the maxims of some of the great imaginative men of the past should give to the lawyer new vistas—new horizons of the grand, majestic sweep of life as it lies before him. The world should seem wider, deeper, longer, broader than ever before. And as he views it, he should feel the thrill of being able to make his own personal contribution to a worthy cause every day of his life *while still earning $100,000 per annum*!

Fighting for Ideals Can Also Bring Rich Rewards

In fact there is no inconsistency in the two—rich monetary rewards and equally rich satisfaction—in ideals rightly conceived and ably achieved. The two go hand-in-hand. They complement each other. It is another way of saying—*find a real need and you have automatically found a fortune, by fulfilling that need*.

No profession other than law, offers such manifold and such striking opportunity for benefiting society—of doing good to your fellow man—and being richly rewarded for your effort and achievements at the same time. In these final paragraphs of this book, I have attempted to give you just a few illustrations of how the average lawyer can figuratively become the Knight in shining armour astride a white horse battling for true justice and for his clients—*and still be well paid for doing it*. Thus, at the end of our days, or at least at the end of our professional career as a lawyer, we may be able to say: "I have fought the good fight! I have finished the course! I have kept the Faith!" Can you conceive of any other philosophy for living more *enticing*, more *entrancing* or more *rewarding*?

INDEX

A

A.B.A. "Disciplinary Rules of the Code of Professional Responsibility," 224, 238-262
"Acres of Diamonds," 321
Active Tray, 19
"Administration Expenses," 116
Administration, Letters of, 117
Admiralty, 196, 198-199
Advance Sheets, 194
Advertisement:
    bank, not attorneys, 111
    becoming public figure, 220
    improper publicity, 226-227
    satisfied client, 65-66, 220
Aerial map, 74
Aerial photographs, 85
Agencies:
    billing, 175
    county and state, 205-206
Amendments to rules, 194
American Bar Association Canons of Ethics, 166
Amount involved, billing, 170
Appearance, 322-323
Appointments, establish ideal hours, 16-17
Appraisal, 65
Appreciation, 27
Assets of client, segregation, 228-230
Assistant Counsel, 206
Associate—partner or sole practitioner, 319-320
Attending physician, 74, 81-83
Attire, 322
Authorization to Obtain Medical Data, 72, 73
Aviation, 196

B

Banks, estates, 111-113
Billing:
    ABA Canons on Fees, 166
    amount involved, results obtained, 170
    attorneys usually only retain 25 percent of fee collected, 174

Billing: *(cont.)*
    combination diary and manual, 180
    consult all available data and statistics, 178
    court regulates contingent fees in some states, 173
    courts, agencies and corporations— hourly basis, 174-175
    daily time charts, 182
    experience, reputation and ability of counsel, 172
    fee certain or contingent, 172
    fees customarily charged in locality, 170
    "hopeless" case, 168-169
    human nature, 175
    improper fees, 227-228
    intangibles, 165
    lack of guide cost 90 percent of fair fee, 176-178
    layman on basis of $50 to $100 an hour, 174
    legal fees substantial—but less than fraction of what they saved, 216-217
    method of furnishing itemized bill, 179-180
    method of time-keeping, 180-181
    minimum fee schedules, 176
    New Jersey Supreme Court, 166-167
    novel case, 168
    philosophy, 165
    psychological rules, 179
    reasonable fees, 327-328
    recent public reaction to lawyers' hourly fee, 175-176
    regular or transitory client, 171
    results count primarily—rather than effort, 166
    "rush job," 171
    33-1/3 percent as fair contingent fee, 172-173
    time-keeper, 178-179
    time—novelty—difficulty and skill involved, 167
    typical recommended schedule of minimum fees, 183-192